CAMBRIDGE LIBRARY COLLECTION

Books of enduring scholarly value

Classics

From the Renaissance to the nineteenth century, Latin and Greek were compulsory subjects in almost all European universities, and most early modern scholars published their research and conducted international correspondence in Latin. Latin had continued in use in Western Europe long after the fall of the Roman empire as the lingua franca of the educated classes and of law, diplomacy, religion and university teaching. The flight of Greek scholars to the West after the fall of Constantinople in 1453 gave impetus to the study of ancient Greek literature and the Greek New Testament. Eventually, just as nineteenth-century reforms of university curricula were beginning to erode this ascendancy, developments in textual criticism and linguistic analysis, and new ways of studying ancient societies, especially archaeology, led to renewed enthusiasm for the Classics. This collection offers works of criticism, interpretation and synthesis by the outstanding scholars of the nineteenth century.

Galen on Anatomical Procedures

Galen was probably the greatest medical writer of antiquity and certainly the most prolific. His *Anatomical Procedures* (c. 200 CE) embodies the results of a lifetime of practical research; it is largely based on verbatim notes of lectures delivered during actual demonstrations of dissection. The work comprises fifteen books, of which only the first eight-and-a-half have survived in the original Greek. An Arabic translation of the complete work has however survived, and this has made possible the translation of the final six-and-a-half books (parts of book 9 and books 10–15). Duckworth's translation was originally made from a German translation of 1906, but for this 1962 edition it was revised by Lyons, working directly from the Arabic text, with the co-operation of Towers. Modern names for the parts of the body are inserted in brackets, and an anatomical index is supplied.

Cambridge University Press has long been a pioneer in the reissuing of out-of-print titles from its own backlist, producing digital reprints of books that are still sought after by scholars and students but could not be reprinted economically using traditional technology. The Cambridge Library Collection extends this activity to a wider range of books which are still of importance to researchers and professionals, either for the source material they contain, or as landmarks in the history of their academic discipline.

Drawing from the world-renowned collections in the Cambridge University Library, and guided by the advice of experts in each subject area, Cambridge University Press is using state-of-the-art scanning machines in its own Printing House to capture the content of each book selected for inclusion. The files are processed to give a consistently clear, crisp image, and the books finished to the high quality standard for which the Press is recognised around the world. The latest print-on-demand technology ensures that the books will remain available indefinitely, and that orders for single or multiple copies can quickly be supplied.

The Cambridge Library Collection will bring back to life books of enduring scholarly value (including out-of-copyright works originally issued by other publishers) across a wide range of disciplines in the humanities and social sciences and in science and technology.

Galen on Anatomical Procedures

The Later Books

Wynfrid Laurence Henry Duckworth
Edited by M.C. Lyons
and B. Towers

CAMBRIDGE UNIVERSITY PRESS

Cambridge, New York, Melbourne, Madrid, Cape Town, Singapore,
São Paolo, Delhi, Dubai, Tokyo

Published in the United States of America by Cambridge University Press, New York

www.cambridge.org
Information on this title: www.cambridge.org/9781108009447

This edition first published 1962
This digitally printed version 2010

ISBN 978-1-108-00944-7 Paperback

GALEN
ON ANATOMICAL PROCEDURES

THE LATER BOOKS

GALEN
ON ANATOMICAL PROCEDURES
THE LATER BOOKS

A TRANSLATION BY THE LATE

W. L. H. DUCKWORTH

Formerly Master of Jesus College and Reader in Human Anatomy in the University of Cambridge

EDITED BY

M. C. LYONS, M.A., Ph.D.

Fellow of Pembroke College and Lecturer in Arabic in the University of Cambridge

AND

B. TOWERS, M.B., Ch.B., M.A.

Fellow of Jesus College and Lecturer in Anatomy in the University of Cambridge

CAMBRIDGE
AT THE UNIVERSITY PRESS
1962

PUBLISHED BY
THE SYNDICS OF THE CAMBRIDGE UNIVERSITY PRESS

Bentley House, 200 Euston Road, London, N.W.1
American Branch: 32 East 57th Street, New York 22, N.Y.
West African Office: P.O. Box 33, Ibadan, Nigeria

Printed in Great Britain at the University Press, Cambridge
(Brooke Crutchley, University Printer)

CONTENTS

BOOK IX

ON THE BRAIN[1]

BOOK X

THE FACE, MOUTH AND PHARYNX

[1] Continuing from ch. 5 of Dr Charles Singer's translation: *Galen: On Anatomical Procedures* (1956). Cf. Introduction, p. xii below.

BOOK XI

THE LARYNX AND ASSOCIATED STRUCTURES

Contents

BOOK XII

THE GENERATIVE ORGANS AND FOETAL DEVELOPMENT

BOOK XIII

ON THE VEINS AND ARTERIES

BOOK XIV

THE CRANIAL NERVES

BOOK XV

THE SPINAL NERVES

INTRODUCTION

I. GALEN 'ON ANATOMICAL PROCEDURES'

The treatise of which the latter part is here presented in English translation has, like some other works of Galen, experienced a chequered history, most of which we learn from Galen himself, in the opening chapter of the work, which is in the nature of a preface, and in a passage at the end of Book XI (below, pp. 107–8). It began as a comparatively brief treatise, in two Books, written at the request of Flavius Boëthus in A.D. 165. Later, after the death of Boëthus (in or shortly before A.D. 169), the work became unobtainable, since Galen's own copies in Rome had been destroyed in a fire, and Galen's friends accordingly pressed him to rewrite it. This he eventually did, but he took advantage of the opportunity to replan it on a much larger scale, and to include in it the fruits of his latest observations. He began this task in A.D. 177, and it is to this year that Dr Singer assigns the entire work. In Dr Singer's view,[1] the treatise is not a literary work, written down as such, but rather 'a shorthand record of actual lectures, though doubtless lightly revised by its author'. It is certainly true that there are numerous passages in which Galen seems to be addressing a pupil or an audience, and the considerable amount of repetition, wearisome to the modern reader, would be readily understandable in a text which is a verbatim transcript of lectures.[2] But there are other passages, in which Galen refers to the planning and progress of the work,[3] which cannot have emanated from the lecture-hall, and which suggest that the composition of this great work occupied a considerable period. We know, in fact, that it was Galen's habit to sketch out a treatise and keep it by him, revising and remodelling it, until he had brought it up to a state fit for publication. And even if the entire work was written down in A.D. 177, it certainly was not all published in that year, for Galen himself tells us that only Books I–XI had been published when a serious

[1] *Galen on Anatomical Procedures*, pp. xiii, xv, xx.

[2] Some of this repetition was certainly intentional on the part of Galen, cf. Book IX, chap. 11 (below, pp. 16–17).

[3] Below, pp. 107–8.

fire in Rome, in which the Temple of Peace and a number of nearby buildings were consumed, caused the destruction of the only existing manuscript of Books XII–XV. This fire occurred in the last year of Commodus (A.D. 192). Galen now had to reconstruct the lost Books, and it was thus only after A.D. 192, not long before Galen's own death, that the work as a whole was at last given to the world.

Misfortune, however, continued to mark its history. Complete texts were certainly available in the Near East as late as the ninth century A.D., since Ḥunain ibn Isḥāq used three Greek manuscripts in his task of translation (see below). But in western Europe all surviving manuscripts derive from a single mutilated exemplar, in which the text broke off abruptly shortly after the beginning of Book IX. Of this frustum of the work the original Greek was first published in the Aldine edition of Galen's works in 1525, and was quickly followed by a Latin translation in 1531. Other editions, both Greek and Latin, succeeded, and the work was therefore widely available to scholars and physicians of the sixteenth century, such as Vesalius, while for Cambridge readers it is interesting to note that a revised Greek text, with notes, was published at Bâle in 1544 by John Caius.[1] The latter Books, however, remained unknown to western Europe until the nineteenth century, when the Arabic version came under notice, and they therefore exerted no influence on the history and development of modern anatomical research.

In 1956 the late Dr Charles Singer published an English translation of the surviving Greek text, namely, Books I–VIII and the first five chapters of Book IX.[2] His lucid and comprehensive introduction serves as a guide to the work as a whole, and the information he provided need not be repeated here, more especially as it is the intention that the present publication and Dr Singer's volume should be regarded as complementary. The present publication follows on immediately where

[1] The British Museum copy of this book (which also contains other works by Galen) belonged to Lancelot Browne, the Cambridge physician; it contains a large number of manuscript notes and readings, many of which are stated to have been transcribed from Caius's autograph.

[2] *Galen on Anatomical Procedures: Translation of the Surviving Books with Introduction and Notes*, Publications of the Wellcome Historical Medical Museum, New Series, no. 7 (Oxford University Press, 1956), xxvi + 289 pp.

Dr Singer's text breaks off, covering the remainder of Book IX and the whole of Books X–XV, and is based on the Arabic translation which now falls to be described.

2. THE ARABIC TRANSLATION

For the survival of the latter part of the work we must be grateful to the great medical scholar and translator of Galen, Ḥunain ibn Isḥāq of Baghdad (b. 809, d. 873). From the fundamental study of G. Bergsträsser, *Ḥunain ibn Isḥāk und seine Schule* (Leiden, 1913), supplemented by the important article by Max Meyerhof, 'New Light on Ḥunain ibn Isḥāq', in *Isis*, VIII (1926), 685–724, we learn that Ḥunain was not only an amazingly accurate and careful scholar and translator, equally at home in Greek, Syriac and Arabic, but was endowed with an almost modern appreciation of the value of textual criticism. The basis of his work was a Syriac translation of the *Anatomical Procedures* which had been made by Ayyūb (Job) of Edessa, probably at the beginning of the ninth century. Ḥunain carefully revised and corrected this Syriac translation, employing as controls three Greek manuscripts of the work. This revised Syriac version, completed about A.D. 850, was later translated into Arabic by Ḥunain's nephew, Ḥubaish. It seems that this translation, though doubtless primarily the work of Ḥubaish, was revised and corrected by Ḥunain himself, and may thus be regarded as the product of collaboration between uncle and nephew.[1] This point is of some importance, since it implies that the interposition of a third language, Syriac, in the chain of transmission is not likely to have seriously affected the reliability of the text.

Although Ḥubaish seems to have been just as accurate and careful as his celebrated uncle, his Arabic versions have been criticised[2] as tending to prolixity, and this is, perhaps, reflected in the present translation. The prolixity of Galen himself has already been adverted to, and this is aggravated by the expansion which the text has undergone in the Arabic. It is necessary to emphasise this fact because of the great and unavoidable contrast of style between the present translation and

[1] This is the view of Meyerhof, *op. cit.* p. 693.

[2] Cf. Richard Walzer, *Galen on Medical Experience* (Oxford, 1944), p. vii.

Dr Singer's translation of the earlier Books. The contrast is all the more marked since Dr Singer has avowedly abridged Galen's wording wherever it seemed to him capable of compression—a principle wholly justifiable where the original Greek is available as a check, but one which could not safely be adopted in the present publication.

The Arabic text has survived, so far as is known, in only two manuscripts, both of which are in English libraries, namely, Oxford, Bodleian MS. Marsh 158 (= Summary Catalogue 9153)[1] and London, British Museum, Additional MS. 23406,[2] which is dated A.H. 887 = A.D. 1482. The British Museum MS. has the better text. On the basis of these MSS. Dr Max Simon, of Leipzig, published, in 1906, a critical Arabic text of Books IX–XV inclusive (beginning at the commencement of Book IX and thus slightly overlapping the Greek), together with a German translation and a very valuable commentary.[3] This Arabic text as established by Simon forms the basis of the present translation.

3. THE PRESENT TRANSLATION

The present work is basically an English translation made by Wynfrid Laurence Henry Duckworth, former Reader in Human Anthropology and Master of Jesus College, Cambridge.[4] Duckworth's active interest in this work of Galen appears to date from 1948, in which year he was chosen to deliver the Linacre lecture in St John's College, Cambridge.[5] For this purpose he selected five extracts from Galen's *Anatomical Procedures*, presented in English translation, each extract

[1] The early transcript of the MS. by Golius is also in the Bodleian, as MS. Marsh 448 (= Summary Catalogue 9446). Both were acquired by the Bodleian in 1714.

[2] Acquired on 14 April 1860 as one of a large collection of Oriental MSS. formed by Col. Robert Taylor (b. 1788, d. 1852), Political Resident at Baghdad 1829–43.

[3] *Sieben Bücher Anatomie des Galen*, J. C. Hinrichs'sche Buchhandlung (2 vols., Leipzig, 1906).

[4] For details of Duckworth's career see the obituary in *The Times*, 15 February 1956, p. 11, and, on his lifetime of service to his College, Arthur Gray and F. Brittain, *A History of Jesus College, Cambridge* (1960), pp. 203–4. An appreciation of his scientific work will be contributed to the Royal Anthropological Society's journal, *Man*, by Dr J. C. Trevor, Director of the Duckworth Laboratory of Physical Anthropology; in the meantime see *Nature*, vol. 177, 17 Mar. 1956, pp. 505–506, and *The Journal of Anatomy*, vol. 90, 1956, pp. 455–456.

[5] This lecture, delivered 6 May 1948, was printed in 1949 under the title *Some Notes on Galen's Anatomy* (Heffer and Sons, Cambridge), 42 pp.

being followed by a detailed scientific criticism. All these extracts were taken from the later Books, which have survived only in the Arabic, and Duckworth's twin aims in making this material the subject of his lecture were to emphasise Galen's remarkable anatomical achievements, and to combat the neglect in which, despite Simon's excellent edition, this portion of the *Anatomical Procedures* had continued to languish. After his Linacre lecture, Duckworth commenced work on a complete English translation of Simon's German version, and this he completed in 1950. At this time he certainly had no thought of eventual publication, though he seems to have subsequently changed his mind on this point. On reviewing the completed translation (in October 1950) Duckworth records that he then realised that he had 'tended throughout to give the meaning rather than the precise translation of Galen's own words', and he thereupon began a second and more literal translation, but he had retranslated less than four Books at the time of his death on 14 February 1956.

The first step towards the present publication was to compare Duckworth's English rendering (using the second and more literal version where available) with the Arabic text, and this laborious task was accomplished, between March and June 1958, by Dr M. C. Lyons, Fellow of Pembroke College, and University Lecturer in Arabic, who in the process prepared detailed notes on all the passages, some three thousand in number, where modification of the English seemed desirable. The necessary changes were effected in the English text by Mr Bernard Towers, Fellow of Jesus College, and University Lecturer in Anatomy, who has also worked through the entire text and brought it into a state ready for publication. The English titles given to the Books, the division into chapters, and the wording of the chapter-headings are likewise the work of Mr Towers. It should be pointed out that no attempt has been made here either to translate the 760 notes which Simon appended to his edition, or to provide any alternative form of commentary. To have done so would not only have seriously delayed the production of the work, but would have enlarged it far beyond the scope envisaged by Duckworth.

A paragraph may be spared at this point to dispose of the suggestion, which has been made by Dr Singer (see below), that in a work such as the present, use should be made of an unpublished French translation of the later books of the *Anatomical Procedures* preserved in the Library of the Royal College of Physicians in London. Simon, indeed, who got his information only at second hand, describes it as an English translation, made by a nineteenth-century student of ancient medicine, Dr W. A. Greenhill.[1] In a note in the *Journal of the History of Medicine* (New York, 1952, VII, 85–6), Dr Singer suggested that the Greenhill version was a myth, and that the MS. in question was a French translation by G. Dugat, which subsequently came into the possession of Greenhill. This is certainly correct, though it is not clear whether Dr Singer ever actually saw and examined the MS. in question. This MS. is, in fact, a French translation, made during 1854–5[2] by the Orientalist, Gustave Dugat, for the great authority on ancient medicine, Charles Daremberg. His covering letter, forwarding the completed work to Daremberg,[3] is dated 17 April 1855 and makes amply clear the provisional nature of the translation—a judgement confirmed by a pencil note (by Daremberg?) on the first page, 'Ceci n'est qu'une ébauche'. Dugat does not appear to have had any familiarity with medical terminology, and there are numerous blanks where the Arabic had defeated him. But apart from this, the salient fact is that his translation is based on only one of the two surviving MSS., that in the Bodleian, the British Museum MS. being at the time still in private hands[4] and unknown to scholars. In fact, Dugat never even saw the Bodleian MS., but used a transcript of it obtained by Daremberg and now in the Bibliothèque nationale.[5] Dugat's translation begins in Book IX, shortly before the point at which the Greek breaks off, and covers the remainder of the work. It now bears the number 133 (a) in the 1928 catalogue of the Library of the Royal College of Physicians.

From the foregoing it will be evident that Dugat's translation cannot contribute any information which is not to be found in Simon's edition, and no use has therefore been made of it for the present

[1] William Alexander Greenhill, M.D. (b. 1814, d. 1894).

[2] Book XIV is dated June 1854.

[3] In this same letter there is a reference to 'notre préface' which suggests that Daremberg and Dugat may have envisaged a joint edition of the translation.

[4] See above, note 2, p. xiv.

[5] Simon, *op. cit.* I, p. 11, note, gives the press-mark as Bibl. nat. MS. Ar. Suppl. 1002 bis.

publication. It is, however, worth noting that, long after Dugat's MS. had passed into Greenhill's possession, its existence came to the notice of Dr John G. Curtis,[1] of Columbia College (now University), New York, who between January and September 1894 wrote a number of letters to Greenhill[2] proposing a joint publication. Some progress was made, but the project seems to have been brought to an abrupt halt by Greenhill's death, and only vague memories of it subsisted when Simon came on the scene.[3]

As already mentioned, it was Duckworth's avowed aim in undertaking the present translation to focus the attention of scholars and scientists on one of Galen's greatest works, and to attempt to remedy the accidental, but disastrous, dichotomy from which it has suffered for so many centuries. It is a fact, remarkable indeed but established beyond doubt,[4] that, although Singer had been engaged on his translation of the earlier books since 1941, and Duckworth on the later ones since 1948, their efforts were entirely independent. Now, happily, publication has brought the two halves of the work as nearly together as circumstances permit, and if this should lead to a reappraisal of the work as a whole, Duckworth's objective will have been achieved. Modern anatomists, with their interest in comparative as well as in human anatomy, and with their experimental approach towards the elucidation of anatomical problems, are likely to be more sympathetic towards Galen than have been their predecessors during the last four hundred years. The eclipse of Galen's reputation at the Renaissance was perhaps inevitable. But if in recent centuries he has been remembered chiefly for his errors, it is possible now to put these into perspective against a background of solid scientific achievement. Ḥunain describes him (p. 264 below) as 'a man who performed marvellously'. It is in support of that estimate of Galen's scientific status that this text is now presented for the first time in English.

It remains to thank all those who have generously assisted in the production of this volume. The vital contributions of Dr Lyons and Mr Towers have already been mentioned. The Wellcome Trust, by a

[1] John Green Curtis (b. 1844, d. 1913).

[2] Also in the Library of the Royal College of Physicians, reference 133 (r).

[3] Simon, *op. cit.* I, p. x, note.

[4] By a letter from Dr Singer dated 26 May 1960, only a few days before his death.

munificent grant, have removed all financial anxieties attending the publication. Dr Singer, alas! it is too late to thank, but he took great interest in the work, of the progress of which he was kept informed, and he had looked forward keenly to its publication. Dr Richard Walzer, Senior Lecturer in Arabic and Greek Philosophy at Oxford, played an invaluable part in enlisting Dr Lyons's aid. The Council of Jesus College have throughout taken a beneficent interest in the project, which they have supported in practical ways. Lastly, the Syndics of the Press must be thanked for undertaking publication on very generous terms, while members of their staff have spared no pains to improve both the usefulness and appearance of the book.

NOTE ON THE METHOD OF PUBLICATION

1. For convenience in reading, the Books have been divided into chapters by the present editors, but it should be clearly understood that there were no such subdivisions either in the original Greek or (except where indicated in Book xv) in the Arabic translation. The Book-, chapter- and page-headings here printed are those of the present editors and do not form part of the text translated.

2. The summaries at the beginning of some of the Books, and the colophons at the end, are those of the Arabic translator; it is clear from the surviving Books that no such summaries existed in the original Greek.

3. With the exception of the headings, summaries, etc., referred to in paragraphs 1 and 2 above, which are left unbracketed for the sake of appearance, all additions to the text translated are enclosed within square brackets. In general, such additions are printed in italic type when they represent anatomical terms, in roman when they form an explanation or elucidation of the wording, though a hard and fast distinction on this point cannot always be maintained. The *Basel Nomina Anatomica* (1895) has in general been used, except where its *Birmingham Revision* (1933) seemed more appropriate.

4. Occasionally, an explanation of some length which would interfere unduly with the continuous reading of the text has been placed as a footnote at the bottom of the page; such footnotes, being clearly additions, are not bracketed. Footnotes which do not bear the initials of either editor are by Duckworth.

5. Anatomical terms which occur in the body of the text, and which in fact are either direct translations of what Galen wrote, or translations employing modern nomenclature, are printed in roman type without brackets. Words and passages within round brackets are parenthetic remarks, etc., by Galen himself.

6. The marginal figures in italic type refer to the pages of the Arabic text as printed by Max Simon, *Sieben Bücher Anatomie des Galen* (Leipzig, 1906), vol. 1.

BOOK IX

ON THE BRAIN[1]

CHAPTER 6. THIRD AND FOURTH VENTRICLES, AQUEDUCT OF THE MID BRAIN, AND PINEAL GLAND.

If you now repeat the movement of that body [*the vermis*] which covers 1
the passage and, simultaneously with this movement, you raise it
upwards somewhat, then you can see the end of the passage which opens
out into the posterior ventricle. This is closed up and covered in by the
vermiform process [*vermis inferior*] which, from behind, forms a sort
of lid for it [*the ventricle*] as soon as you draw back the whole of the body
which covers the passage towards the rear, and it [*the ventricle*] opens
itself as soon as this body goes forwards. This is the moment to introduce from in front into the posterior ventricle whatever smooth
cylindrical instrument you have available, the calibre of which corresponds to the opening of the passage, whether now the instrument be
made of wood, copper, iron, silver or gold. Should it be of wood, then
it should be first and foremost of boxwood, since this wood is strong
and very smooth. The Greeks are accustomed to name all instruments
of such use with the generic term sounds. For my part, I have sometimes in the past, when I had no other thing at hand, inserted into this
passage from the middle ventricle the writing reed, though I did not
introduce the tapered end with which one writes, for this is sharp, but
the other rounded-off end, and I pressed it steadily and gradually
onwards, until I brought it into the posterior ventricle without boring 2
through any part of the surroundings. Do you now turn your attention
to and consider particularly what I am about to describe for you. It is
that the posterior ventricle is bare in the region where it borders upon
the first origin of the spinal marrow, and has no sort of body which
overlaps it, as is the case with the three other ventricles and those

[1] The text continues from the end of Dr Charles Singer's translation of chapter 5 of Book IX, given in his *Galen: On Anatomical Procedures* (O.U.P., for the Wellcome Historical Medical Museum, 1956).

portions of this fourth ventricle which apply themselves to the passage between it and the middle ventricle. As for what relates to that portion of this [fourth] ventricle which lies at the upper end of the spinal marrow, it is completely free from any structure of which the substance resembles this [*spinal marrow*], except that it is covered by the dura mater only. When you have seen all this, now remove the whole body with which two vermiform processes are connected, after you have previously taken care for the undamaged preservation of the membrane covering the passage in order that you may have a clear view of it. You will then be in a better position than on the first occasion if you wish to introduce an instrument to penetrate through the passage, and you can also open it up by means of a cannula. When you have done that, now is the time to cut into the membrane or to open it up, so that the passage may be laid open to view. The density of its inner surface, which you perceive, indicates its nature and its function. In this place also you will see another passage slanting downwards and forwards [*the inferior horn of the Right or Left lateral ventricle*] which you will presently have to dissect in order to see where it ends.

But now withdraw the pineal body, and raise it up from the channel, then take hold of it in the hand, examine it carefully and thoughtfully and notice how it consists of 'spongy flesh' like the 'spongy flesh' which is found in many bodily structures, and which one calls glands, this being brought as a cushion and padding in order to support and prop the vessels which are distributed to those bodily parts. It constitutes a part of the brain which is denser than all other brain substance. Observe also how there exists in its cavity a hard substance, similar to a date-stone or a cartilage, which you do not find in the remaining
3 glands. This substance is found very clearly in the large animals, that is to say, in the horse, ox, ass and other suchlike. On this matter instruct yourself in your own way, as it appears good to you, since this is an object that lies outside the bounds of all anatomy.

CHAPTER 7. LATERAL AND THIRD VENTRICLES.

What you should carefully study is the reciprocal symmetry of the four ventricles in the brain. For if you proceed carefully, you find that the part which the anatomists have compared to the sharpened end of the

writing reed is fashioned similarly to an outflow which discharges into the spinal marrow. Further you see how, above this part, a passage opens out from the posterior ventricle, which extends itself to the middle ventricle. Then you see how the two anterior [*R. and L. lateral*] ventricles open themselves, discharging into the middle ventricle, as I have described above [Book IX, chap. 4]. And you see how the anterior end of each of the two anterior ventricles [*inferior horn*] goes to each one of the two nasal cavities like a hollow horn, wide at its commencement from its upper part and then steadily narrowing itself. You must now detach and remove all that surrounds these two horns, and go on uninterruptedly along them until you arrive at their termination. Now this is something that it is most desirable for you to see in the brain of a starved and emaciated animal, such a one as starvation and exhaustion have afflicted so that it has become lean, being emaciated by disease. For when you set about this examination, it is necessary that the substance of the brain be exceptionally hard and desiccated. Previously also, if you will, inspect thoroughly the discharging effluents on the two sides [R. and L.] of the anterior ventricles, and remove completely all the parts lying around them, so as to get a fair view of the duct which comes out from the end of each of the two ventricles, noticing how for a wide stretch it descends in the same way as the commencement of the spinal marrow [*central canal*]. However, the top of that duct does not resemble the point of the calamus scriptorius. For it has
in this spot no sort of vaulting; on the contrary each of the two ventricles 4
steadily narrows and diminishes, so that the duct comes into being thereout.

You find here, at the side of this duct, a part of the brain of a peculiar kind, different in boundaries and in circumference from the other parts of the brain and so singled out from the others [*lateral geniculate body*]. Direct your efforts to this part, and loosen away from it that which surrounds it and follow it in its course towards the front. There you find it firmly connected with and intimately united to the two nerves of sight [*optic nerves*]. For speedy discovery of its union and its contiguity, it will help you to draw these two nerves from below upwards towards their upper parts, their specific roots. That point I have not yet mentioned. Later on I will say something with reference to their roots,

where it is necessary to re-introduce a discussion of this point, but beyond that I will remain silent thereupon. At present now examine carefully in this spot how the outgrowths of the two anterior ventricles stretch themselves out towards the nasal cavities [*olfactory bulbs*] and seek to ascertain that fact from the ventricles themselves, as I will describe for you. Betake yourself to the part where each of the two ventricles, stretching towards the front, is narrowed. Into this part insert the head end of a thick sound. For the place itself is wide at its commencement. When you have done that, then point the sound a little upwards, cut or tear through the part stretching itself upwards, and again go gradually forwards until you come to the first part of the nose where the bone lies which the anatomists name the 'cribriform'. When you have fully set free all this offshoot, in such a manner as described, then there reveals itself clearly the rigid quality of the [interior] surface of the duct. Also you see that in this region the brain is softer, more like the nature of mucus. Often indeed, when I have wished to attain to a complete knowledge of the nature of this region, have I met with no slight uncertainty. And so will you likewise feel uncertainty, and see grave difficulties confronting you. The reason for my difficulty was that it was not possible for me to ascertain by the eye whether both those two
5 cavities come finally to a single orifice, as is the case with the cavity of the place named the 'pool' [*infundibular recess*], or whether the two come to an end, closed up and blocked, or whether fine apertures and effluents are present in the duct. The very nature of the thing makes it necessary for the ducts not to be closed up, since you often see that from the brain there flows down very abundant thick mucus into the duct opening into each of the two nasal cavities. And this mucus cannot be poured out explosively without an effluent orifice of a certain diameter. Nevertheless it is not here my purpose to derive the knowledge of the nature of the things which I wish to understand from analogy; for this is not the aim of anatomy. Rather I am simply trying to give an account of those things which manifest themselves to the eyesight. And it is not possible for you to perceive with the eye how the canals leading from the brain to the nose terminate. For the matter is as I explained, that is to say, in this region the brain is soft. For the rest, I do not believe that the outlet of the two effluent ducts is a single one [i.e.

common to both], because you see plainly that that substance which envelops those two hollow spaces is a brain structure of which the individual parts on both sides, right and left, are united to one another in one and the same manner. I have often investigated and explored this in well-lighted surroundings, and have continued until I have come close to observing clearly enough to allow me to state definitely that the ending of each of the two prolongations is pierced by numerous openings. That which surrounds these processes is the more delicate of the two meninges of the brain, and this meninx itself lies in the middle between the two processes, passes on beyond each of them, defines its limits, and separates it clearly from the other zone. And the middle part of this delicate meninx ends opposite the portion to be found here of the thick meninx, which likewise intervenes between these two processes, together with a very thin bone [*crista galli*]. These are things *6*
which I have repeatedly seen quite clearly. And when I detached and cut away from the bone the portion of the dura mater found at this spot [i.e. overlying the cribriform plate] and then with my hands stretched it out towards the sunlight, I saw clearly that in certain parts of this membrane the sunlight penetrated to a greater extent, as if there were in them fine perforations, whereas in other parts it shone through to a lesser extent. These again are details from which a man can by surmise reach a correct solution, to the effect that the ends of the two hollow spaces are furnished with perforations, except that these two endings, as demonstrated, are not accessible to the eye.

As for what relates to the other two 'outlet' ducts, the ones at the middle ventricle, of those you can see that which flows out of the duct connecting the middle with the posterior ventricle, of which I said that it [*inferior horn of lateral ventricle*] travels obliquely downwards and forwards. First you can examine properly the union of the two, then see how both are picked up by the single duct, which goes straight downwards, and into which both discharge. Then you can see afterwards how that delicate meninx covers over the duct externally. Next see how this meninx also is perforated, in the place where the brain finally ends. You can see here how the dura mater lies beneath its base [the lower aspect of the brain]. Begin the examination of these things by introducing the sound from out of the oblique duct, and carry it

onwards to the duct descending downwards from the middle ventricle, and then, as you wish, strain it upwards as strongly as you may be able, so that all that which lies above the oblique duct may be cut through, and it may be completely uncovered, as far as to the spot where it unites itself with the duct travelling directly downwards. When you have executed this exposure, then it is clearly seen that the hardness of its inner surface is not something which came into existence through
7 our stretching of those bodies which we strained, but on the contrary it was in this state previously. Also, the duct into which both the two open out will give you a better indication of its own nature, and thereupon convince you of what, in fact, the position is with regard to both of the two. That is, what surrounds it is the pia mater, and beyond, a pair of arteries, which ascend upwards from the basis cranii, lie upon the pia mater [*middle cerebral arteries*].

CHAPTER 8. THE REGION OF THE OPTIC CHIASMA AND THE PITUITARY GLAND.

If you follow the distribution of these two arteries, you thus see all the external portions of the brain filled with arteries which resemble these, and which, by means of the pia mater, are bound up in the same way as the veins. There are other arteries which descend into the cavity of the brain, while others contribute to the chorion-like vessels which I began to mention above [Book IX, chap. 3]. Also you see that just as two arteries, one on each side, ascend from below and reach the brain and unite themselves and pass over the one into the other at the place called the 'pool' or the 'cistern' [*infundibular recess*], similarly at that place, still other numerous structures lie partly on the anterior, partly on the inferior subdivisions, partly at the sides. That is to say, the two passages that lead to the eyes—many anatomists call the two nerves that go to the eyes by this name, I mean that of 'passages', as alone of the nerves they contain two narrow perforations—the two passages, I say, at the place where they are preparing to pierce the cranial bones, are to be found conjoined at a point near the anterior region of the pool or cistern. From above they cross over from opposite places of origin, as I have already described. And further, you also find here the other pair of nerves, that is the hard ones which go to the eyes [*oculomotor nerves*].

Adjoining the pool [*infundibular recess*] and lying below it there is 8
found a flabby spongy flesh, similar in formation and size to a lupine bean [*pituitary gland*] (that is to say in the head of the ox; in the head of other animals the form of this structure is the same, but its size corresponds to that of the body of the animal.) Further, you find that the retiform plexus which surrounds this, being set together from arteries, extends backwards over a wide expanse, but occupies a restricted space towards the front and at the sides. In the bone above the palate [*sphenoid*] upon which the spongy glandular flesh rests and supports itself, you find narrow perforations. All this lies in this place. The first part of it that you see is the duct of which I said that it descends from the brain, and the pia mater envelops it here. Its structure resembles that of a sieve or a strainer with which one strains and clarifies turbid beverages—by which I mean everything to which the name 'sieve' or 'strainer' is applied. After that, in the place where this duct vanishes, sinking into the depth of the dura mater which is perforated in exactly the same manner as the pia mater, you see the lupine-bean-shaped spongy flesh. And at this flesh [*gland*] ends the effluent of the pool or cistern. When you have reached this place, then cut away the portion of dura mater which lies here below the site of the brain and above the pituitary. The substance of this gland is flabby and, round about it, is the so-called reticulate tissue, in which innumerable arteries travel entwined about one another in manifold fashion. Nor do they resemble a simple plain network, but rather numerous nets, laid the one upon
the other, and moreover interwoven and plaited with one another. 9
And the whole of that mass is produced from the two arteries of the neck which one names 'the vessels of stupor' [*carotids*]. Of the constitution of the passage through which they enter the skull, and the region towards which they wend their way on their entry, I shall speak in that section of this treatise where I take in hand the dissection of the foramina of the skull. Here it suffices for you, in connexion with the dissection of the brain as opposed to that of the skull, to go as far as this place which you have reached. You must apply yourself to the study of the nerve-origins, of which by reason of necessity I shall presently have to deal more thoroughly than here, when I come to the description of the manner in which one must dissect the brain while it remains in its

place in the corpse of a dead animal. In that mode of proceeding you must follow up all the nervous origins from their exits from the skull. But here it suffices for us to enumerate the origins of the nerves.

CHAPTER 9. THE CRANIAL NERVES.

Thus, as the first pair of nerves, you find the two large nerves [*optic*] of which each one lies on one side of the two outgrowths which lead from the brain to the nose [*olfactory bulbs*]. Next you find, as the second pair, the two nerves which ramify in the eye-muscles [*oculomotor*]. And you find that this second pair, to the extent to which it exceeds the first in hardness, is inferior to it in size. After this pair there is a third pair [*trigeminal*] which, as soon as it comes into view at its first point of origin, you see resembling a plait of numerous fine nerves, except that these nerves do not interlace, interweave, entwine, and interlock with one another as in genuine plaits, but, rather, come closer to being mounted one on the other. And in general, through their combination, their aggregate mass is greater than the two nerves of the first pair, while you see that the measure of the thickness of the second pair [*oculomotor*] amounts to one quarter or one fifth of the measure of the thickness of this [*trigeminal*] pair. Now this third pair immediately after its origin, when it emerges, sinks into the dura mater, so when you see that, you believe that it is hastening to pass through the cranial base, and to make its way to the inferior parts of the body, whereas in regard to the first two pairs you see how they travel straight forwards till they reach the hollow space of the ocular socket [*orbital cavity*]. Yet not even the third pair passes out from the skull for all its swiftly descending course, and in fact it does not penetrate the whole thickness of the dura mater, let alone that of the skull. On the contrary, it splits the thickness of the dura mater longitudinally into two halves, so that of the two halves one supports and cushions it from beneath, while the other half takes the form of a vault and a covering for the nerve, and so it proceeds onwards between the two to where it reaches the back of the eye. When I say back, I mean the place where the skull has perforations whose size corresponds exactly to the diameter of each of the two optic nerves, that is the nerves of the first pair. And when the third pair of nerves has reached this place, then leave it there. For it is not here our

intention that the skull be perforated for you so that you can pass through to its exterior. Your wish should be to follow up each single pair from its first origin until you arrive with it at the bone, and do you restrict yourself for the present to that. After this, the third pair, you find there another pair [*motor root of trigeminal*] lying close to it, more slender than it, approaching in thickness the second pair. Its origin and source are at the hinder part of the base of the brain, like the source of the third pair. Its source lies in front of this and it unites itself to that pair [*trigeminal*] forthwith, and proceeds together with it through the dura mater. You see both nerves clearly if you cut away all of this meninx [*dura mater*] which lies above them. After these pairs you find,
following in succession, if you go backwards with your dissection, 11
another pair of nerves of which each unit consists of two component parts. But as the origin of each nerve of the two components of that unit lies close to the place of origin of the others, Marinus came to reckon these four nerves as a single pair, although we clearly see that two nerves come to both sides of the head, the right and the left, opposite the ears, and enter into two foramina, one anterior, that is the auditory canal, and the other in the petrous bone. Of these two pairs the one which lies at the back is the auditory pair. But concerning the other [*facial nerve*], that one which enters into the blind foramen, it was believed previously that it did not reach through to the exterior. And the same opinion was held of the foramen itself. Consequently Herophilus and his supporters named this foramen the 'blind' one. But in the discussion on which we will embark when we take you to the stage of dissecting the brain while it is still in its place within the body, you will learn that this foramen is not blind, and that the nerve passes on through it outwards. But for the present do you restrict yourself for your part to designating both these pairs [*facial and auditory*] as a fifth pair, in agreement with the method of nomenclature of the modern surgeons, counting both these pairs as one, lest any careless and idle reader of our book believe that we differ from Marinus in our account of these nerves because we have not said that the nerve pairs springing from the skull are not seven, as those men claim, but eight, through a difference in the actual nature of these things. For many surgeons do not know that in his work on the roots of the nerves Marinus has

12 enumerated only those same roots which Herophilus specifies, but Marinus has concluded that there are seven pairs, whereas Herophilus says there are more than seven, regardless of the others. Whoever does not know this is, as the proverbial expression goes, like a seaman who navigates out of a book. Thus he reads the books on anatomy, but he omits inspecting with his own eyes in the animal body the several things about which he is reading. And because of such folk, we say, like the supporters of Marinus, that the fifth pair of nerves goes to the auditory canal and the 'blind' canal. Similarly, in regard to the sixth pair of nerves, neither one of its two units consists of a single nerve springing from either side of the brain, but each of the two consists of three nerves which come off from three roots [*glosso-pharyngeal, vagus and accessory nerves*]. We treat it, however, as we did the fifth pair and reckon it as a single pair, corresponding to the conception of Marinus. For to count these nerves as forming a single pair seems more reasonable and more convincing than to reckon the nerves of the fifth pair as a single pair. For its three component nerves make their way through a single one only of the foramina of the skull, and, in the dura mater, all these nerves are wrapped up together just as if they were a single nerve. There now still remains for us one of the nerve pairs springing from the brain, that is the pair [*hypoglossal nerve*] which runs to the two processes of the skull which intrude upon the two cavities of the first vertebra which many anatomists call the trough-shaped. Here then you should end this first dissection which I recommend should be made upon the brain removed from the animal's body.

CHAPTER 10. EXPOSURE OF THE BRAIN, WITH AN ACCOUNT OF THE INSTRUMENTS USED AND OF THE TECHNIQUES EMPLOYED AT OPERATION.

13 Do you now proceed to the next stage, for here is the place where I must describe to you the method of dissecting the parts of the brain while it remains in its place in the animal body. The dissection is best made in apes, and among the apes in such a one as has a face rounded to the greatest extent possible amongst apes. For the apes with rounded faces are most like human beings. When you have procured a newly-dead ape of this sort, then first of all carry two incisions

which lead in a straight line lengthwise over the skull, at the sides of the line which runs from the most highly-situated place on the head, straight towards the mid-line of the nose. For the median suture lies on this line, whereas the two scale-like sutures pass on their way a little above the ears. Thus I recommend the laying-out of this incision between the two sutures. And together with the skin, draw off the bulk of the sheath [*pericranium*] encompassing the skull so as to expose the skull and to strip off from it, as far as possible, all the parts investing it. Go on until you come to the sagittal suture and to the two limbs of the suture which resembles the letter Λ of the Greek script. For in this place the enveloping cranial membrane and the dura mater enter into close partnership. Their combination and partnership are clearly recognisable at the meeting-place of any two bones, and between them a suture is interposed. In these places only should you leave the skull unstripped and unbared. Next cut away the whole of the bone between the two sutures. That is the bone called the parietal, one on each side. Four lines limit it and mark it out, two of these travelling in the longitudinal diameter of the head, and two in the transverse diameter. As for the two lines running in the longitudinal direction, these are the so-called median suture [*sagittal*] and the scale-like [*squamous*] suture. The trans- *14*
verse ones are the lambdoid suture and the coronal. If you cut away these bones, as you are accustomed to do when you pierce through the skull, either with the perforator or with the instrument called the lens, then you see, when you take stock of and apply your intelligence to what is visible, how in the whole of that region round about, the dura mater is pressed down upon the brain, and you see how in the region of the suture running straight in the longitudinal direction it [*the dura mater*] attaches itself to the skull. And if, in addition, the animal is already very aged, then you see also that the part of the dura mater which I said may be pressed down upon the brain has also fallen away markedly from that part of it which is fused with the median suture. Similarly when you cut away the whole of that part of the skull behind the suture which resembles the letter Λ of the Greek script, and after you have preserved in this region the attachment of the dura mater to the skull, you see that all the remaining subdivisions of the dura mater have fallen away from the part at [attached to] the suture. This then is the first dissection which

you can carry out, in order to convince yourself that, in its circumference, the brain is smaller than the internal cavity of the skull. The other operation by means of which you can reach this conclusion—and it is a sounder and clearer method than the first—should proceed in the following way. Take away all that lies above upon the skull, without leaving anything at all adhering to it, with the sole exception of the sheath investing it at the two sutures, I mean the straight lengthwise suture and the suture resembling the letter Λ of the Greek script. Then cut into the skull together with the dura mater in the longitudinal direction above the squamous suture, and hereafter draw its upper part a little upwards. Next introduce beneath this the broad head of the spoon-shaped sound, and you will thereby realise how extensive is the space below the overlying bone to which the dura mater is firmly fastened. You can also hold the cut portion towards the sunlight, and draw slightly upwards the upper bone in the same way, and thus you will discover the vacant space between the skull and the brain, not by means of the touch only, but also by means of the eye-sight. You see this most clearly when you turn to the upper portion of the bone, which you have incised and split, and shift it from beneath upwards with the ossifrageous instrument, the so-called lens, as with the variety of instruments which you have previously seen in my possession ready prepared for tasks like these. I prepare these instruments, though, and use them for a different task, one which requires still greater attention than this one, namely for trephining a skull that is broken. But now, since readers of this my book—not my friends and colleagues only, but all those who love knowledge—should derive profit from it, as I said before, I will not abstain through idleness from describing the nature and the form of these instruments.

I will start my description, then, and say that you should understand me clearly, and construct for yourself in imagination this osteoclastic instrument which is commonly used and which everyone knows. Picture to yourself that its front end, that with which one makes cuts, forms a straight line. Then imagine that the end of one of the two extremities of this line is a thing resembling the form of a lens. This projects outwards from the whole line which cuts, and it is very round and smooth, so that when it penetrates the clefts in the fractured skull,

it brings together and adjusts the parts of the bone that are broken without piercing anything. Introduce then downwards at the place of the cranial fissure, the region of splintering, the smooth rounded part of this instrument, the part of which I said that it resembles the lens, until with this portion you feel the dura mater of the skull of the man whose skull is perforated, and, in the head of the animal whose brain *16*
has been subjected to this process of dissection which we are now describing, you feel the brain itself. But now beware that you do not then press the convex portion of the instrument downwards. Slope it sideways, and ensure that its wide smooth part encounters the structures that lie there underneath, and that it lies resting upon them so as to serve you in the place of the instrument which is known as 'the protector of the dura mater'. But press forwards [i.e. not downwards] the front part, that rounded part of lens-like shape, together with the whole of the cutting edge, and this you do by tapping the blade with the hammer which one is generally accustomed to employ. This is a method of procedure by means of which you are in a position to chisel out from the skull whatever you please, so as to open up a place for inspection, through which you can make an entry and so inform yourself accurately on the gap between the dura mater and the brain.

Should you have become practised previously in this mode of procedure on the carcase of a dead animal, then it will not prove difficult for you to carry it out well and correctly on a living animal, all around the greater part of the bones of the skull, without tearing away the dura mater along with the bone of the skull. And when you do that, then you see that this part of the brain together with the meninx sinks away to a considerable extent from the uplifting of the skull, so that you suppose that the whole depression downward of this region comes about solely by reason of the falling and sinking of the meninx upon the brain, especially when you omit to inform yourself by means of experiments carried out in this way of the variation in conditions to be observed here. For when you carry this out on newly-born animals, you then find the skull almost completely filled up. And if you carry it out on emaciated feeble old animals, then you find there a large vacant space. A little further below, I will describe to you what part of this *17*
condition is to be seen if the animal is a living one. But in the dead

animal you see clearly, in this dissection which we are now describing, all that of which I said previously, that you see it when the brain has been taken out of the skull, and you see additionally, how all the individual nerves emerge from the skull, and further, you see the posterior ventricle, and you find that the end of it resembles a reed which one trims down in order to write with it. But although some have asserted that it extends downwards as far as the third vertebra, yet nevertheless no one is in a position to demonstrate that this ventricle descends visibly as far as the second vertebra, let alone as far as the third vertebra. But in many animals it descends as far as the site of the sockets of the skull [*condylar fossae on first cervical vertebra*], in many as far only as the interval between the first vertebra and the skull, that is the place at which the persons called the 'slaughterers of oxen' insert the small knife. Only in very few animals does one find this ventricle reaching as far as the first vertebra, but it does not go beyond this vertebra and reach as far as the second vertebra. It is understood that you must cut clean away all the bones, on this side of the skull, after you have exercised yourself previously in the dissection of the skull in a dead ape. When you have cut away these bones, then pay particular attention to that spot where the two meninges alone lie over the end of the posterior ventricle, since this is one of the most useful points for you in connection with the dissection which you intend to carry out in the living animal body. Pay attention also to the middle ventricle which the cupola or vault-like structure roofs over. This ventricle is situated in the upper regions of the head. Observe further, very thoroughly and carefully, the
18 two anterior ventricles at the sides of the longitudinal suture, and search out and remember well the position of each of the two as you see it. Then, when you have also seen quite clearly how the two optic nerves mount upwards towards the two anterior ventricles, and how this takes place at each side of them, preserve this also in your recollection. For in the course of this operation which I have described for you, you will have to investigate what takes place in the body of the living animal when one compresses or severs all these single structures. Moreover you cannot help seeing by the way as you perform the operation just described that in many places veins emerge through the sutures, and that they combine and unite themselves extraordinarily

intimately with the external veins. When you have seen all this, then begin on the foramina of the skull, in order that you may teach yourself, as to which bodily structures each single one of the nerve pairs which we have enumerated betakes itself.

CHAPTER II. EXPOSURE OF THE BRAIN IN THE LIVING ANIMAL.

But I have formed the opinion that I should construct the scheme of this work and the ordination of the subjects reviewed in it according to the principle and the scheme of the work 'On the Uses of the Bodily Parts'—a work to which this one is a successor—conformably to the sequence of the matters reviewed in it. Since in the Book VIII of that work the description of the parts of the brain is set out, and in Book IX there were dealt with the processes growing out from it [the brain], so I have believed that, on this ground, here also it would be best to include in this Book that which, in the dissection of the living animal, can be seen in the brain itself, in order that the review might be restricted to the brain alone, and be comprehensive. I say, then, that for this purpose you must procure either a pig or a goat, in order to combine two requirements. In the first place, you avoid seeing the unpleasing expression of the ape when it is being vivisected. The other *19*
reason is that the animal on which the dissection takes place should cry out with a really loud voice, a thing one does not find with apes. Make this experiment, of which I wish to tell you, upon a young fresh animal and afterwards upon old and decrepit ones. For in that way you will discover a remarkable contrast and a great difference between the young and the worn-out animals. But as for what concerns the vivisection itself, it should proceed on both animals in all details after the same fashion. That is to say, every cut that you impose should travel in a straight line, just as it travels in the dead animal, and the cut should without pity or compassion penetrate into the deep tissues in order that with a single stroke you may lay free and uncovered the skull of the animal. That comes to pass by this means, that together with the skin you also cut through the membrane [*pericranium*] enveloping the skull. Now with this incision, it frequently happens that the outflow of blood is such that the operator can be disheartened from renewing and

finishing his dissection. But that need not make you timid. For the outflow of blood from these structures can easily be arrested by this means, that you stretch upwards and towards the sides the two margins of the divided skin. At the same time you can also compress with the fingers the vein from which the blood is flowing by stretching the skin, inasmuch as you stretch the skin and evert it sideways. Very useful also is an assistant who co-operates with you, and in the manner described compresses for you the places in which you are in need of it. Furthermore what is also helpful is a hook with which you grasp the part from which the outflowing blood is coming and twist it round. In such dissections also, you may not restrict yourself solely to this, but in addition you may turn over the part, roll it up, invert it, stretch it or set to work on it in other ways, as it pleases you. This is a thing which you can do with the hook as well as with the fingers. When you have now manipulated the margins of the divided skin in the manner described, then proceed to peel off the membrane around the skull [*pericranium*] from the bone, and for that employ the myrtle-leaf-like knife. Next cut away from the skull the bone lying over the crown of the head without perforating the dura mater. Then turn your attention to what you see plainly happening in the brain together with the dura mater. For you see that the whole brain, so long as the animal does not cry out, rises and sinks slightly with a movement which resembles that of the pulsation of all beating blood vessels, that is of the arteries. And if the animal cries out, then you see that the brain heaves itself up further, so that it is quite clear to observe that it rises up higher than and overtops the skull. In fact the upheaval, the ascent of the brain, appears to the eye to be augmented for two causes. The first is that whoever looks at it is looking at the cut margins of the bone, and he does not realise that the bone which has been cut away was higher than the margins. The other is that the recoil, the shifting of the brain to the position which it takes up, is easier for it, inasmuch as before you cut the bone away, the skull formed the barrier at which the brain stopped and came to a standstill.

I have now explained to you the real cause of this condition in an abbreviated fashion. However I know that it often happens that the abbreviated and condensed statement detracts something from the

confirmation of the intended meaning. And therefore it is necessary that I should still submit something in addition to that which I stated in regard to these two points. I say, then, that the whole bony skull is outwardly convex and within concave. It follows that each portion that one cuts out from it is higher and more elevated than the part which remains behind, in the same proportion as the surface of a sphere is more strongly curved than a level surface. And on this ground, it does not become perceptible to the eye that the cut edges of the bones are higher than that portion of the meninx which you have laid bare. But now, in consequence of its softness, the brain rises upwards when the animal cries out, and encounters those parts of the skull which have not yet been cut away, and presses against them. So they press upon
it and push it towards the place which can receive and accommodate it. 21
For at that moment the brain can only be received by that place where there was the part of the skull that has been taken off. And when owing to pressure from all the other parts the whole brain moves towards this place, it must necessarily appear from time to time that it both rises higher, and projects further upwards when the animal cries out, and that occurs especially with young fresh animals, corresponding to the degree to which, with them, the brain more completely fills up all the cavity of the skull than does the brain of others. In very old animals, since the brain is much too small to fill the cavity of the skull, it never rises above or overtops the bones surrounding the excised area, not even when it is enlarged and rises as the animal cries. This now should be the ending and conclusion of your work.

CHAPTER 12. EXPERIMENTS IN BRAIN SURGERY.

Next begin another task, in the following manner. Insert a hook into the dura mater and draw it upwards. Then first cut through the piece of it that has been raised, so that it may not make contact with the part of the brain lying beneath it. Next insert two hooks, one on each side of the first hook, from the ends of the margins of the incision; also with these two hooks draw upon the dura mater found above, and cut through the whole raised portion of it, without touching any of the underlying parts of the brain. If you do this well, you can also introduce your fingers upwards beneath the part of the dura mater which

you have incised, and you can split it until you have uncovered the whole of the brain lying beneath it. For the meninx as I described it is in all its parts separable from it, as I have shown, except at the sides of the sutural lines which I indicated, where the meninx becomes folded into two layers as described, and sinks downwards penetrating a considerable distance further into the parts of the brain lying beneath it [*falx cerebri and tentorium cerebelli*]. I said earlier that there in that region
22 lies the parietal bone one on either side, and that in the space at the back of the suture resembling the letter Λ of the Greek script is the whole of that portion of the brain found in those parts, which one calls the hind-brain or occipital brain [*cerebellum*]. Now you can cut away these three parts of the meninx[1] [*dura mater*] and thus expose the underlying portions of the brain. Two of these three parts lie in the region beneath the parietal bone, the third is the portion overlying the hind brain. When you have done that, then make an inspection and ascertain for yourself whether the animal is being deprived of respiration, voice, movement or sensation, or whether none of these defects is showing itself in it, either at the time when the incision was made upon it or else soon afterwards. The latter may quite well be the case, when it happens that the air is warm. But if the air is cold, then in a degree corresponding to the amount of the cold air streaming in upon the brain, each single one of these functions of the brain that we have mentioned weakens; the animal remains for a certain length of time unconscious, and then expires. Therefore it is best that you should take in hand the detachment of the dura mater from the skull in the summer time, or, if you perform it at another season, no matter which that season may be, you should heat the room in which you intend to dissect the animal, and warm the air. Should the dissection be thus performed, then after you have laid open the brain, and divested it of the dura mater, you can first of all press down upon the brain on each one of its four ventricles, and observe what derangements have afflicted the animal. I will describe to you what is always to be seen when you make this

[1] Simon interprets the three parts as the right and left cerebral hemispheres and the cerebellum. But the three parts are of the dura mater, not the brain itself. If we understand the falx cerebri and the right and left halves of the tentorium cerebelli as the three parts referred to, the text specifying the meninx as due to be removed seems more intelligible.

dissection, and also before it, where the skull has been perforated, as
soon as one presses upon the brain with the instrument which the
ancients call 'the protector of the dura mater'. Should the brain be
compressed on both the two anterior ventricles, then the degree of
stupor which overcomes the animal is slight. Should it be compressed
on the middle ventricle, then the stupor of the animal is heavier. And 23
when one presses down upon that ventricle which is found in the part
of the brain lying at the nape of the neck, then the animal falls into
a very heavy and pronounced stupor. This is what happens also when
you cut into the cerebral ventricles, except that if you cut into these
ventricles, the animal does not revert to its natural condition as it does
when you press upon them. Nevertheless it does sometimes do this if
the incision should become united. This return to the normal condition
follows more easily and more quickly, should the incision be made
upon the two anterior ventricles. But if the incision encounters the
middle ventricle, then the return to the normal comes to pass less
easily and speedily. And if the incision should have been imposed upon
the fourth, that is, the posterior ventricle, then the animal seldom
returns to its natural condition; although nevertheless if the incision
should be made into this fourth ventricle, provided that you do not
make the cut very extensive, that you proceed quickly, and that in the
compression of the wound in some way or other you employ a certain
amount of haste, the animal will revert to its normal state, since the
pressure upon the wound is then temporary only—and indeed especially
in those regions where no portion of the brain overlies this ventricle,
but where the meninx only is found. You then see how the animal
blinks with its eyes, especially when you bring some object near to the
eyes, even when you have exposed to view the posterior ventricle. Should
you go towards the animal while it is in this condition, and should you
press upon some one part of the two anterior ventricles, no matter which
part it may be, in the place where as I stated the root of the two optic
nerves lies, thereupon the animal ceases to blink with its two eyes, even
when you bring some object near to the pupils, and the whole appearance of the eye on the side on which lies the ventricle of the brain upon
which you are pressing becomes like the eyes of blind men. 24

With this matter we have now dealt sufficiently. And should any person consider that there still remains something for us to say about it, he should know that what remains over is clearly explained from the connection with the things that have been discussed, as for example that the animal, when one pierces or incises the thin meninx, sustains no derangement as a result, just as none such befalls it if the brain should be incised without the incision reaching as far as to one of its ventricles.

CHAPTER 13. EXPOSURE OF THE SPINAL CORD, AND THE EFFECTS PRODUCED BY SECTION OF THE CORD AT VARIOUS LEVELS.

What has been discussed previously is to be followed by and connected to an account of the spinal marrow. Your dissection of this should be made in the following manner. Provide yourself with a large strong knife. My advice is that this knife should be manufactured from exceptionally good steel, because I prefer that all such instruments with which you provide yourself should be of excellent steel. The animal which you vivisect should not be aged, in order that it may prove easy for you to cut through the vertebrae. For the bones of fully mature animals are, on account of their hardness, difficult to cut. So the animal should be young. Lying upon its face, it will be stretched out upon a board, the feet being secured either by means of strong straps, in the manner in which as you know I am accustomed to make them fast, using a board with holes bored in it, or by the hands of assistants. Next, carry an incision longitudinally from above downwards on both sides near the spinous processes of the vertebrae. Then with the blade of the knife cut into the flesh and scrape it to both sides. Upon the flesh laid bare, lay a sponge soaked in cold water, in order quickly to check any haemorrhage. Next, with the instrument called 'bone-breaker', cut out, at the roots of the dorsal ridge on both sides of the vertebrae, the piece of bone found there. When you do that, then occasionally a sheath [*ligamenta flava and posterior longitudinal ligament*] becomes visible, wrapped around the spinal marrow over the dura mater, which resembles this meninx in thickness, colour and strength. Yet the dura
25 mater enwrapping the spinal marrow is intimately combined and connected with the dura mater which surrounds the brain, just as the thin meninx [*pia mater*] lying upon the spinal marrow is intimately com-

bined with the thin meninx upon the brain. For the spinal marrow has two meninges which take their origin from the meninges of the brain. And wrapped around them the third structure, which serves the marrow as a preservative and a covering and a protection, surrounds both of them outwardly. The place from which this structure grows out, its site of origin, is on the skull, and its nature is that of a ligament, since it grows out from the bones, just as is the case with the outgrowth of the rest of the ligaments. Besides this, it binds together the vertebrae in front, since, folded up, it breaks in upon the spaces between them. When you have cut away the bones from behind, at the place at which, as I said, lies the root of the dorsal ridge, and you see this ligament lying exposed to view, then insert at that place which you have laid open, a broad tool of the class of the instrument which one calls a spatula, between the third outer covering, of which I said that by its nature it is a ligament, and the vertebra enclosing it. Then place the so-called bone-breaking instrument upon it [i.e. upon the spatula]. When you have done that, you then cut freely loose, from whichever vertebra you please, by a smooth, rapid, cautious incision, that portion which extends as far as the vertebral basis. By the expression 'vertebral basis' I mean that part of it which is inclined forwards, there where I said that the ligament is folded up and breaks in between the vertebrae. And here, in accordance with the sequence of the vertebrae, the nerves spring out on both sides of them, and the nerve-roots pass out through perfectly rounded foramina, the width of each single foramen corresponding to the thickness of the nerve which passes out through it. In the cervical vertebrae, this foramen is formed by two vertebrae, each one of which has a semicircular groove forming one half of the foramen. In all quadrupeds the cervical vertebrae are seven in number
just as is the case in mankind. But in the thorax, the first vertebra is *26*
somewhat more strongly curved than the one lying beneath it. That peculiarity becomes more marked towards the lumbar vertebral column until finally in the last vertebrae the whole nerve emerges solely through the foramen in the upper vertebra, which is always to be found at the root of the process at the side of each single vertebra.

When you have thus uncovered the spinal marrow, on whichever vertebra you please, then introduce a hook upwards and only super-

ficially into the ligament described, so as to pierce it easily and by itself alone without cutting into any part of the meninx lying beneath it. Make the incision as you wish, either lengthwise or crosswise or in both directions. The cutting into this ligament brings no injury to the animal, just as it does not harm it at all if you distend and cut into the dura mater in just the same manner. Now assume that you have already done what is here described, so that the spinal marrow, protected only by the pia mater, lies exposed. Now this sheath [*pia mater*] is laid upon it [*the spinal marrow*] absolutely tensely and intimately, and in it are numerous veins just as in the pia mater enveloping the brain. You see these veins in the large animals very clearly, plunging down into the substance of the spinal marrow, and sinking into the depth of it. Were you to expose this sheath round about the spinal marrow then no harm would befall the animal on that account, or even if you made a longitudinal cut into the spinal marrow itself, since all the respective nerves branch off at the places where the vertebrae meet one another at the sides, the right-sided nerve on the right side, the nerve of the opposite side on the left. Should you wish to bring the region below the incised portion [of the spinal marrow] into the paralytic state, and to arrest its movements, then carry the incision transversely, and sever the spinal marrow with a cut running completely through so that no sort of
27 union remains between its parts. This is a matter which you can accomplish without cutting through the bone, that is to say in young goats, dogs or pigs. For this purpose you must have at hand the long 'palm-leaf knife', which must be strong. After you have introduced this instrument vertically and straight from behind forwards between the vertebrae towards the spinal marrow, cut this through transversely. Do your best to contrive the insertion of this instrument at the meeting-place of two vertebrae. That you will do only if you pay particular attention to the end of the spinous process of each of the two vertebrae. For the meeting-place of the two vertebrae lies just in the middle of this place. So when you have cut this, and have brought the instrument to the site of the spinal marrow, then at this stage you must so manipulate it, that thereby you may feel about with your hand on it in the depth [of the wound] and rock it to and fro so as to leave no part of the spinal medulla undivided. After the incision, in all the nerves which

lie below the place where the transection has been made, both the two potentialities are lost, I mean the capacity of sensation and the capacity of movement, and also all the bodily parts of the animal in which they are distributed become insensitive and motionless, a result that is inevitable, clear and intelligible. If now you cut through the spinal marrow at the neck between two vertebrae, then the nerve arising and emerging at the meeting-place of the two will be severed. In the lumbar vertebral column on the contrary, when you cut through the spinal marrow alone, without making the slightest contact with what lies on both sides of it, the nerve will not be cut through. But if you lead the knife crosswise a little, outwards from the vertebra, you then cut through the nerve because this travels obliquely downwards. If you have directed the knife towards the meeting-place of the vertebrae in
the way in which I said you should do it, not in a newly-born animal *28*
but in an aged animal, then in such a case it is unavoidably necessary that some part of the vertebrae must be cut through. After the spinal medulla has been exposed, you must then make the cut somewhat above the origins of the nerves. For when you do that, the sensibility and the power of movement of the nerve which springs off below will be annulled.

Should you now, by research on some particular function, desire to inform yourself as to what happens when you cut through [at the level of] a single vertebra, it is enough for you either to make the cut with a knife, or to cut through the vertebra in the way in which I described it. But should you wish to concern yourself solely with training yourself, and to combine thereby the search for truth with its discovery, then you can perform that incision on a larger number of vertebrae, according to the degree of what the animal tolerates, and of its endurance. Accordingly commence at the meeting-place of the so-called 'greatest' bone or 'broad' bone, that is the 'cross-bone' [*sacrum*] with the last vertebra, where a massive nerve-shoot grows outwards so as to distribute itself to the lower limb. Next, go upwards to the vertebra above this, then further upwards. And on the several [nerves, one by one] you will see, as I have informed you, that the first structures which paralysis affects and which will be deprived of movement, are the ends of the legs, the second, next to the end, are the parts which

come in front, then the parts of the thigh and the hips, then those of the lumbar region. When you come to the thoracic vertebrae, then the first thing that happens is that you see that the animal's respiration and voice have been damaged. The injury, and the damage which befalls it [the animal] is slight in the case in which the cut is applied to the false ribs, and greater when the cut falls further up, and very great indeed when the cut runs yet further above these parts. But the animal sustains the most extreme degree of damage when the transection is made above the first rib. In an ape none of the bodily parts, which in
29 other animals form the two fore-limbs, sustains any damage when the spinal marrow is cut through, unless the cut reaches the first of the intercostal spaces. But if you cut the marrow [*spinal cord*] behind the first thoracic rib, that then damages the hand of the ape. And should the cut follow a line behind the second thoracic rib, then that does not damage the arm, except that the skin of the axillary cavity, and the first subdivisions of the region of the upper arm turned towards the trunk become deprived of sensibility; and you also see, similarly, that the extent of sensibility which the region indicated is going to lose is small when you make the cut behind the third rib. If you cut through the spinal medulla behind the fifth vertebra of the head [*fifth cervical vertebra*] so that you dissever the origin of the nerve next following it, then both arms are paralysed and their movement will be completely abolished. And if you cut in behind the sixth vertebra then the nervous functions persist in all the subdivisions of the upper arm, being maintained in their normal state, with the exception of a small part. But the cut which falls behind the seventh vertebra, makes the forearm devoid of sensibility and of motion.

CHAPTER 14. SUMMARY AND CONCLUSIONS, WITH OBSERVATIONS ON THE EFFECTS OF TRANSECTION OF THE CERVICAL SPINAL CORD.

To sum up briefly, then, the matter is as I described it before: the parts of the body which have become paralysed, and from which their movement has been taken away, are those of which the nerve proceeding to them has its root, its head, below the dividing incision through the spinal marrow. Hence, from the anatomy of the nerves, you can easily infer the derangements which will befall the animal as the result of the transection of the spinal marrow in all its several parts. Similarly, when you have read the book 'Of the Causes of Respiration', and the book 'On the Voice', you understand what degree of damage falls upon the respiration, and upon the voice, at the transection of each single vertebra. In both those two works we explained that breathing [stertorous expiratory breathing] comes about by means of the muscles between the ribs, and we explained that respiration is the material as well as the instrument of speech. For in inspiration, without obstruction, the animal inhales the air by means of the diaphragm alone, until the time when, should its inspiration meet with resistance, it brings into use the intercostal muscles besides the diaphragm. And when it is inhaling to the greatest possible extent it uses in addition those upper muscles which descend from the neck to the upper parts of the thorax [*Mm. scaleni*]. If now you know from their anatomy where the nerves of these muscles arise, then you also know for certain when any single one of these muscles will be paralysed.

But I should like to add more to what I have mentioned here, namely, that should the spinal marrow that lies between the skull and the first vertebra be severed, or the meninx which protects the end of the posterior ventricle of the brain be cut through, then at once the whole body of the animal becomes deprived of movement. It is just here that you will see, in the temples of the gods, the oxen receive the stab when the so-called sacrificers of oxen cut into them. But as for the incision which is made behind the first vertebra, it inflicts on the animal just the same manifestations, not because it lays open the first ventricle [*fourth* in modern terminology] but because it paralyses the feet of the animal, and arrests the whole of its respiration. And this is found also with regard to the incision which is made behind the second, third, and fourth vertebra, when in making the cut you go to work thoroughly, so that you divide the nerve which springs off at its [the fourth vertebra's] junction with the fifth vertebra. However the first [i.e. upper] segments of the neck still move themselves in the animal on which the cut has been made in such a manner. Transection of the spinal marrow behind the fifth vertebra paralyses all the remaining parts of the thorax, and arrests their movements, but the diaphragm

31 remains almost unscathed, and so also does a small portion of the upwardly ascending part of the musculature of the thorax [*Mm. scaleni*]. The transection which takes place behind the sixth vertebra damages in the same way the upwardly ascending thoracic musculature, and the diaphragm meets with less damage than that which followed in consequence of the preceding cut. But after the transection which takes place behind the seventh vertebra, and more particularly after that made behind the eighth vertebra, the whole of the mobility of the diaphragm remains unscathed, and indeed in most instances still more so than is the case after the cut behind the sixth vertebra. Again the mobility of the upwardly ascending musculature, and the mobility of the whole neck will remain quite free from damage, but the intercostal muscles do not at the same time remain uninjured thereby. For the mobility of this musculature is destroyed and becomes totally lost when one imposes the cut upon any one of the vertebrae of the neck, and the whole hind-brain is cut off from the first thoracic vertebra. Amongst the proofs of that is the fact that the activity of the intercostal muscles becomes totally lost when one carries through the spinal medulla behind the first thoracic vertebra a cut which completely divides it, whereas a slight proportion of this activity stays retained when the cut takes place behind the second vertebra. In connection with that there is the fully analogous point that those intercostal muscles which lie higher up than the situation of the incision preserve their activity, whereas the activity of the muscles lying below the site of the incision will be abolished.

End of the Ninth Book of the work of Galen on Anatomical Dissection. Praise be to God.

BOOK X

THE FACE, MOUTH AND PHARYNX

In the name of God the compassionate, the merciful. The Tenth Book of Galen's work on Anatomy. In this Book, the eyes, tongue, lips and the movements of deglutition will be surveyed.

CHAPTER I. INTRODUCTION. DISSECTION OF THE ORBIT AND ITS CONTENTS.

In the immediately preceding book we have described the particular 32
parts of the brain and of the spinal cord, and the damage which can befall both. This should suffice in order to make clear the method which, when followed in dissection, reveals best to visual inspection those parts and the injuries which they suffer. As for these latter, they are to be seen by vivisection, while in other respects the descriptions apply in part to dead animals alone.

In this Book I now describe the method of dissecting the structures of the face, and of the whole of the head, including the symptomatic changes which are to be observed in each one of them. I make my start with those parts where symptomatic changes follow when one divides them, bruises them, ligatures them with a cord, presses them with the fingers or twists them or stretches them unduly far. For when they are exposed to such conditions, the [normal] activity of such organs will be either completely or partially suppressed.

Let us assume now that the brain has been exposed, in that the enveloping bones have been removed, as we have previously explained.

Next proceed with the work, and first detach the bone called zygomatic.[1] Then remove from the skull the M. temporalis until you approach the [*optic*] nerve where it enters the skull. If you do not
perceive the nerve when you have cut away the uppermost fibres of 33

[1] If, as is possible, this description applies to the pig or dog, the absence of a postorbital wall must be recalled, as the orbital contents come more closely into contact with the M. temporalis than in Man, or apes.

the M. temporalis, then pass on to the skull, and work back along the path pursued by each of the two nerves as they leave the optic chiasma each going towards its own side. Work along that line, without deviating to either side, until you have reached the eye itself.

Now precisely in the place where you see the nerve approaching the skull, divide the bone with the tool called the osteoclast (and this must itself be strong), making an incision passing from above downwards, until you encounter the nerve. The foramen which this nerve traverses leads and brings you to the orbital cavity, and in the interior of the bottom of that space you find the cranial wall pierced by a circular foramen [*optic*].

Should you wish to perform this operation, it is best to have at hand the skull of an adult ape which has been macerated so that no remnant of tendons, fasciae, vessels or ligaments remains on it, and that the bony substance alone remains clean and bare after all the organic tissues have decayed and wasted away from it. In my possession you have seen many skulls in this condition, some of them intact, others having had the upper parts of the cranium removed in the same manner as from the skulls used here in connection with the anatomy of the brain. Should you thus examine a mature macerated skull as it lies before you, this will ensure for you guidance to the orbital position of the optic nerve as far as the spot at which it emerges from the optic foramen.

The best procedure is that you should make a thorough examination of an eye removed from the skull. For in this you will view the optic nerve as though it constituted a root for the whole organ. Regarding the eyeball thus, you will form the opinion that those anatomists who compare the whole eye with its nerve to the seed-capsule of the poppy have used an apt comparison.

Now when you have cut free the bone surrounding the nerve, and
34 especially its upper parts, notice how closely it is connected throughout that sunken space by ligaments to the muscles surrounding the eye, as far as the bases of the eyelids. Here there is actually no muscle origin, but a membranous layer which emerges from the bases of the eyelids and ensheathes the whole of the muscles, enveloping them from without and applying itself firmly to them.

This is in fact the membrane which clothes the bones of the skull [*pericranium*] inasmuch as it and the membranous fascia are brought, in the substance of the eyelids, into continuity of the closest and most intimate kind.

Leave this, however, until you have time to observe it later. At the present time, detach the bone from the muscles and try to find, close to that foramen which we have mentioned, another [*superior orbital fissure*] from which emerges a 'hard' nerve smaller than the preceding one. It goes to the muscles already indicated as surrounding the orbital globe. Thus there betake themselves to the region of the eye [*orbital cavity*], passing through these two 'foramina', of which the one lies alongside the other, two nerves which are much more massive than accords with the relative dimensions of the orbital cavity. Next observe the connection of this nerve, how it is joined to the eye, so as to make out later in another larger eye, removed from the carcase of an animal, how its branches are distributed. I have already remarked, and may here recall it to your memory, that in the six classes of animals, the form of some organs is [constantly] one and the same, while the form of others varies in one particular class from that in others. And this contrast is either great or small. But the eye belongs to those organs whose form is the same. Since, however, we have often been compelled to excise the cranial bones of the human skull in the manner which we have described, so here I recommend you on similar grounds to train yourselves on the bodies of apes. But as regards the study of the strength of the optic nerve, all the various animals are equal in suitability and fitness.

When you have divided the frontal bone so as to reach the deep cavity beneath it, you will be met by the two nerves that go to the eye. If you divide the larger of the two, then the visual sense of the animal 35
will be impaired. And if you divide the lesser of the two, you will see the eye immediately remain motionless. The defect of the eye-movement is a sign you can very easily detect and recognise. But that the animal can no longer see when in such a condition of injury as you have inflicted on it is something which you can only appraise by deduction from the fact that you find that it does not blink with its eye at anything which you bring near it, pretending to be about to stab home with it. In the dissection of the eye in the living animal there are things which

require further operations in addition to the foregoing. In the recently dead animal, on the contrary, you can observe the ophthalmic artery and vein, each traversing one of the two apertures. The artery distributes its blood to the muscles acting upon the eye. As for the vein, in addition to 'branches' to the muscles, there are others to the body which surrounds the humour compared to molten glass [*corpus vitreum*]. This is a body whose name is derived from its appearance. Consequently it is called the net-like [*retina*, from *rete*]. You will study it later on when you are in the course of dissecting the globe of the eye itself separately for its intrinsic structures.

So long as the eye remains attached in continuity with the skull you notice how the artery and the vein together with the nerve go down into the eyeball, and you will perceive numerous vessels which go to the eyelids and to the fascial membrane that covers the eye externally and is connected to it. They come from the structures that surround the eye and from its interior angles. This sheath, enclosing the whole of the musculature of the eye and blending with it, comes to the eyeball from the surrounding bones. And on this account some have termed the membrane periosteum, just as others name it pericranium, while others again content themselves with naming them in Greek 'epipephukōs',
36 which indicates enveloping or adhering. The idea whence these several names derive is obvious.

Now I have described to you the relationship of the eye to the surrounding structures, and you must train yourself in their recognition when the eye retains its place in the body. Should we however have extracted the eyes, you must acquire knowledge as regards their nature by dissecting out their component parts. First of all then, you will encounter the delicate fascial sheath which envelops the musculature and blends with the muscles. This [sheath] you follow until you see how it reaches the eyeball and attaches itself there. The place where it meets and blends with the eyeball is the place in which the white coat meets the large circular margin which it surrounds externally. I called it the large circular margin because another smaller circular margin is found within it, and this is the circle through which anyone inspecting the eye perceives an image. It is called 'the pupil'. The area of which the larger circle is the anterior margin is white in all eyes, though its

whiteness is variable, that is, more or less intense. The large circle, however, is never white in any eye, but it is coloured in many different shades in different men and beasts. For in some this whole part of the eye is black, in many it is blue or grey, and in others again it is some shade a little removed from black. Many people are in the habit of calling eyes of this colour 'goats' eyes'. Furthermore, the marginal line separating the cornea from the surrounding white coat is called by anatomists the rainbow or corona. It is also called a circle, though it is *37*
not a circle but a line which encloses a circle. But it does not matter if you call it a circle as they do. Now there extends to this line, whether you want to call it a circle or a line surrounding a circular area, the fascial sheath which envelopes the musculature of the eye, blending with it. This sheath stops here and does not pass beyond. It attaches itself at the corona to the subjacent tunic. Many [anatomists] describe this fascia not as such, but as a tunic, just as they designate the other tunics which belong to the eye. In reference to names, however, I wish here to impress upon you what I continually advise, and that is to attach no great importance to them. But since of necessity the significance of objects can only be understood from their names, in your use of them you should follow the majority of the physicians. Now all those who have written on anatomy have applied the term 'tunic' to all the protective sheaths of the moist bodies in the interior of the eyeball. The tunic which covers from the front the whole of the superficial aspect of that circular area mentioned resembles horn. You must, therefore, in that detail follow the common usage of anatomists. So long as this tunic remains stretched around the interior tunic which surrounds the moist tissue resembling molten glass and the moist tissue that resembles hail-stones, you cannot observe correctly what its colour may be. But when it is removed then one sees that it is white. You should however postpone dealing with that till a little later when you have dissected all the muscles surrounding the eyeball. The musculature is slight, and at the back of the eyeball it forms a single muscle which covers and surrounds the optic nerve. And the musculature itself consists either of three united muscles, or of one muscle with three layers. Again, sometimes it is held that there are not three layers but only two.
When you have disengaged this muscle from around the nerves, then *38*

turn to the remaining muscles, and remove the fat which is lodged between them and clear it completely away. In the event of a delicate fascial sheet being left, enveloping part of these muscles, then clear this away also, so that the direct course of the fibrillar bundles of each muscle may be brought to light [view]. For these are the fibres which will guide you in the correct separation and distinction of the various [individual] muscles from one another. You must stretch each muscle between its two 'heads', by which I mean the head attached to the eyeball where it ends by becoming tendinous, and that other head which lies over against the former and which gives the place of origin of each individual muscle. It is this which you detached from its first origin when you dissected out the eye from the recess in the skull surrounding the eye, while it was still in its natural situation. And when you have found this place to which you can pull and stretch the muscle-mass, you will be confronted clearly enough by the need for deciding about the segregation of each muscle, how you may best free it from its connected tissues. You will observe in each individual muscle the [exact] site of its attachment after it has changed its character and become tendinous. And just as at this stage you find fat amidst the muscles, so also you discover between them some glandular tissue, in the interstices of which is a slightly glutinous fluid resembling albumen. You will further find there a structure of elongated form, hollow and resembling the structure of a vein from which the blood has been drained, and taking origin from each of these two glandular masses. For this glandular tissue, the lachrymal glands, consists in most instances of two glandular masses or glands. So it is with the duct that resembles a vein, whose origin from the glandular mass is double. And these two vessels discharge their fluid contents into the [cavity in the] fascial tissue which covers and blends with the eye-muscles through two outlets, whose lumen yields on inspection the evidence that its size is such that a hog's
39 bristle can [just] be introduced into each. No anatomists have mentioned these two glandular masses or glands, or the ducts which emerge from them, and neither have they recorded the 'puncta' which are situated in the two eyelids.

As you now dissect these muscles and separate them from each other in the manner I have described to you, you find that each of them ends

as a slender tendon, which is however stouter than the fascial tissue, and is inserted close to the corona [*corneo-sclerotic junction*] at which I have said that the fascial layer which lines the bones [*periosteum and conjunctiva*] terminates, although that fascia is securely joined to the corona, whereas the terminations of each of these tendons merely approaches it. Of the tendons one reaches the eye from the upper regions [of the orbit], and the other lies opposite the former. One of these two muscles, that is the larger, draws the eye upwards, the other draws it downwards. There are here another two muscles, of which each is attached in corresponding fashion to one of the two angles of the eye. Of the last two, one draws the eyeball towards the lateral [temporal] side, the other draws it medialwards towards the nose. Now these four muscles produce rectilinear movements of the eyeball. Further there are in the eyes two other muscles [*superior and inferior oblique muscles*] which confer on the eyeball obliquely inclined movements, one might say [movements] on arcs of a circle. That is because these muscles encircle the eyeball obliquely, and do not attach themselves directly to it, like the other four muscles, and each of the two [*oblique muscles*] exercises traction towards its head and origin and so it rotates the eyeball. One of them rotates the eyeball upwards, the other rotates it
downwards. They are connected on either side [above or below] of 40
the lesser palpebral angle, above the insertions of the four muscles previously mentioned. When I say 'above' I mean in relation to the corona [*corneo-sclerotic junction*] since those [the first four] come close to the corona, while these [the other two] form insertions somewhat remote from the former. When you have cut away these six muscles, then you will see that the eyeball really does resemble the seed-capsule of the poppy in constitution. But before you have cut loose the muscles notice the smaller nerve that comes to the eye from the brain, and how it breaks up into branches together with an accompanying vein and an artery.

CHAPTER 2. THE EYEBALL: (1) SCLERA AND CORNEA

Now proceed to investigate carefully and intensively, the tunic surrounding the whole of the eye, so as to determine its substance. This tunic is itself laminated, and moreover its components are not all alike.

Consequently some [observers] have regarded it as a single tunic, while others say there are two layers. The tunic is itself perforated within, at the place where the optic nerve comes to resemble a sort of root of the whole eye. Here the optic nerve passes through the aperture in the tunic and so makes its entry within it. This nerve is bound up with the enveloping sheath, and connected by a definite bond and union which are difficult to unravel. This tunic is hard and gristly, so that some anatomists call it the cartilaginous covering, others again [call it] the tunica albuginea. Thus constituted it extends as far [forwards] as the corona [*corneo-sclerotic junction*]. From the corona onwards its front part becomes softer, and now, as I have explained, it becomes called the corneous tunic [*cornea*]. I remarked already, in connection with other details, that the whole of the interior portion of the corona is coloured grey or blue, brown or black. An observer looking at the cornea in a living animal might perhaps conclude that its composition is identically the same in every detail up to its superficial surface. But the matter is not so. On the contrary, when you examine horn, which one can split
41 into fine layers, or again crystals and again alabaster which one sets in windows, you will notice as each slice is removed the colour of that which lay behind it. So in the eye you will look from this layer to the colour of the layer which lies beneath it. When you free this and detach it from the subjacent structures, you will see that it is white [transparent] after the fashion of horn which one can split up into delicate laminae neither coarse nor thick. For this reason therefore this layer is called the cornea [horny]. In regard to its tenuity, the cornea does not resemble the fascia which envelops the muscles, and of which I remarked that it originates in the periosteal membrane ensheathing the bones. Rather it can be divided into four laminae, each as thick as that fascia. You must first train yourself so that on the first occasion on which you apply the scalpel you incise the dense mass of the periosteal membrane. And further, the incision should run in a straight line, passing the centre of the cornea and reaching to its outer margin. Next, draw the two margins of the incision apart with two sharp hooks. Then undercut and separate with the scalpel, and divide off that portion by itself. That manipulation should be carried out with a scalpel designed specially for such a purpose, sharp-edged and thin. The best

model is that resembling a myrtle-leaf. The easiest method and procedure for peeling-off this superficial layer of the corneal substance is to make a second incision passing across the centre of the cornea, at right angles to the first, so that the whole area is subdivided into four symmetrical segments. And now, when you pull each one of these four parts from its apex at the centre of the cornea, which is the point common to each of the four, you will then find it easy to separate them completely. And just as you incise this layer, which is a sort of covering for the cornea, and set it apart by itself, similarly you will be able to *42*
set free a second and then a third layer (by removing in each layer which you strip off all its parts) right up to the corneo-sclerotic junction.

But as for the last remaining stratum of the cornea, it ruptures immediately if you apply the scalpel in the same way as before and endeavour to separate it in its entirety with a clean-cut margin. And when it is ruptured there flows out from [behind] it a liquid, which in the eyes of living animals resembles the fluid contained in eggs, which fluid we employ in the treatment of painful eyes. In dead animals that fluid is colourless.

When it has escaped, you will now see that the cornea is superimposed upon another layer, of which the colour is the same as that of a 'front view' of the eye, before you dissect the eye. When you draw [forwards] this fourth layer of the cornea, and separate it from the layer beneath it, then you find that these four layers are each distinct from the other in all parts of the cornea, and you find that they adhere firmly to the corneo-sclerotic junction. We call these four subdivisions of the cornea leaves, since our forerunners held it as appropriate so to name them in view of their similarity to slices of horn. And again they [our forerunners] named the second subjacent layer the grape-layer [*uvea*]. This [latter layer] resembles grape-pips on account of its smooth outer aspect, and its corrugated deep surface. Some [other] authorities do not give it this name, but they speak of it as 'the perforated layer' since it has a central aperture. This aperture is circular in many animals as in Man but in some animals it is slit-like, as [for example] in cattle. It is within this aperture that you can see the ice-like humour of the lens. This name has been given to it because its appearance resembles that of ice. But if you handle it, you perceive that it is much less hard *43*

than ice. Further, you can see that the grape-like layer is attached to and blended with the cornea only at the corneo-sclerotic junction. But as for all the other parts of the grape-like layer these are free from it [*the cornea*] as we have described. To both, again, the lens attaches itself, blending with them at the corneo-sclerotic junction. Now just as the outlying layer, composed as it is of several dissimilar parts, is nevertheless firm and consolidated throughout, so some [anatomists] have reckoned as a single independent layer that second layer which the outer one envelops. Starting from the latter assumption, some authors conclude that the layers which surround the lens of the eye are four in number, while others say they number two only. We have already in another place set out in order these and similar differences of opinion. That portion of the sheath which is to the front, that is to say that which is found immediately below [? behind] the cornea, is completely separated from the corneal layer. But that portion which extends behind the corneo-sclerotic junction as far as the [*optic*] nerve is connected with it [*the sclera*] by means of fibrils and slender threads, which are somewhat darker in colour than the whole of this layer. These threads and fine fibrils I have always been able to observe in the eyes of the ox, since this animal has dark eyes. Their attachment to the corneo-sclerotic junction is strong, and difficult to sever. In this region the continuity of the layers is not effected by means of a fibrous tissue nor by slender threads separated from one another. But nevertheless, by using a sharp scalpel you can separate these two layers here, conserving the second and protecting it from damage. That you can achieve by working from both sides, and you can carry the work through by a twofold procedure, at one time making your approach from the side of the cornea, and at another time from the side of the sclerotic coat, that tough cartilaginous structure extending behind the corneo-sclerotic junction as far as the attachment of the optic nerve to the
44 eyeball. But you will not be able to divide that structure [*sclera*] into several laminae as you were able to do with the anterior part, that is, the cornea, and you must confine yourself to making an incision from the point of entry of the nerve to the corneo-sclerotic junction. And lest in incising the first layer you divide the second at the same time, you should make your incision slightly oblique and not vertically

towards the deeper parts. For should the incision pass perpendicularly into the deeper parts, then the scalpel tends to penetrate downwards at one stroke the thickness of the outermost structures, and, simultaneously with the division of the first layer, to cut not merely the second, but also the third layer, that is, the retina. If the incision is made to slope, and is inclined more obliquely, that course is more prudent and better calculated to give a safe result.

So now, as one separates the first layer, entire, from the second, that is the dark layer, it will become apparent that the second layer is of a composite nature. There is a single aperture in its anterior portion, through which one who looks into the eye sees his image in the crystal lens, as though he was looking into a mirror. Should you have reached this stage of the dissection, you will then be able to separate the second layer in turn from that layer situated beneath it. After you have raised this portion from around the pupil, then cut away all that portion of it which extends as far as the corneo-sclerotic junction. For in this region it is not blended with that which lies subjacent to it, any more than it attaches itself in its outer portions, namely where it encounters the cornea. When you have freed, from in front, this second layer as far as the corneo-sclerotic junction, you will see clearly its connection in that junction itself.

At that stage, when you recall the [presence of the] fluid which flowed out after the removal of the deepest layer of the cornea, you
can search for the place in which it was accumulated, and you will see *45*
that this was in the space between the cornea and the iris, and also in the space between the iris and the crystalline lens. For you see the iris [the 'second sheath'] on its anterior aspect, up to the corneo-sclerotic junction, [equally] free from the crystalline lens and from the cornea. And indeed in this region, it [*the iris*] is naturally free and unattached, without any instrumental interference on your part. But those of its component parts which reach from the corneo-sclerotic junction and to the junction of the optic nerve are connected with the first layer [*sclerotic*] by means of delicate and independently separable fibrils.

You must remember that in dissecting an eye that is connected to the bone structure, when you trace the blood vessels connected to the first layer, you should try to free them properly, without any portion

being cut away, even when vessels running in the first layer pass from here out into the second layer [*chorioid*]. And should you not achieve this aim the first time, repeat the process a second or a third time, in the hope that you will eventually succeed. Seek to perform that dissection on an animal recently killed, from which all the blood has not been drained off. Should it so happen that a horse, free from disease, collapses because of much racing (and this occurs quite frequently), try to free these blood vessels in such a specimen. Should however no blood remain in them, they will be invisible, after the fashion of these
46 vessels in this animal. But in inflammation of the eye, they often become clearly and visibly recognisable. Now if you are one of those who like to enquire into such matters with the intention of observing for themselves the natural processes, then you yourself should at some time choke an animal to death, either by using a noose or by immersing it in water, and you will then gain reliable information about those small veins, no matter which part of the animal's body you choose to examine. Should it happen that the death of the animal has been caused by suffocation, then the small veins are fully engorged throughout the whole of the head. All those veins which enter into relation with the eyeball are larger in their proximal parts, finer in the region of the actual eyeball, and they arise and travel from the veins which are in the brain. You must employ this very same method of investigating the eye in order to grasp the position of the vein that comes to the eye with the nerve. For this is the only one of the nerves to have a perceptible channel and through passage. It is compounded of three parts, as are the other nerves. Of these, the first is its actual substance, which is connected to the brain. The second is the thin membrane which is wrapped around it, and the third, the exterior portion which comes after this, is the hard membrane. For both the membranes that envelop the brain spring off with the nerves. The dura mater does so obviously enough, but the emergence of the pia mater is not obvious, so much so that frequently it cannot be seen. If you are able to free both of these together from the substance of the nerve, you will see that the thick, hard membrane is connected to the first tunic, and the thin membrane which underlies it is connected to the second tunic. What lies in the
47 interior of this, that is, the substance of the nerve itself, released from its

constriction, widens out and becomes like a layer spread within the second tunic. You can most often arrive at a knowledge of these points by dissecting the animal immediately after its death. If you do that, you must remove this layer, which is spread within the second tunic, beginning from the nerve junction. For you see that the nerve has broadened out to the extent that it has become a single compact body travelling transversely, whose limit is slender in the extreme.

CHAPTER 3. THE EYEBALL: (2) RETINA, LENS, VITREOUS HUMOUR.

This structure [*retina*], with the 'tunic' enveloping it (of which I said that its interior is of a dark brown colour), is connected to the corneo-sclerotic junction, for it serves as a ligamentous band for every tunic of the eyeball. That is, the two components of the first 'tunic' [*cornea and sclerotic*] interlock here and become a single 'tunic', and so it is with regard to the components of the second 'tunic', and of the third, which is called the net-like one [*retina*]. For the nerve which spreads itself out becomes in shape like a net. The fascia, also, which surrounds the muscles from without, inserts itself similarly in this place. The crystalline lens for its part, too, is attached to and united at the corneo-sclerotic junction with the adjacent structures. Furthermore, there emerge from the second 'tunic' [*chorioid*] fibres resembling the delicate capillary hairs of the eyelids called eyelashes, and these spread to the humour which is covered by the net-like 'tunic' [*retina*], blend intimately with it and join it to the enveloping parts. On account of its tint and the consistence of its structure, this humour is called the 'vitreous', because the consistence of its structure resembles molten glass and its tint is the same as that of clear glass. As regards the crystalline lens, however, this is an even clearer white in colour than the vitreous humour, to the same degree that ice is whiter than glass. The form of this humour [*vitreous*]
is spherical, with the exception of its anterior part which encloses half *48*
of the vitreous humour. This latter, also, corresponds in form to a sphere which is however slightly flattened transversely. And consequently many anatomists have called it lentiform, wishing thus to compare its form to a lentil-seed. And since it is so formed, it is understandable that whereas one circular 'section' passing through its centre is found to

correspond to its maximum circumference, yet there are not infinite numbers of such circular 'sections' as are distinctive of a perfect sphere.

By means of its maximum circumference, the lens enters into relation with the corona [*corneo-sclerotic junction*]. At this margin a delicate sheath which envelops the lens externally comes into being [*anterior layer of lens capsule*]. Some physicians count this sheath as one of the 'tunics' of the eye, and that is because it surrounds and clothes the lens. By reason of the delicacy of this tunic some have termed it 'arachnoid' others 'froth-bubble-like', namely, because the bubbles which arise in froth expand as a delicate substance over the steamlike gas contained within them. It is most correct to say that the substance which has this structure spreads itself only around those regions in the lens with which the vitreous [humour] is in direct relation, and to describe as a delicate sheath that which lies at the gap in the iridic tunic. And it is in this that we observe our image, just as when we see it in a mirror, when we look into the eye of any person who is close to us.

Similarly, with regard to the vitreous humour, the thickness of the layer which forms its outer covering does not resemble that of its more
49 deeply placed parts. That is, all its outer covering can be seen to be more coherent and compact than what is within it. For this reason you might well believe of this covering that it is nothing more than a sort of condensation of its intrinsic substance and is not [derived] from another source of a generically different nature, after the fashion of the sheath which overlies the crystalline lens on its anterior surface at the aperture in the uveal 'tunic', where you see the image of the pupil.

In this place the two structures are clearly distinct from each other, since the one which encloses the lens is merely a thing of the class of fascial sheaths, [whereas] the humour itself resembles moist cheese. As regards the substance of the vitreous body, its consistence resembles that of moister and softer cheese. It is as if it had only half solidified. That [sheath] clothing the crystalline lens on its hinder aspect is on the contrary comparable to what the Greeks call 'epipēxis', which means coagulated. We have often seen it [*posterior lens capsule*] thicker than that which envelops the vitreous humour, to a degree comparable to that in which it is thinner than the structure enclosing the crystalline lens at the pupil. And often also we have found it resembling the dis-

tended membranous wall of a froth bubble. Consequently one is using
the correct expression in calling this a cystic [*vesicular*] 'tunic', and that
[other] which lies in front an arachnoid sheath. For indeed that
which forms the surrounding wall of the bubble is far thinner than the
spider's web. Anyone who wants to apply terminology with exhaustive
care must know that the cuticle of a bubble is not one of the stable and
complete substances, but is rather something of the nature of water
itself, distended so as to surround steam-like vapour. Perhaps if one
draws a more accurate comparison one may say that the external 50
surface of the vitreous humour is of this description. As for my remarks
about the superficial tissue drawn around the posterior aspect of the
lens, the affair here is as I have said. This [tissue] does not enclose it
completely, and it does not possess the smoothness which, as we have
indicated, is found in the arachnoidal 'tunic' [*anterior capsule*] at the
pupil, and in the surface layer of the vitreous [humour] on either of its
two surfaces, that with which it is related to the lens, or that with which
it encounters the vitreous [humour]. 51

Similarly you find also that the arachnoid tunic is completely smooth in front but rough behind where it is applied to the lens. Now to investigate and research into this structure, as to whether it should be thought of as being one of the fascial sheaths or a coagulum or the gelatinous surface of a fluid, is to investigate and enquire into the essence of the thing. For the fascial tissue is formed of a solid substance, and consequently you can stretch it on all sides to a moderate degree without perforating it. But the coagulum which forms on curdling fluids does not submit to stretching in any degree. And in regard to gelatinous surfaces, these undergo no transformation, from the group of substances they clothe, to a group of another substance. But since the body lying near the pupil is in the state which I described as applying to its substance, you know clearly what kind of a condition that is. As to what relates to the difference between it and the other tissues which still encompass the exterior parts of the 'humours', the investigation and enquiry must now be concentrated on nomenclature and its significance, not on the object itself. For we enquire whether we should call this thing a sheath or a 'tunic' or an expansion as some [anatomists] have done. Should you believe that we should give some

sort of exposition of the sense of this nomenclature, accordingly we say of the 'hymēn' ['fascial sheath'] that it denotes a single substance, one of the primitive corporeal elements of which the components are like one
52 another. In this it resembles such nouns as stone, wood, bone or nerve. But as regards the designation 'tunic', notwithstanding that it denotes clothing and investment, the physicians have diverted its meaning, and transferred it to those bodies which serve this purpose and perform this useful task. The name itself, then, as given, is applied not to a substance but to a relation of its surroundings to that which is surrounded. And since such is the case, then this name, I mean 'tunic', means nothing more than clothing, enveloping and ensheathing. Then you will find that it is correct to describe as 'tunics' of the optical 'humours', all that which surrounds the eye-humours externally, even when these are things differing from and contrasted with each other in respect of their substances. The [capsular] sheath of the lens near the pupil is called a 'tunic', and the nerve that has spread out over the vitreous humour is called its tunic. I remarked previously that this body [structure] is called the net-like 'tunic' [retina]. And so it is also with regard to other 'tunics' which have their places outside this last [retina], I mean the first and the second, of both of which I explained clearly in my work 'On the Variations between the Anatomists', that it is permissible to reckon these 'tunics' as two or as four, as one likes. In that work I exposed and distinguished which points of dispute between the anatomists were concerned with the actual knowledge of anatomical parts. For it may be said of one of those [involved] in that dispute, that he understands the nature of the thing, and of a second that he too understands it, while the [real] dispute between them is concerned only with nomenclature and the teaching system. We have given a sufficient account of all such points in that book. But here, however, I only report on the things that come to light in anatomical dissections, and I include
53 in that the methods of dissection. So I will explain clearly what those parts are which, as the result of faulty dissection, are either completely unknown, or whose real and essential state is not known, or the extent of whose overall dimensions has not been discovered. There are other anatomical parts to be dealt with, of whose openings, structure, attachments, connections, and, in fine, of whose local relations to their

related structures men are in ignorance. An instance of that is what we have seen in this modern age, when a physician, influenced by his method of dissecting the eye, was led to state to those concerned with the study of anatomy who attended his lectures that the uveal 'tunic' is imperforate. Meanwhile another tried to show that the heart has three chambers, and yet another demonstrated that the foetus lies outside the uterus. I have already described before how that lecturer who declared that the chambers of the heart are three in number deceived and misled those who attended his dissection. And so again, when we come later to speak of the dissection of the reproductive organs, we shall prove how that other [teacher] misled the spectators of his dissection when he tried to show that the foetus lies outside the uterus. Here, however, it is time to mention how it is that many have declared that there is no aperture in any one of the optical 'tunics'. I say that if you remove the first and the second tunics, starting at the back, and then, after the second tunic, you denude the net-like tunic [*retina*], next to this removing first the corpus vitreum, and then the [crystalline] lens without tearing the arachnoid layer [of the lens capsule], you will see no special [peculiar] opening in the eye when you look at it from behind, since the perforated [defective] part of the iridic tunic [*uvea*] is screened and veiled at the back by the arachnoid 'tunic', and at the front by the corneous 'tunic' [*cornea*]. Whoever 54
treads this pathway of illusion, should he in the course of his professional work meet with an ignoramus who has not before seen an eye being dissected, can in fact deceive and mislead him. Should he, however, in the same way encounter a person who has seen the eye dissected, he cannot in the least degree deceive him.

CHAPTER 4. DESCRIPTIVE AND APPLIED ANATOMY OF THE EYELIDS.

I have now thus far almost completed for you the description of the several parts of the eye. And it is here, in this place, that I have to commence with an account of the eyelids, together with those parts externally attached or closely associated with them. Their investigation can only be sound and exhaustive if you have previously cut loose the two eyebrow-bones [*supra-orbital parts of frontal bone*]. But before you

cut away these bony parts, you must observe carefully the continuity of the pericranial membrane with the eyelids. Therefore I begin with their consideration from above downwards from the commencement of the forehead, where that part of the head [*scalp*] ends at which hairs are found. You must set about this work in the ways I am about to describe. Make an incision which is parallel to the line which marks the margin of the hairy head [*scalp*]. Take care to make your incision in such a way as not to divide the pericranial membrane. To achieve this end, it is best that at first you make an incision with a light pressure, then [next] with two hooks draw apart the two margins of the skin which you have incised, and afterwards cut through the whole of the remainder of the skin down to the pericranial membrane. Between this sheath and the skin there is now a substance resembling flesh, and this substance extends over the whole frontal area. It contains fibres which are directed in the long axis of the body, from above downwards, from the place where the hairs end, as far as the brows. And the substance of
55 these fibres resembles that of the fibres which are found in muscles, and their function is the same. That is, when they contract upwards towards their root and their origin, they draw with them the skin connected to them, that is all the skin of the forehead as far as the brows. With this skin there is continuous the skin which overlies the eyelids, which are also moved at will by an animal. Accordingly you [can] see quite clearly and plainly that, at times, the skin of the forehead, from the hair margin to the eyebrows, can be drawn upwards without any simultaneous movement of the eyelids. Again, the eyelids alone of animals are often moved at will while the skin of the forehead remains motionless. That is because every single cutaneous part of the frontal skin and the palpebral skin possesses a point of departure for a movement peculiar to itself. Furthermore, in a dissection which you carry out in a living animal you can cut through the whole [thickness] of the skin of the forehead, making an incision carried transversely, and dividing the skin as well as the subjacent tissue of muscular nature. When you do that, the skin connected to the forehead curls downwards. And the animal which has been thus vivisected is subsequently unable to raise this skin up again. The same result often occurs as a sequel to wounds which have affected this region, should they have reached the mem-

brane investing the skull and cut it in that way. That is, afterwards, when they [the wounds] have healed, the sufferers of such injuries are unable to raise the eyebrows. Furthermore one sees in this injury that the eyebrow on the side which met with the injury is stouter than the other, because the skin contracts on it and shrinks, with all such muscular tissue as underlies it, in conformity with the characteristic of all musculature, that is, that when it [a muscle] has been divided transversely, it contracts towards its ends, so that each one of the parts separated by the incision draws away from the other, [being] separated by an interval of considerable degree. *56*

Now this muscle [*M. frontalis*] is wide and thin, and it lies under the whole of the frontal skin, to which it is most intimately bound and united. In the dead animal you must incise it with the whole of the overlying skin, without cutting into the subjacent periosteum, in order that you may clearly recognise the connection of the latter with the eyelids. In some animals we have already seen that this bone-investing membrane [*periosteum*] goes so far that it reaches to the convex cartilage-like body [*tarsal plate*] which is peculiar to the eyelid, and there, with the exception of a minute portion, it is all strongly and solidly attached, although a slight part of it, namely that which lies superficially, comes to resemble a fine spider's web, and passes onwards over the 'cartilaginous' component of the eyelid. And as you observe the main part of this [periosteal] sheath blended with the 'cartilaginous' part of the eyelid, so also you will see clearly how a second sheath, similar to the foregoing, grows out from the lower surface of that sheath after its first coalescence, and that from this second sheath there springs the other portion of the eyelid. To this sheath is immediately connected and united the free superficial part of the periosteum, that is to say, what binds together the pericranial membrane with the eyelid. It is from this fascial sheath that the eyelid derives and, for its part, it derives from the common stock which is shared between it and the process arising from the frontal bone, since that layer is reflected on itself. That is to say, this fascial sheath when it comes to the margin of the lids—when I say margin of the lids, I mean the place in which it ceases—reflects itself there also and, since it is compounded layer upon layer and blended on its inner surface to form an extremely compact

unit, from it originates the peculiar substance of the eyelid. Here you
57 must use a sharp knife, with which the complete skin of the eyelids can be dissected off as far as its end from which the eyelashes spring. As by 'lashes' I mean the hairs on the lids, so also by the expression 'margin of the lids', I understand their ends [free margins] on which the lashes grow. In the lids these hairs are embedded in a substance whose nature is more solid than that of skin. Anatomists call it the 'chondroid' substance, and it overtops the margin of the lid. Many [anatomists] speak of it unequivocally as cartilage.

When now this manifold 'tunic', of which, in conjunction with the skin, the eyelid consists, has ascended from the margin of the lid upwards and made connection with the end of the muscle [*M. levator palpebrae superioris*] which draws the whole lid upwards, it is no longer folded on itself, but its two parts, I mean its two laminae, diverge and separate the one from the other. And the lower of the two laminae goes to the corneo-sclerotic junction, [while] the upper takes the direction towards the brow-ridges. The place in which the [first] one of the two [fascial] layers diverges from the other you must depict to yourself as being a sort of root or head for the peculiar substance of the eyelid. And it is with this 'head' that there unites and binds itself the tendon of the muscle which moves the eyelid, and upon the dorsal aspect of which the diseased condition known as the 'cyst' has its site. But often when the animal is obese, because of the quantity of the fatty mass, it is the only thing that can be seen as soon as there has been drawn aside from it that overlying fascial sheath, of which I said that it descends from the brow-ridge. And frequently the substance of the muscle is clearly visible under the fat when this is small in quantity. Should this fat increase to an unnatural degree exceeding its normal amount, it produces the disease called 'hydatid' [or cyst]. The removal of this superfluous fat, the so-called 'hydatid', is very easy. But not inconsiderable
58 mistakes often occur, as they do in blood-letting in the arm. For this [blood-letting] is likewise a curative operation out of which, provided it proceeds properly and correctly, no grave detriment arises. But should it miscarry, then it exposes the patient to injuries of three kinds. That is because, together with the median vein, which is the dark vein in the elbow-bend, a small nerve lying there may be divided; or else

together with the large median vein, that is the basilic, the artery lying beneath it may be incised; or again together with the shoulder vein, that is the V. cephalica, the head of the tendinous muscle[1] may be cut through.

The situation is the same in regard to the excision of superfluous fat, that is the 'hydatid'. For when you stretch the skin of the eyelid in all directions, and when at one stroke you divide the skin and the fascia lying beneath it, the fat rises up, and from the opening of the wound the artery emerges, as indeed it does when you exert pressure on the lid 59
with the fingers which you have placed around the skin of the part in order to remove the fat. For your hand will be encircling the eyelid which you are incising, and be pressing [upon] it. And if you incise this [the skin of the eyelid] more deeply than to the limit of the fascia lying upon it, and the incision extends somewhat into the fat within, then that damages nothing. But if you insert the knife so that it passes further than this point and perforates the muscle, it occasionally leads to the sequel that there an inflammatory swelling with pain may develop, and often, besides this, a remnant of the persistent inflammatory swelling becomes indurated, or else in the first incision a considerable part of the levator muscle may be severed, so that this muscle consequently weakens and atrophies, and is no longer able to move the lid or to raise it in the proper way. And consequently there is for the surgeon disgrace and infamy and, for the person whose muscle is affected, serious damage.

These remarks have been made in a superficial way, though I am aware that there can be no deception in these studies with which we are concerned. It is an account, and not a very long one, whose value should be considerable now with regard to the object at which we are aiming. I say, then, that this small muscle extends down to the place where the two fasciae join each other, I mean the fascia which descends from the brow-ridges, and the fascia which ascends upwards from the corneo-sclerotic junction. As regards the clarity of expression at which we are aiming in our account of the dissection, there is nothing to

[1] Ḥunain the translator says: 'We must here pause and see whether the expression of Galen is "head of the tendinous muscle", or else "tendinous head of the muscle".' But either end of a muscle may be termed its head, so far as I can judge.

prevent us from saying of one and the same part at one time that it is
the natural beginning of the structure whose description is being
summarised here, and at another time that it is not the beginning but
rather the end, adopting the custom of Herophilus in the use of words.
This junction also is the true head [upper origin] of the substance of
60 the lid, since everything which extends from this site upwards to the
brow-ridge has been created only for this place. When you have seen
these things as I have described them to you, next split the lower
portion of the fascia, beginning at the corneo-sclerotic junction, until
you reach the 'head' of the eyelid, of which I spoke. If you carry that
out well, then it will appear to you clearly that the musculature which
moves the whole eyeball is enclosed in one sheath. When you have
seen that, return to the eyelid, and free it all around until you come to
its two extreme points, that is, the greater angle of the eye which lies
near the nose, and the lesser angle of the eye which is close to the
zygomatic bone. When you do that, you can see that the muscle which
raises the eyelid upwards possesses a head and a band of the fascia type,
which is attached to the bones surrounding the eye, up to which
extend the heads of all the muscles that move the eye. They are joined
to it by bands of the fascia type. And in proportion as the muscle of the
eyelid is far thinner and slighter than any one of those others, so is its
sheath thinner and more nearly approximating to the fascia type. You
can only acquire an adequate view of these things when you previously
have removed the brow-ridges. Now although this muscle [*levator*] is
in a high degree thin and slender, yet you will nevertheless find here
two other muscles which are still thinner and weaker than it, one at
each of the two angles of the eye [*M. orbicularis oculi*]. They lie, however,
not externally, but concealed in the cavity of the orbit, and only by
hard work does one obtain a view of them. Whoever desires to see them
must cut away the bone which bounds the orbital aperture below.
Nevertheless he must not remove all, but only so much as adjoins the
two angles of the eye. These two fine and delicate muscles commence
there and pass towards the margin of the upper lid, and the end of each
61 of them becomes very attenuated. Their utility is considerable although
they are thus attenuated. For when either of them draws to itself that
portion of the palpebral margin that is united and blended with it, at

once downwards and sideways, then through this activity, the upper lid will be drawn downwards as a whole so [far] that it meets the lower lid, touches it, and 'closes the eye'. For the lower lid possesses no [faculty of] movement, and consequently is not competent to take part in the closing or opening of the eye. And when we do close and open the eye, that occurs solely because [first] the upper eyelid descends and so encounters the lower eyelid, and again it ascends and is separated from the latter; only, when we open the eye, this is brought about by the activity of a single muscle, the one which passes down to the head of the eyelid, but when we close the eye this occurs from the combination of two muscles acting at the same time. Now should any damage befall one of these two muscles at any time, then the eyelid will become crooked and distorted because only one of the two muscles is drawing it down. The damage which then befalls the muscles [i.e. if only one is impaired] will be one of two kinds, namely either Relaxation or Contraction. When the muscle near the greater [medial] angle of the eye relaxes, then the eyelid advances towards the opposed muscle, and one sees then the eyelid spread out towards the lateral angle of the eye. And when the muscle near the lateral angle of the eye relaxes, then that part of the eyelid where the muscle is inserted will be drawn towards the greater angle. The case is the same in respect of the oblique inclination and the eversion of one of the eyelids when both these muscles relax. But when one of them contracts more than is natural for it, then that part of the eyelid closely connected with the contracting muscle will be pulled over towards that muscle itself. And since this is so, in fact no harm is done if you tear out or cut or split away the whole of
that part of the eyelid which consists only of the periosteal layer folded 62
up. But should you sever one of the muscles acting on the eyelid, there results painful swelling, contortion and paralysis of the eyelid. And indeed there is found in the middle of the eyelid a very considerable quantity of this substance. When I say middle, I refer to that mid-point which lies between the upper and the lower parts of the eyelid, [and] not the mid-point between the limiting parts at the greater [medial] angle, and the limiting parts at the lesser [lateral] angle along the length of the [free] border of the lids. That pleated fascial sheath extends from this mid-point to the junction and attachment of the smallest muscle

[*levator*]. But on both sides of the mid-point of the border of the lid lies the terminus of those muscles which draw the eyelid down. As for this part and what lies above it, when you start to go upwards in the direction of the eyelid, no part of it that lies close to the angles of the eye has any contact with the muscle that raises the eyelid. But whatever is raised upwards in the upper parts of the eyelids is in contact with this muscle, since it combines and unites with the upper border of the ground substance of the eyelid. As for what relates to the two separate muscles which draw the lid downwards, these behave differently. For they do not reach to the upper border of the eyelid. On the contrary, since they are spread out along the margin of the lid, and are incorporated and bound up with it, they draw it with themselves in a downward direction, each one acting from the side of the eye on which it is found. Since that is so, you must be assured, when you undertake curative operations with the knife on the eyelids, that there is safeguarded and free from danger that component which extends from the
63 middle of the margin of the eyelid to the region above, until it comes to the place where the end of the muscle which opens the eye [*levator palpebrae*] is attached.

As for what relates to those components of which the place in the eyelid is on both sides of this intermediate zone towards the angles of the eye, you must realise that those of them which lie closer to the margin of the eyelid are more endangered than those which lie further from that [margin].

Of the upper eyelid, we have now presented ample details. As for what relates to the lower lid, on this there is not one single muscle. On the contrary, it is only the periosteal layer that is pleated, after it has mounted up from the so-called malar eminences in the manner I have indicated, [namely] that the periosteal layer descends from the brow-ridges, and extends itself so widely that it comes to the margin of the eyelid, and then wends its way from there back again, and is folded on itself layer upon layer. Afterwards it opens out again and ensheathes the muscles up to the margin of the corneo-sclerotic junction.

CHAPTER 5. HIATUS IN TEXT. SUPERFICIAL STRUCTURES IN THE FACE.

[*Hiatus in text*]

These are the details which you can clearly see in all men's eyes even before dissection. And in the dissection of animals you will notice them likewise, by inserting a fine hair into one of them. These apertures [*puncta lachrymalia*] are inclined slightly inwards. Consequently they become more accessible to inspection when you draw the lesser angle of the eye in an outward direction. Amongst the things which are also to be seen at the greater angle of the eye is the structure called the core of the angle, a cartilaginous mass of flesh fully exposed to view before dissection. And here in dissecting you see an aperture in the bone adjacent to the nose. This aperture that I have indicated leads through, passing down into the interior of the bone. In addition to this you will
see in the orbit other small apertures, in no regular pattern, through 64
which the veins and arteries of the orbital cavity communicate with and are connected to the veins and arteries in the brain.

When you have seen all this, then draw away the whole of the skin covering the periosteum which lies in the region of the malar eminences. This skin here contains a thin sheet, of muscular nature, which lies spread out underneath in the same fashion as the Musculus frontalis. And this [the former structure] combines and blends with that muscle which is called the muscular carpet, that is a muscle which we have already described previously [*M. platysma myoides*]. Further, you see that the cutaneous elements of the head are connected with the cutaneous elements of the forehead, and that a very thin structure of fleshy nature underlies them. As for the skin of the head, this can very easily be detached from the pericranial membrane. And when the pericranial membrane becomes thus freely exposed, then it is also very easy for you to investigate the association of this pericranial membrane [*periosteum*] with the thicker one of the two meninges at the cranial sutures. For the pericranial membrane is connected with the thick one of the two meninges solely through the medium of the cranial sutures. Together with the thick membrane, delicate vessels make their way through the sutures to the exterior.

Now as for the parts of the face, there is there the musculature which we mentioned previously. Furthermore in the book 'On the bones' we have already dealt with the nasal bone, and have said that at its terminal margin there are found the two emplacements of what are called the two leaves [*alae*], two separate bodies of the nature of cartilage, and then also in Book IV, where we have dealt with the anatomy of the muscles, we described the muscle which acts upon them.

CHAPTER 6. THE TONGUE, MOUTH AND PHARYNX.

Since we have now completed our account of these things, it is time for us to begin to give an account of the tongue. Its substance consists of spongy flesh, paler and poorer in blood than the muscular flesh.
65 Muscles enter into connection with the tongue on behalf of its voluntary movements. You can bring about paralysis of these muscles during the life of an animal and deprive them all of movement, on both sides of the tongue, provided you sever both nerves of the seventh pair [*hypoglossal*] of those arising from the brain. They [the nerves] pass in between the two muscles which come to the tongue, and they make their way towards the thin part of the mandible where the molar teeth lie, and indeed their path runs beneath the mandible. I have already advised you, in all dissection operations that you carry out on the bodies of animals, first of all to learn to know the nature of the organic parts, and their positions in the dead animal, and again I advise you here to do the same. Whoever has been present and has seen how I lay bare with a single stroke of the knife the tough nerve of the tongue [*hypoglossal nerve*] while the animal is still alive, that person can do the same after he has memorised the place in which the incision was made. But if anyone has learnt that and studied it only from my words and my descriptions, he must exercise himself first on the body of a dead animal in order to expose in it that nerve of the tongue by means of which the movement of its muscles proceeds. For there are in the tongue other nerves which approach this one as they pass beneath the deep surface of the mandible, and they are much softer than the nerves which break up in its [the tongue's] muscles. In fact, that nerve which goes to the muscles of the tongue is tougher than almost all the other

nerves springing from the brain, and on its way it draws near to the side of the special mandibular muscle, that is, the muscle of which many anatomists speak as 'the one which is tendinous in the middle' [*digastric*] namely because this muscle unlike all others has a tendinous middle part and two fleshy ends. The heads of this muscle are, in the 66
bodies of apes, narrow and also up to a certain degree rounded—rather rounded than flat. They also possess a sort of ligament below the root of the ear. The whole of their intermediate portion is fleshless in the highest degree. Nevertheless a slight difference and contrast exists between their mid-parts and their ligaments and the other parts which alone are without flesh, although these resemble them in respect of their lack of flesh. For you see that their middle part is harder than the tendons and weaker than the ligaments. These two muscles, one on each side, extend to the end of the mandible, where the part lies that in the human body one calls the chin, and their ends join and attach themselves chiefly to the actual bony mass of the chin. Since now the condition of each of the two muscles is such as this, it follows that their two ends adhere to each other. Additionally to these parts, fascial fibres which reach across there from one to the other bind together and unite them. But, in other animals, the muscle which exerts traction on the mandible does not reach the end of it, but terminates far behind, [that is], before it has arrived at that spot. The reason for that is that all other animals have a longer mandible than the mandible of Man and apes. And the larger the mandible is, the larger will be the area left over to which the muscle is not attached. The head of this muscle does not lie in precisely the same place in the bodies of all animals, as we shall explain later on in reference to its dissection. But as for what is shared in common by them all, a point of value to us in our present discussion, I have described it before and will describe it here also. For I say that the position of the nerve of the tongue muscles is after that of this nerve. You must reflect the skin and the muscular carpet from it, and you 67
must direct your attention to where you have seen it very clearly and distinctly in the body of the dead animal, and you must remember it in order to make the incision precisely in the same place in the body of the living animal, so that the nerve may be exposed. This spot is where that part of the mandible begins which ascends towards its [*temporo-*

mandibular] articulation. If here you expose the tough nerve of the tongue—and there is one of these on each side of the tongue—and then tie a ligature round it, or sever it, then you deprive the whole tongue of mobility but not of sensibility. For it is the 'soft' nerve which passes by the bone of the mandible and goes to the tongue which, coming from the brain, conveys sense-impressions of taste to it [and does so] without distributing itself in a single muscle, or in the substance of the tongue; rather is it distributed to the covering of the tongue which envelops it completely on its surface.

This covering is firmly united with the one which clothes [lines] the whole of the oral cavity uniformly as far as the fauces. When I say fauces I understand by it that portion within the mouth up to which the head of the oesophagus and that of the larynx extend. The same covering passes downwards into the oesophagus and the larynx, as a continuous, firmly woven single structure, yet variable in its different parts. Its essential structure does not change, and it differs only in respect of its thickness or attenuation. That is to say, the mucous lining, so long as it passes down in the oesophagus to the stomach, continues to increase in thickness, and when it comes to the stomach, there it is even thicker. For the inner one of the linings of the stomach is the one which is continuous and conjoined with that of the cavity of the mouth.
68 And just as this layer becomes here thicker than it was, so it diminishes in thickness gradually while it passes down through the fauces into the trachea. You know that it is the larynx which lies between the fauces and the trachea, and it is through the larynx that that lining passes to the trachea. Its position is as I have described it, that is to say, it is common to and envelops all these organs, namely the tongue, the whole oral cavity, the epiglottis, the fauces, the larynx, the trachea, the oesophagus, and the stomach. Because of the position of this covering, it is best that you should cut away the mandible as a whole from its connection with the upper jaw and that you should divide the mandibular symphysis at the chin. In the mandibles of apes this union is so difficult to divide that you may regard the mandible as a single bone in which there is no single joint that can be perceived by a careful examination, unless you boil it till it softens and then you forcibly break it in two. So far as relates to other animals, this symphysis is less easy to

divide in some than in others. For in the bodies of dogs it is very quickly divided.

When the symphysis of the mandible at the chin has been divided,
you must cut away everything which connects it with the tongue,
leaving nothing attached to it. Then you pull on the two separate parts
of the mandible, and prize them forcibly apart so that they diverge
widely the one from the other. In this way the inner cavity of the
mouth will be brought clearly to light, and lie exposed for inspection.
By means of this artifice you are also suitably placed to inspect the
whole of the mucous membrane extending in the interior over the
parts in the mouth that we have mentioned, and to convince yourself
that it is applied to all these parts as a single [continuous] sheet, and
spreads itself over the upper aspect of the tongue as far as its site of
attachment to the mandible. Then it passes upwards from here to the
higher portions of the mouth and it covers the whole of them. Furthermore you see how it spreads itself over that deeply placed region *69*
following the mouth, in its inner recesses which are markedly narrower
than the mouth [*oral cavity*], and which may be compared to what the
Greeks call an isthmus, by which they mean a piece of land between
two seas, and on this account many [writers] have distinguished this
region by this name. Again on the same grounds, they have named
'paristhmia', a name derived from the foregoing noun, those two
lateral pieces [of the fauces] called the almonds. Others have not so
named the sides of the fauces, but the tumours arising there, while some
name the faucial nuclei the two spongy fleshy bodies [*glands*] lying at
the head of the hollow of the fauces, and others again indicate with
this name the tumours arising in them.

You can also examine such things while the tongue remains attached to and hanging from the mandible, if previously you have divided the mandible at the chin and split apart each of its two divisions. But as for the parts which lie within the fauces, you cannot see them clearly enough without cutting the tongue freely away from the mandible. When you cut and draw apart the two portions of the mandible towards the joint that divides them, or when you split it or tear it out, you can see all the parts situated in the fauces. Here lies the epiglottis, and, behind it, the openings of the two ways which diverge from the passage which we mentioned and which is what the anatomists indicate by a name meaning 'gorge', because it ascends to the upper end of the oesophagus and the upper [orifice] of the larynx.

CHAPTER 7. EXTRINSIC MUSCLES OF THE TONGUE.

Should you now wish to search for the heads [attachments] of the tongue musculature, commence with the dissection of the outward parts first. But should you wish to search out the general association of the coverings investing the tongue you must deeply dissect the
70 larynx and the oesophagus. For the time being, however, abandon this region when you have seen how the same covering [*mucous membrane*] spreads over the whole mouth and extends over the epiglottis and the fauces, and when you have seen that this covering reaches as far as the head of the oesophagus and the larynx. At another time you can return to it and study it again, so that you may observe all that is associated with the tongue which you have not previously noticed.

But in regard to what lies outside the mouth, you find where the bone which is called 'that which resembles the letter Λ in the Greek script' [*lambdoid*, but now called *hyoid* from the comparison with *hypsilon* in Man] there this bone stands in relation with the tongue through the muscles, and in many animals, as for instance in apes, with the skull also. In these [latter] animals on each of the two sides, there runs up in the direction of the tongue a muscle which springs from the cranium near the process which Herophilus calls the 'pharoid' ['lighthouselike', now *styloid*]. But if you dislike to call it by this name, you can call it the awl-shaped or needle-shaped process. It is here that the two muscles begin that pass outwards from the fauces [*M. styloglossus*]. Its path runs laterally, where lies the muscle peculiar to the mandible, of which I said that it is called the one which is tendinous at its midpoint [*digastric*]. When you have previously reflected the transversely directed muscle [*M. mylohyoideus*], and the obliquely directed M. hyoglossus, you see clearly and distinctly this muscle, which commences at the base of the styloid process, joining and associating itself with the tongue.

Should you wish to dissect all the tongue muscles separately in the body of a dead animal, as I am about to describe for you, then you

must, I say, commence by reflecting the skin over the neck and the lower portion of the mandible. Next remove the muscle which is 71
called the muscular carpet [*M. platysma myoides*]. And if you have already previously examined this muscle, you can remove it together with the skin. When you have reflected it you will see the peculiar muscle of the mandible, which is the one that is tendinous in its middle portion [*M. digastricus*], and simultaneously with it there will appear firstly the muscle of the tongue that is called the 'transversely directed' one [*M. mylohoideus*], whether you like to call it one muscle with two parts, or else two muscles associated closely and united with one another. Their point of origin is a straight line extending along the middle of the tongue. The line terminates at one end, where it approaches the mandible, at the head of the chin, and at the other end, where it approaches the neck, at the head of the bone resembling the letter Λ of the Greek script. But the source and origin of this bipartite muscle which we have mentioned commences from this head [*medial process* of the *hyoid bone*]. Possibly this muscle is best regarded as two muscles, both of which have a common site where they join each other. This site is the mid-line of the tongue, extending from the head of the bone which resembles the letter Λ of the Greek script to the mid-point of the mandible along the mid-line of the tongue. For along the whole length of this line the two muscles combine and unite with one another. At this spot also there [come to] lay themselves near each other the two peculiar muscles of the mandible, that is the two that are tendinous in the middle. Then pass on to the 'oblique' muscle [*M. hyo-glossus* with *M. chondroglossus*] which in apes has its source and origin on the lower rib [*greater cornu*] of the bone which resembles the letter Λ of the Greek script [*hyoid bone*], one on either side of the neck. In all other animals, however, it springs, for the most part, from both sides of the head of the bone which resembles the letter Λ of the Greek script and from the structure attached to this, which forms the terminal point of that bone, which it supports and fixes one on each 72
side. Furthermore again, this [particular detail] differs in the remaining five animal classes, namely those other than the apes. For the ape has certainly not got these two supports, which are lacking in man as well, but in the place of these are two ligaments, one on either side, which

couple together the end of the styloid process itself with the upper 'rib' of the lambda-like bone. That is a thin cartilaginous 'rib'. This oblique muscle [*M. styloglossus*] which we must mention here begins, as we previously remarked, on the cranial bone and runs into the side of the tongue. If you dissect it, together with that other oblique muscle [*M. hyoglossus* with *M. chondroglossus*], which we have already pointed out, you can now see the second of the two nerves of the tongue which is 'soft' [*N. lingualis*]. It [this nerve] is present on both sides, and distributes itself in the outer covering of the tongue. Every tongue of an animal from one of the six classes which we have already distinguished possesses the so-called bilateral muscle-pair which we have mentioned, that is to say the pair which runs upwards from below, being the two muscles which form, as it were, two sides. These animals have also a pair of obliquely directed muscles, which [*Mm. hyoglossi*] come from the bone which resembles the letter Λ of the Greek script. Their origin [attachment] does not in all animals proceed from one and the same site of commencement. In the subsequent course of this exposition you will learn what is the source and origin of this muscle, that is, the point which we have to regard as its head, in each one of these six classes of animals which we mentioned previously. But of that pair of which we have also talked before, that is to say the transversely directed muscles, their nature and their site of origin is one and the same in all the six classes.

There now remains before us still another pair found in all animals,
73 of which the origin lies on the head [*median process*] of the Λ-like bone [*hyoid*], and of which the course goes to the chin where that band [*frenulum*] of the tongue is, of which I shall presently be speaking. In many animals these two muscles are a single one with two parts. And the line which divides the two, and separates the substance of one from that of the other, is the [line of] union of the two transversely directed muscles [*Mm. mylohyoidei*] previously pointed out. This is again the median region of the whole tongue which as a whole is completely united and [in its substance] continuous, although one may say of it correctly that it consists of two parts, since you will certainly encounter and see on its left side all that which is to be found and recognised on the right side. Now this pair of muscles [*M. geniohyoideus*] extends

along the length of the tongue, and both its component muscles are more strongly rounded, and the state of both of them is nearer to the nature of [? muscular] flesh, in contrast to the aspect of those two muscles which lie superficially to them, that is the muscles of which I said that they are to be seen and discovered first. In point of fact, these last two can be seen to differ for the most part from the former pair inasmuch as their transversely directed fibres have a diametrically opposed position to the longitudinal fibres [of the others], and the tenuity and breadth of these muscles stands in contrast to the rotundity and thickness of those [others], except that the transversely directed muscle shares, with the longitudinally directed one, a common attachment at the mid-line of the whole tongue, of which we have previously spoken.

With these muscles [*mylohyoid*] the arrangement is such as I have explained, namely that they are to be seen before the main mass. Then
immediately after that you can see the muscle passing longitudinally 74
[*geniohyoid*] and the obliquely directed [i.e. *hyoglossus* with *chondroglossus*] whose origin in other animals is not the same as this. In the apes, however, the natural state of this muscle resembles my description here.

I say that from the lower rib of the bone which resembles the Λ of the Greek script (which is wider than the rib lying higher up, and stands closer to the nature of bone) a fleshy outgrowth projects from which a muscle sprouts forth, of which one part joins and connects with the mandible, while to the other part another outgrowth approaches and combines with it, [coming] from the upper end of the mid-line of the bone which resembles the Λ of the Greek script, laterally [in relation], and it goes to the tongue. After this pair of muscles comes another, which consists of the two laterally situated muscles [*styloglossi*] coming from the head [*cranium*]. Thus there are, in all, four pairs [of muscles] if you count in with them the two transversely directed muscles [*mylohyoid*]. And should you not include these in your reckoning as a pair, then there are three.

When you dissect away both these muscles which we have mentioned,
then you will see two other pairs of muscles, which run at the sides of 75
the middle pair in two parts closely bound together as one [*genioglossi*].

When you have removed these and then arrived at the root of the tongue, and you search for their place of origin, you will not consider that they are [? extrinsic] muscles, but you will think that they are [? intrinsic] parts of the tongue. For you are not in a position to discover any part whatsoever from which the tongue has arisen, just as each muscle has a head [origin] which grows out either from a bone, or else inevitably from some sort of a firmly fixed static substance. On the contrary, when you remove from it all these muscles described here, then there remains nothing left over with the sole exception of the covering which invests it and which itself connects the nearby structures to which it is joined with the tongue. Should you cut through these, you will then clearly see the faucial passage to which, as I said before, you will come afterwards. For the moment, however, let it be your concern to convince yourself, in the first place as to the tongue, after removal of its muscles, how soft it is and how scanty is the amount of blood in it. That part of it which lies in the mouth reveals itself freely and visibly in its entirety from above, but from below you do not view it as a whole, but you see only that part which is outside its band of communication with the mandible [*frenulum*], which is found in its outer covering. This band frequently shrinks considerably, and then does not permit the tongue to perform its various movements. Because of this defect we are forced to cut the frenulum and subsequently liberate the tongue, so that when it is used for speaking it can extend itself and reach to the uppermost part of the hard palate and the sides of the mouth.

CHAPTER 8. SUBMANDIBULAR SALIVARY GLAND. ARTERIES AND NERVES OF THE TONGUE.

On both sides of this band [*frenulum*] you find the orifices of ducts called salivary [*ducts of Bartholin* or *Wharton*]. On the tongue of an ox a thick sound [probe] may be able to penetrate into any one of these orifices, but with the tongues of small animals, the use of a fine sound
76 is required for that purpose. The origin of these ducts is near the root of the tongue, where the spongy flesh [glandular mass] attached to the tongue lies, since the origin of these ducts is from that part. Their aspect is that of the pulsating blood-vessels, that is the arteries, and often

when you see the artery of the tongue running in this place you think that you are simply looking at these ducts, regardless of the fact that their structure consists of a single layer. However, should you now have previously detected their first [foremost] ending, which lies externally at each side of the frenulum, then insert a long slender sound [probe], whether of wood or of bronze, follow the sound and trace its course until you reach the gland which I have mentioned to you. But should you wish to begin and approach it from the glandular tissue which I mentioned to you, and which lies on the tongue, then incise the gland tissue through its sheath, which invests all its several lobes [fleshy parts], and observe the roots of those vessels which discharge the saliva. Their original source is that spongy flesh [gland], and they are in fact like numerous fine rootlets, which unite with one another, and from these arise other rootlets larger than the foregoing. Should you investigate the nature of this spongy flesh, and apprehend it clearly and with diligence, then you will see that from those rootlets two large ones emerge, and when the two have united and become conjoined the one with the other, there then proceeds from them a single duct, after the fashion of the trunk of a tree with a tap root [single shoot], and moreover there is such a stem on both sides of the tongue.

This vessel, which is called the salivary outlet [*duct of Bartholin* or *Wharton*], possesses, as I have remarked, two large rootlets on each of the two sides [of the tongue]. You see also that to this spongy flesh which I have mentioned are joined and connected a vein and an artery together. This is something which you must memorise in relation to
all spongy flesh [glandular tissue] which has been created for the 77
generation of some fluid from which the animal derives some use. For this is a matter which is common to it all. Again, the nature of this spongy flesh set apart for the generation of fluid is other than the nature of the spongy flesh which has been accumulated as the stay and the support for blood-vessels where they branch. That also I will describe later on.

Now you must direct your attention [to ascertain] that in the tongue there are arteries which, when you measure their calibre comparatively, are much larger than they should be by rights. In it also are large veins, but their arteries are, as described, far larger than the extent of the tongue warrants. And moreover with them are soft [sensory] nerves whose proportions also are much greater than is justified by the size of the covering of the tongue in which they branch out. For these nerves are distributed only to the covering which envelops the tongue, without mounting upwards to the higher subdivisions of the mouth. Those subdivisions also have very fine nerves of their own which go to them specially, not from the root of the nerve which goes to the investing covering of the tongue itself. This soft nerve is very much greater in mass than that which the covering of the tongue should by right receive. But in regard to what specially concerns the intrinsic body of the tongue, there is found in it a very small nerve, attaining such a degree of minuteness, that all anatomists overlook it and do not know of it. This small lingual nerve [*N. glossopharyngeus*] is joined and united only to the root of the tongue, and it distributes itself in that region without extending itself forwards, so far as can be observed. I shall mention it again in the description of the anatomy of the nerves springing from the brain.

CHAPTER 9. THE PHARYNX AND OESOPHAGUS, WITH A DISCUSSION ON THE NOMENCLATURE OF 'COVERINGS'.

You have now observed sufficiently all that pertains to the tongue. So keep the oesophagus, the larynx and the trachea, and take away the parts surrounding them. Do you then cut open the thorax in [the
78 direction of] its length from above downwards. The incision that you make in it should traverse the [costal] cartilaginous parts, as I have described to you in the dissection of the respiratory organs. Now draw a transverse incision across, and separate the sword-like cartilage [*xiphoid*] from the organic parts connected with it. Next force the sternum upwards. For then you are in a position to note the continuity of the covering membrane of the tongue with the inner investing membrane of the larynx and the trachea. For this membrane, which is smooth, passes down and through the interior of the larynx and covers the interior of the pulmonary tube, that is, the trachea, and continues to divide itself concurrently with the divisions of the trachea until it reaches the extreme limits of the lungs. And so just as [here] it does not cease to become more attenuated gradually, so that each one

of its successive parts is thinner than the preceding one, even so [by contrast] in the whole of the oesophagus until it reaches the stomach you see it [*the mucous lining*] incessantly and gradually increasing its thickness, so that each one of its successive parts is thicker than the preceding one. And even when it reaches the stomach it still never ceases to increase in thickness, from its mouth [*cardiac orifice*] up as far as its fundus. You see that all its fibres pass for the most part spread out from above downwards, though in the membrane which invests them externally there are fibres which run transversely round it. This externally lying membrane—the first which you encounter in your dissection—stands closer to the nature of flesh, but the inner layer approximates to this less closely, since the blood in it is scanty, and it [its substance] is harder [i.e. tougher]; but in the outer layer the blood is more abundant, and it is softer, its substance being very close to that of muscle. You see that its upper head [commencement of mucous layer] has its origin at the skull [base], at the anterior margins of the suture which is found at the lower part of the cranium. This is the suture which runs transversely, and unites together the two ends of the suture 79
which resembles the Λ of the Greek script, I mean the two end-points at which the nerves of the sixth pair of those arising from the brain emerge [*glossopharyngeus, vagus, accessorius*]. After it [*the mucous membrane*] has taken this origin, it connects with the larynx, at the anterior portions of this, and with it there combine themselves and unite the fibres of the muscles [*Mm. thyropharyngei*] which join together at the mid-line dividing the two halves of the oesophagus posteriorly. For these muscles connect with the oesophagus only at this place. But on its anterior parts, they come to lie on both sides of the great cartilage of the larynx, that is the cartilage which lies in front and is called the shield-like one [*thyroid*]. Many [anatomists] have indeed believed that these muscles are parts of the oesophagus; but they had not thoroughly investigated their peculiar substance, and so they supposed that the whole oesophagus was a muscle.

With reference to the muscle which binds and couples the oesophagus with the thyroid cartilage, you will learn when I come to the description of the anatomy of the larynx that it is really a muscle and what its activity is. Here however take notice of what I wish to say. Each one

of the two coverings shared by the oesophagus and the stomach—for the coverings of the one are identical with the coverings of the other—is joined and united so as to coalesce into a single sheet. And also the course of the fibres upon the oesophagus and the stomach is one and the same. For in the whole external covering the fibres run transversely, whereas the fibres of the inner layer are spread out longitudinally from above downwards. Neither the stomach nor the oesophagus possesses another substance [? investment] besides these two coverings. And when you reflect on the name which the anatomists have used, you will come to the conclusion that they are right when they call a covering that which is on the surface of the tongue even if it interlocks and combines with the covering of the interior of those organs. But as this so-called covering extends to the inner [surfaces] of the oesophagus and the stomach, then you will no longer think that
80 in applying this name, they employed the correct word, since we Greeks are accustomed to apply this name, I mean cover, only to the uppermost [superficial] bodies [tissues] which invest and clothe other bodies [structures] externally. Whoever, then, calls that part which lies in the interior of an organ a cover differs in his use of the term from the custom of those who speak this language, I mean Greek. The case is the same with regard to the eyes. For when you consider the name applied by the anatomists to the structures that surround the gelatinous parts of the eye constituting for this a sort of mantle, then you find that they were right when they called these covers. But when you turn to look at the oesophagus and the stomach, then you find that the case is not so, and neither is it so for the intestines, the urinary bladder, and the uterus. For the 'substance' of these organs is again nothing more than their covering, a containing wall and a protective sheath for that which accumulates in their cavities. And since this is so, then others have done better, and judged more correctly, when they named such organic structures as these 'leaves'.

What we have said in regard to names is fully adequate. And you must remind yourself of the point I made to the effect that you should lay no high value upon names, nor should you ponder upon them, but rather you should follow Plato on that point. But notice that the slight significance which one assigns to nomenclature is not the same thing

as if one were to pay scant attention to explanation and interpretation. For my part I do not advise you to neglect and underestimate explanation and interpretation, and neither did Plato, who showed by actual fact the lengths to which went his care to explain and interpret things well. None the less, I advise you to follow normal practice in the use of names, without investigating whether they are employed correctly or incorrectly. You should try to organise your terminology with the 81
object of conveying to your interlocutor the clearest possible conception of the thing about which you are talking. That is the course which I adopt myself, and I follow the usage of the anatomists even though it differs from common usage. So I say that the intestines also have two coverings, but their fibres run transversely. The uterus, however, has only one covering, as has also the urinary bladder. As for those who believe that these organs have only two coverings, but that the stomach and the intestines have three, they are merely in error, as I have shown, since the peritoneum is wrapped round them completely, although it is outwardly applied to all the organs situated below the diaphragm. And in reference to each one of these organs you will need to make sure that you inspect it carefully after the removal of the peritoneal layer clothing and covering its essential substance.

But in the elaboration of this matter I have been more diffuse than is justified by the point which I wished to make, because of the ambiguities of the terms. And now, so far as the external covering wrapped round the oesophagus is concerned, your interest should now be directed to severing in the body of a dead animal this covering alone, without incising the inner layer simultaneously. Then in a living animal try to incise the oesophagus with a single cut which runs in a longitudinal direction from above downwards so that you divide the whole of the fibres. When you have done that, see now if the animal is able to swallow or not. It is necessary that the animal should be hungry and thirsty before it is vivisected, so that although afflicted by the experimental wounds, it will nevertheless be stimulated to eat or to drink even though at first it can scarcely do either. But when the wound [in the skin] has been closed with threads, you see that it takes 82
food and laps water, and when it does so, you see that it swallows. The evidence of that teaches you that the action of swallowing is always

completed and brought about by the inner of the two portions of the oesophagus. This you may call a 'leaf' if you like, or if you prefer, a 'cover'. This will become more clear to you through [the study of] the movements of the larynx in the upward and downward direction as that occurs at the time of swallowing. Of that I shall speak in [connection with] the anatomy of the larynx.

The end of the Tenth Book of Galen's work on Anatomy, translated by Ḥunain ibn Isḥāq. To God alone be his due of praise, and on the Prophet, his family and all his companions be blessings.

BOOK XI

THE LARYNX AND ASSOCIATED STRUCTURES

In the name of God, the compassionate, the merciful, whose aid we invoke. Summary [of the contents] of the Eleventh Book of the work on Anatomical Dissection. There will be discussed the parts of the larynx in the bodies of apes; the structure of the muscles of the larynx; the organic parts which adjoin the larynx in the bodies of swine; what sort of form, in the bodies of swine, has the bone resembling the letter Λ in the Greek script [*the hyoid bone*]; the root of the tongue, the activities of the tongue, and its uses; the nerve [*vagus*] of the neck in the living animal.

CHAPTER I. SUPERFICIAL DISSECTION OF THE NECK, ANATOMY OF THE LARYNGEAL CARTILAGES, AND OBSERVATIONS ON BILATERAL SYMMETRY IN THE BODY.

Insofar as the organic parts of the larynx are concerned you must dissect *83*
them in the following manner. First, it is necessary that you remove the M. platysma, the thin muscle called the muscular carpet. In this way you will be able to observe the muscles that go from the larynx[1] and the hyoid bone[1] to the sternum, and you will see the spongy flesh [*submandibular salivary gland*] lying on each side of the wide part of the mandible. On each side there is this 'flesh' which forms a single unit of considerable size.

After this flesh, when it has been removed, and all the fascial coverings reflected which clothe and veil the entire laryngeal region, there appears the muscle of the mandible which one rightly calls 'tendinous', since its intermediate part is tendinous and fleshless [*M. digastricus*]. Follow well, listener, what I say and expound to you. I inform you only about
what lies on one side of the body, but everything which you see on *84*

[1] The Arabic phrase is the same in both cases. M.C.L.

this, the right side of the body, resembles what lies on the left side in number as well as in mass and form. The state of this muscle I have already demonstrated above. And here, in connection with it, I will explain this further point, that its root [origin] adjoins the root of that part of the skull which Herophilus calls the 'columnar' process, [*processus styloideus*; also called '*pharoid*' from the Pharos] and which we call 'awl-like' or 'needle-like'. That is the process which starts from a broad base and stretches out to a slender extremity, after the fashion of the end of an awl or of a needle. Now the muscle of which we said that it is tendinous in the middle, and is called by this name [*M. digastricus*], and adjoins this process, has its root at the upper end of this process.

If, now, you do not set a [strict] limit to the incision through the muscular carpet [*platysma myoides*] and the sheaths underlying it, you will here destroy a very small muscle which has its origin just at the place at which the laterally placed muscle of the tongue [*M. styloglossus*] commences, passes in the direction of the lower end of the hyoid bone, and is inserted on its infero-lateral border, one on each side, on the right side, and on the left [*M. stylohyoideus*]. Between the two lies the muscle which makes its way downwards in the direction of the sternum, that is the [muscle] which arises from the lower aspect of the hyoid bone [*M. sternothyroideus*]. And when you also remove these four muscles, then that slender muscle shows itself to you clearly, which proceeds onwards in the direction of the two [right and left] scapulae [*M. omohyoideus*]. You can see that it has its origin on the side of the hyoid bone, there being one of these muscles on each of the two sides. When you cut through them, then you see all the individual structures lying beneath them quite freely.

85 But since you will now gain very great benefit from a thorough understanding of the conformation of the hyoid bone, for the clear comprehension of the subject which we propose to discuss I shall pass on to give an account of its condition, starting from another point which will be clear to everyone. I say, then, that the body lying beneath the mandible in the mid-line of the first part of the neck, that is to say the part projecting forwards, is a body which everyone knows and designates by the name larynx. Among wrestlers, one will often be

thrown by the other when the latter grips that structure [*larynx*] and dislocates and fractures it, when the two competitors are exerting themselves violently in wrestling a fall and one slips in below the armpit of the other. That is because when this structure is ruptured or crushed, the animal is choked forthwith because the passage of the air through which it passes here, being expelled or breathed in, is very narrow. For the musculature which lies there, and opens and closes the larynx is of considerable size. Later I will explain clearly the condition of these muscles, and I will describe to you how you must expose each of them fully, one by one. I say that when you clear away from the larynx and from the hyoid bone the muscles descending down to the sternum, then the larynx appears, and you see clearly, that it includes a large cartilage, whose shape in its front parts resembles that of a shield. Therefore it has had this name bestowed upon it, namely 'the shield-shaped' [*thyroid cartilage*]. The dimensions of length and breadth can be clearly seen from its surface when one examines it by handling. The very best thing to do, if you wish to understand fully the point which I am making, is this. Remove this cartilage from the body of
another ape, and after you have cleared away all that surrounds it, *86*
uncover it separately by itself and study it thoroughly from every aspect, and instruct yourself thereupon. You will find that it is attenuated to such a degree that it is possible to bring it into manifold and diverse shapes, when one presses on it with the fingers. It has four margins arranged opposite one another. Of these, one, the lower, is directed towards the lower portions of the neck. The second is the upper one, which encounters the mandible as soon as it mounts upwards when the animal swallows. But the two remaining margins lie on its two sides, one on either side.

Now this cartilage is slightly convex in the place in which you encounter it and take hold of it. In the middle it has something like a crest extending in the middle in front from above downwards, commencing at the place which is the true mid-point of its upper margin, and ending on the line which borders its lower portion. This crest [*crista cartilaginis thyroideae*] goes in a straight line from above downwards, is quite distinctly to be seen, and comes to be a boundary which distinguishes between the right and left sides of the larynx, and likewise of the neck.

It is astonishing to see how Creation acts in the distinction of the right side of the body from the left, through straight lines. As for the head, its two sides are divided by the median suture, and directly in the same meridian as this is the line in the middle of the nose, where is found the bone which separates the two nasal fossae in the manner of a partition wall, making the two of them like two limbs. Thereafter a line passes downwards to the upper lip. It lies precisely in the mid-point
87 between the front teeth, of which there are four, the so-called 'incisors', I mean the two medial and the two lateral cutting teeth. For of these teeth two, that is to say a medial and a lateral incisor tooth lie to the right of this median line, and two to the left. Similarly the mid-line of the lower jaw goes further onwards, that is the line which extends onwards in the middle of the incisor teeth till it reaches the head of the chin [*spina mentalis*] exactly at that region where the two bones of the lower jaw meet. Another clearly evident line connects with this one and runs in the long axis, dividing the tongue on its lower surface in the mid-line. And this line extends to the actual mid-point of the bone [*hyoid*] which resembles the letter Λ of the Greek script. Straight at the end of this line is the mid-point of the thyroid cartilage, on which there is a slightly projecting process called the 'ridge' [*crista*] of this cartilage. And if you imagine that this line runs onwards in a rectilinear direction, and extends to the middle of the sternum until it reaches as far as the xiphoid cartilage, that is [to say that cartilage] that projects itself over the stomach, you will find that it is joined also from below by the line which travels in the middle of the umbilical cicatrix [*navel*], and the region of union of the two pubic bones. As for the dorsal side of the animal body, in the mid-point of the head there lies a line extending itself straight in the line of the vertebral bones exactly where the processes called spines are. At the bottom end of these is found the bone which is called the 'cross-bone' [*sacrum*]. If, consequently, you wish to cut up the body of any quadruped and to divide it into two halves, you make your section along these lines which I have mentioned. And you will find the whole of the bodily parts in the two halves of the body resembling one another, that is in the right and left halves. Their
88 similarity consists not only in their number, but also in their mass and form, and their whole nature with the exception of the liver and the

spleen. Admittedly when you look at the measurements of their structures you find these two organs resembling one another, as we have shown before. However, if you consider their form and disposition, then you find them unlike one another, inasmuch as the liver is not like the spleen. You have now heard what I have said on this point incidentally, without entering upon it directly, and you should always keep it in your memory. But now, I go on past it, and to the discussion of the larynx, and I will instruct you as to how its constitution is made up.

I say accordingly, that if you wish to dissect the larynx, then first cut it completely out in the way which I have described and remove from it the surrounding tissues, so that you see clearly that it is composed of three cartilages. Of these there is one in front, that of which I broke off the account, and two others right against it and behind, set out in the longitudinal direction of the neck. The front cartilage, the one of which I said that it is called the shield-like one, is in contact in most of its parts with the larger of the two cartilages. You see that of its margins those which mark the limits of its two flanks [*lateral thyroid laminae*] continuously adjoin the margins of the second cartilage [*cricoid cartilage*] and you see that the whole of its lower portion is fastened to the lower part of that [second] cartilage, and is connected to it by means of muscles. But as for the upper ends of both cartilages, that of the one stands opposite to that of the other. Their shape resembles that of two elongated shields, which confront one another with their obverse faces so that they overlap each other, and between the two a cleft, a wide open space, persists. At this place is a third small cartilage, seated upon the second, the shape of which is like that of a drinking vessel. Consequently it derives its name from the name 'drinking vessel', and it is called the drink-vessel-like, or drink-vessel-shaped [*cartilago arytenoidea*].

When you have seen all these things which I have described, and 89
those things also which I wish subsequently to describe after you have removed the whole larynx, then your understanding and comprehension of the dissection of which I am about to tell you will be clearer. The things of which I said that I wished to speak to you are as follows. I say that the thyroid cartilage has four angles [*cornua*], at the meeting places of the four lines which bound it. Those two angles which lie below are attached by an articular ligament to the second cartilage

[*cricoid*]. But the two upper angles are united to the lower margins of the lower [i.e. greater] ribs [*cornua*] of the bone which resembles the letter Λ of the Greek script [*hyoid bone*] by a ligament of which the nature [substance] is intermediate between tendon and cartilage [*cartilago tritice in the thyrohyoid ligament*]. For the hyoid bone lies above the upper margin of the first cartilage [*thyroid*] and its vertical median line stands opposite to the median line of the underlying parts of the tongue. But its two lower ribs [*cornua*] go back towards the two upper angles [*cornua*] of the first cartilage: it is the same whether you call this cartilage 'first' or 'thyroid'; just as it makes no difference whether I say 'third cartilage' or 'arytenoid cartilage'. But so far as the 'second' cartilage [*cricoid*] is concerned, this has no special name. But you and I must all remember that there are six classes of animals, that is to say those of which the older [former] [anatomists] speak in their publications, and to which they refer when they say 'Animals which are not far removed from the nature of Mankind'. You must know that in all
90 these animals alike you find these three cartilages of the larynx similarly placed. As I have said just now, the hyoid bone in the bodies of these animals lies above the thyroid cartilage, and in fact these six classes of animals differ from one another in regard to its size and its shape. Later on I shall mention the remaining classes of the six. At present, however, what we say concerns, first of all, those animals which resemble Mankind most [closely], among them the Ape, and the animal called the Lynx.[1] My intention is to describe how the form of the hyoid bone appears in these animals nearest in resemblance to Man. Endeavour likewise to understand the whole of its nature [structure] when you have already removed all the muscles which adjoin it. For in this way it will be easy for you to grasp what I shall describe to you.

CHAPTER 2. THE HYOID BONE, THE STYLOHYOID LIGAMENT, AND THE SUPERFICIAL MUSCLES OF THE NECK.

I say then, that you find in these animals, and particularly in those apes which most closely resemble Man, the constitution of this bone [*hyoid*] as follows. You find its middle portion [*body*], that is the portion across

[1] ? a variety of Cynocephalous Ape.

which runs the line which divides into two halves [R. and L.] the neck and the whole of this bone, of small length. You will find it deficient also in breadth and depth, a deficiency which is even greater than that of its length, as you will find when you compare its three dimensions. Two ribs spring from the two sides of its lower margin, which pass in a sloping direction towards the upper angles [*cornua*] of the thyroid cartilage, as I [have] described previously. And on its upper margin this hyoid bone has two other 'ribs' which grow outwards parallel to the lower 'ribs'. Now these two upper ribs are slender and cylindrical like two stout needles, or the ends of two awls, and the substance of these two ribs, which are likewise slanted and inclined slightly down- 91
wards, is pure cartilage. From the end of each of the two [*lesser cornua*] goes a cylindrically shaped ligament [*stylohyoid ligament*] like a nerve, and each of these two [ligaments] extends itself to one of the two processes of the skull which are called 'awl-like' [*styloid processes*]. These two processes also have two margins which resemble the upper ribs of the hyoid bone. For their substance is cartilaginous and the form of them all is one and the same. But as to the length, here the two styloid processes are shorter than the two ribs [? *lesser cornua*] of the hyoid bone.

Should you now have come so far, and have seen with your [own] eyes what I have described, I will now revert to the exposition upon which I was engaged, and say—when you remove the muscle which is called the muscular carpet [*M. platysma myoides*] together with the underlying fasciae, you see first two muscles fused into one,[1] which reach to the sternum from the lower margin of the hyoid bone [*Mm. sternohyoidei*] where lie the joints of each of the two clavicles with the sternum. The clavicles lie at the two sides of the two joints. As for the muscle to which I referred, it grows on to that bone of the breast-bone [*sternum*] which lies between the two joints, and its ingrowth [attachment] is at the upper end of its superficial portion. When you cut through these two muscles, then you see two other muscles, which lie as it were beneath and close to them, and which commence at the lower part of the thyroid cartilage, from the whole of the line here marking it out, with the exception of a small portion. These two muscles [*Mm. sternothyroidei*] grow upon just the same part of the

[1] Fused at their upper ends, at their origin from the hyoid.

sternum. Now when these four muscles contract they compress and constrict the trachea, and draw downwards the larynx and the whole hyoid bone. Furthermore here are four other muscles, confronting
92 these [others], whose mass is inferior to theirs. Two of them make traction on the thyroid cartilage, and the other two raise upwards the hyoid bone as a whole. The site of origin of both these two muscles, and of both the preceding two muscles is in exactly the same place as that at which the downwardly-running muscles begin. As for the two muscles which raise upwards the hyoid bone [*Mm. geniohyoidei*], their place of origin is at the upper margin of that bone, and their end point the lower region of the mandible. Then the two muscles which raise the thyroid cartilage [*Mm. thyrohyoidei*] have their origin on the whole of this cartilage, with the exception of a small portion, and their insertion is on the two lower ribs [*greater cornua*] of the hyoid bone. I remind you who read my book that in the course of my description of the dissection it makes no difference whether I say that any single body arises [and] extends itself outwards from a body, or if I say that it is connected with that body and grows firmly on it.

CHAPTER 3. DISSECTION OF THE LARYNX *IN SITU*.

If now you have examined all these things thoroughly, and if you wish to dissect a larynx in its place in the animal body, together with the hyoid bone, and also to observe the muscle which is tendinous in its mid-portion [*M. digastricus*], and the small muscle of which I said that it has an attachment at the side of the hyoid bone [*M. stylohyoideus*], that is the muscle that overlies the one which is tendinous in the mid-point, then remove the spongy flesh of which I said that it lies beneath the expanded part of the mandible [*submandibular lymph glands and salivary gland*]. Thereafter, dissect away the muscle tendinous in the mid-point [*M. digastricus*]. In this way you will be able to get a good
93 view of the hard nerve of the tongue, I mean that nerve which comes from the hinder part of the brain and passes over the upper regions of the neck [*N. hypoglossus*]. The path of this nerve goes first transversely. Then it bends downwards, and extends in an oblique direction to the muscles of the tongue, in which it distributes itself. During its ascent, two branches separate off from it, of which one [*R. descendens n. hypo-*

glossi] goes to the four muscles of which I said that they descend to the sternum, their origin being on the hyoid bone and the thyroid cartilage, and to the plexus of nerves of which the greater number are distributed in the muscle [*sternomastoid*] which comes from the auricle [*ear*] towards the breast-bone. One of these two branches [of the hypoglossal nerve] goes out and terminates as I have described. Beyond it lies another second branch, which distributes itself in the muscle which fastens the lower one of the ribs [*greater cornu*] of the hyoid bone to the thyroid cartilage [*M. thyrohyoideus, Ramus thyrohyoideus n. hypoglossi*], and so connects the two to one another. Occasionally in the bodies of some animals you see that this branch splits itself into two parts, from which extremely small offshoots pass upwards to the larynx, especially in apes, because all the parts around the larynx of these animals are small, delicate, and weak. And consequently, these nerves can easily become mixed in disorder among the other nerves if they are not well dissected out.

The pair of nerves which goes to the muscles of the tongue [*N. hypoglossus*] is the seventh of the nerve-pairs that descend from the brain. But that pair which lies close to this [the seventh pair] at its place of origin, and which has three roots [main divisions], comes off in front of this pair and is the sixth in the reckoning. Occasionally, in some bodies, you see a branch from it going to the four muscles which we have mentioned and of which we said that they extend to the breast-bone. These nerves are very slender, as are those which enter into the muscle which binds together the thyroid cartilage with both the [right and left] lower ribs [*greater cornua*] of the hyoid bone [*M. thyrohyoideus, Rami thyrohyoidei n. hypoglossi*].[1] Endeavour to *94*
acquaint yourself with the position [relations] of these nerves in the body of a large, emaciated, lean ape. For in such an ape you will find them [the nerves] of greater size, and you will also find them devoid of fat which, when it envelops the nerves in obese animals, causes the nerve to be hidden, so that it cannot be seen clearly.

[1] Note that there is an error here in attributing these nerve-twigs to the sixth pair. It arises because the XIIth nerve is so closely approximated to the Xth nerve [*vagus*] immediately outside the skull, and the two, X and XII, run close together for some distance, sometimes a considerable distance. In the latter event, nerve-twigs might easily seem to arise from X (sixth pair) which careful dissection upwards would trace back to XII (seventh pair).

Now the nerve which comes to the whole musculature of the larynx, and which is peculiar to it, comes to it from the sixth pair [*vagus*] as two branches [*N. laryngeus superior*]. Of these two branches, one goes to the upper region of the larynx [*Ramus internus*] where the two lower ribs of the hyoid bone connect themselves with the two upper 'angles' of the thyroid cartilage. But the other of the two branches of the nerve, that which lies beneath the first branch, you will see coming to the side of the larynx, where the thyroid cartilage connects with the oesophagus, and the transverse muscle binds the two with one another [*M. thyropharyngeus, Ramus externus n. laryng. sup.*]. And this branch splits and breaks itself up in the muscle here indicated, of which I said that it is disposed transversely, as well as in that muscle [*M. crico-thyroideus*] which binds the first cartilage [*thyroid*], at its end, with the second cartilage [*cricoid*]. But the upper nerve, of which I said that it grows inwards at the upper angle of the thyroid cartilage, one on either side, distributes itself in the covering [*laryngeal mucous membrane*] which is found within the larynx, that is the covering which combines itself with that of the tongue in those parts from which the epiglottis takes origin (I mean by epiglottis the body suspended [or attached] in the laryngeal orifice).

Now as for the nerve which ascends from below, that is the nerve which I discovered and distinguished [*N. laryngeus recurrens*], this is the place where I must mention as much as you need to know about it, from which you may gain benefit in the anatomy of the larynx. My
95 purpose is to write two Books on the Anatomy of the Nerves, one on those nerves which spring from the brain, the other on those which spring from the spinal cord [Books XIV and XV]. In those two Books I shall set out how all the nerves in the whole animal body should be dissected. But here, as I have said, I will only deal with what you require in the dissection of the larynx, and what will be of use to you in it. I say, then, that where the two lower angles of the thyroid cartilage lie, by means of which it [*the thyroid cartilage*] articulates with the second cartilage [*the cricoid*] so that between it [*the thyroid*] and that [other, the *cricoid*] two joints are formed, you find two small nerves which come from below upwards, and are clothed in the sheaths surrounding the trachea. As to how you should investigate the place of

their ascent from the trachea, you must look for that at the point where its cartilages end which resemble the letter sigma of the Greek script—and that [form] is this—C—and the lower region commences, with which it [*the larynx*] encounters the oesophagus. Both of these two nerves [*Nn. recurrentes*] connect with the larynx at the lower angles of the first [*thyroid*] cartilage. In fact each of the two approaches one of its two joints not from the front, but from behind. When you have found them and properly acquainted yourself with them, then dissect away the transversely directed muscle of the larynx [*M. thyropharyngeus*], and commence at the middle [line] of the posterior oesophageal [*pharyngeal*] region, till you reach the thyroid cartilage upon which this muscle grows [is attached]. And if you like, then cut this muscle out, and take it clean away. Should you do that, whichever of the two you like, then you see that the oesophagus is attached to the hinder subdivision of the second cartilage [*cricoid*]. After you have examined that, cut the oesophagus loose, and dissect the two muscles which lie upon the second cartilage. These are the two which border upon one another, and they separate at a swelling [*process* or *ridge*] which projects
from the second [*cricoid*] cartilage, and descends in it in the long axis *96*
from above downwards [*Mm. cricoarytenoidei postici*]. This swelling on this cartilage you may call its ridge, just as the swelling which is on the first cartilage [*thyroid*] is called the ridge [*crista*] in order that the designation may be appropriate and at the same time brief as well as clear.

After this muscle [*M. cricoarytenoideus posticus*] dissect the larynx together with the hyoid bone, and this dissection should take place while the larynx is still in its place in the body. On the first occasion it makes no difference if you cut it [*the larynx*] out as a whole, together with the hyoid bone, the community of which with the tongue we have already established in the preceding Book. But it is best if, first of all, you investigate very thoroughly all the points of contact of this hyoid bone with its associated structures before you cut it away from the tongue. For it is very small, particularly in apes, and so, if you remove from it everything that is conjoined with and united to it until it remains isolated, free, and exposed, its small size which you now see will lead you to disbelieve that so many muscles spring off from it.

For besides the muscles of the tongue, with which I have dealt already in the preceding Book, there go out from it other, not small, muscles, which extend to the breast-bone [*sternum*], and those are the muscles with which I dealt not long before this. From it [*the hyoid bone*] two other muscles, slender and long, proceed to the scapulae [*Mm. omohyoidei*]. Two more muscles, bound together, proceed from it to the lower jaw [*Mm. geniohyoidei*] and besides these, two other muscles connect it with the head [skull] at the roots of the awl-like processes [*styloid processes; Mm. stylohyoidei*]. The anatomists have not seen them because they are small, and have often cut them up or destroyed them
97 when they have set free the whole of this region from fasciae. Two other muscles proceed to the broad portion of the lower jaw, and their place of origin is on the two lower ribs [*greater cornua*] of this, the hyoid bone. At the same time, two other muscles spring from these two lower ribs and connect it with the thyroid cartilage [*Mm. thyrohyoidei*]. I said already in regard to these muscles that the nerve-twigs from the two 'hard' nerves of the tongue [*Nn. hypoglossi*] go to them. In addition to these muscles, there is yet another here, a single one, unpaired. It springs from the end of this bone which directs itself towards the tongue and blends with the back [*lingual aspect; submucous*] of the epiglottis [*M. levator epiglottidis* of many mammals: carnivores and ruminants]. In a number of individual animal bodies you see this muscle folded into two layers. I have already said previously that rounded slender ligaments connect the ends of the two upper ribs of this bone with the ends of the two styloid processes.

If now you have removed the musculature which binds it [*the hyoid bone*] to the jaw, and the muscles which ascend upwards to the scapulae, as well as the muscles which descend to the sternum, and you have furthermore detached the small muscle of which I said that it rides on the muscle peculiar to the lower jaw [*M. stylohyoideus* adjoining *M. digastricus*], and have removed, together with it, the ligaments of which I stated that they connect the two upper ribs [*lesser cornua*] of the hyoid bone with the head [skull], then it becomes easy to inspect the underlying structures which we have not yet mentioned or dealt with at all. You can also cut out the whole larynx together with the hyoid bone, and if you wish you can cut it [*the larynx*] out

together with the hyoid bone alone, or together with the tongue and the epiglottis, or with the oesophagus as well. You should then examine intensively the parts of the larynx peculiar to it and *98*
acquaint yourself thoroughly with their whole nature. As for the structures lying beneath, which you must consider before you see these, they consist of the slender nerve which goes to the root of the tongue [*N. glossopharyngeus*], and the muscle which attaches itself and grows into the side of the tongue [*M. styloglossus*], which likewise has its origin on the head [skull] between the origin of the muscle that is tendinous in the middle [*M. digastricus*] and the root of the awl-like [*styloid*] process.

This slender nerve which grows into the root of the tongue is found on both of its sides. From it, on its way up to the tongue, a small offshoot goes to the wall of the pharynx, that is the muscular wall. It must be clear that when I say 'pharynx' I mean the region which lies between the oral cavity and the commencement of the oesophagus. The mouth [*inlet*] of the larynx also extends upwards to this part. Already, in the preceding Book, we have said that here lie also two other 'soft' nerves which split themselves up in the covering [*mucous membrane*] of the tongue [*Nn. linguales*]. You must remember this point, that to this organ alone, that is, the tongue, three pairs of nerves make their way, so that the aggregate number of its nerves amounts to six. And if you say that three classes of nerves go to it, you are quite correct. For the class of the 'hard' nerves and the class of the 'soft' [nerves] are distinct, a point on which all surgical anatomists are in agreement. And as for the third class, which they, the surgical anatomists, have not recognised, this stands in respect of 'hardness' and 'softness' between the other two, since it is surpassed by the 'hard' nerves by the extent to which it surpasses the 'soft' nerves.

When you have observed these things and come to the stage of cutting out the larynx, look for its association with the covering [*mucous membrane*] common to the oesophagus and the tongue, of which I spoke in the preceding Book, and stated that it lines the whole *99*
of the cavity of the mouth, and going further it extends to the pharynx, and then it descends to the lung, passing down in the larynx and the trachea; and it descends to the stomach making its way right through the oesophagus. In this dissection at which we are now present, you

can inspect it thoroughly by itself alone and see how it is situated in the place at which I said that the muscle [*M. thyrohyoideus*] springing from each of the two lower ribs of the hyoid bone connects with and joins the thyroid cartilage of the larynx. If you cut through this muscle, and with the one hand draw upwards the hyoid bone, and with the other hand draw the thyroid cartilage downwards, you find the place [interval] between the two occupied by the structure that is common to those organs which I mentioned. Of that we shall speak later on. But now I assume that the larynx of the animal has been detached and completely removed, and I will begin on the elucidation of the nature of its particular [special] parts, and make them clear. I say that the first, that is the thyroid, cartilage has four borders as I described, which go along it in four lines. Two of these are vertically upright in the direction of length, one on each side, and I will call these two the sides of this, the first cartilage. The two others go transversely, one of them above, where the hyoid bone lies, and the other below, where the end of the cricoid cartilage is. But the second cartilage [*cricoid*] has two sides, which affix themselves to the vertical sides of the first cartilage [*thyroid*], and in fact they are correspondingly vertical, precisely as the two sides of the thyroid cartilage. It [the second cartilage]
100 has a third side, above, extending sideways like the upper border of the first cartilage, and situated as it were correspondingly over against that, and it stands back from that [the first cartilage] at a considerable distance, thus producing the hollow space of the larynx. But at its lower end, the second cartilage has no second line which marks its border and courses along it as is the case in the first [cartilage]. That is because from each of its two lower angles by means of which it is articulated with the first cartilage through an articular ligament, an obliquely directed process juts out, which is twisted and inclined in a direction inwards and forwards. For that reason each of these two processes soon meets its counterpart, and from them is derived a three-sided figure, the base of which is the lower line of the [second] cartilage. The mid-space between the three sides of this triangle is filled up by two muscles [*Mm. cricothyroidei*], whose function is to draw the ends of the two laryngeal cartilages towards one another when they both contract. Try to make yourself adequately acquainted with these two muscles by

cutting first through those of their fascicles which lie superficially and then those which are in the depth. For those muscles comprise two layers, as their fascicles embrace [enclose] the lower border of the thyroid cartilage on both aspects, I mean the outer and the inner. On the further side of the line which passes from below round the thyroid cartilage, their fibres occupy no great space either without or within. On the contrary, they take over only so much [space] as they require for their firm attachment at the union of the two muscles. If you dissect or cut these two muscles [*Mm. cricothyroidei*] clean away, and in addition you cut through the muscle going transversely, of which I said that it binds together the first cartilage with the oesophagus [*M. thyro-pharyngeus*], then you can clearly see the two muscles which attach themselves behind to the second cartilage [*Mm. cricoarytenoidei postici; cricoid cartilage*]. A sharp median ridge separates the two, and parallel to *101*
the sharp ridge there is yet another line by each of the two of them, which goes from above downwards, opposite to the other side of each of them, where you see the first cartilage adjoining the second throughout its length from above downwards. Of the lines which limit these parts one may consequently say that they go straight from below directly upwards, and again that they travel from above downwards. That is because in things outside the body you find that what you mean when you use the notion of a path leading somewhere is a single thing and a single notion, in that you can use the term 'travelling' of those who traverse it both upwards and downwards. The position is the same with the lines which bound the muscles along the length of the neck. For you find that they can be said to go from above downwards, and from below upwards. Whoever thinks of and pictures in his mind their lower endings first, for him they will go from below upwards. And whoever assigns priority to their upper ends, for him they will go from above downwards.

CHAPTER 4. THE RECURRENT LARYNGEAL NERVE (OF GALEN) AND ITS DISTRIBUTION.

Now the nerve, of which I said that it comes from the thorax, proceeding along the neck until it reaches the larynx, is the nerve which the anatomists have neglected to record, and have left without attention

[paid to it], and with which I was obliged to deal in a long exhaustive discussion in the books in which I treated of the Nature of the Voice. It adjoins that part of the larynx, and enters it where the lower border of each of the two muscles that I have mentioned terminates, and at just that spot are also the [R. and L.] joints between the two large laryngeal
102 cartilages. I call these two nerves 'the recurrent nerves' and 'those that come upwards and backwards', on account of a special characteristic of theirs which is not shared by any of the other nerves that descend from the brain. For there is amongst the nerve pairs that spring from the brain one that descends to the thorax, travelling in the neck, and that is the sixth pair [*vagus*]. When the nerves of this pair reach the thorax, from each there arises another pair, and these are two small nerves which mount upwards, travelling in the neck to the side of the trachea, and, at the place described by me, they enter the larynx. Beyond this both nerves pass slightly aslant and come to the inner and upper part of the larynx. And first, there springs off from them a twig which divides itself in the two muscles mentioned [*Mm. cricoarytenoidei postici*]. Then a second twig springs off from them, which divides up in two other muscles which come into position after those, and which take their origin from the upper margins of the second cartilage [*Mm. cricoarytenoidei laterales*]. Afterwards it branches out into two other muscles, of greater dimensions than those mentioned, which take up the principal part of the inner space of the larynx [*Mm. thyroarytenoidei*]. After its ramification in this muscle, it branches out again in those muscles which envelop the base of the third cartilage [*right and left arytenoid cartilages*]; these are very small muscles, and they approach each other so closely that anyone who sees them believes that they are a single muscle [*Mm. interarytenoidei obliqui et transversi*].

Should you wish to examine all this thoroughly, then try to make your dissection by freeing the second cartilage from the first at the two lower joints. It will not prove difficult to recognise these joints and to make their acquaintance, even though they are covered by stout ligaments, as soon as you cut through the muscles which I have described
103 to you, which bind together the lower regions of both cartilages, and the muscles behind the cricoid cartilage. You must aim for the place where you see the two first [the first and second] cartilages attached to

one another. At that spot you move the two cartilages about by making them rotate in a circular fashion about their junction, and by drawing each of them up and down and then in two diametrically opposed directions, then once more let them spring back one against another. You must make for the place where you see the part between the two which expands and contracts. There you now draw apart the structures divided by that part, and you cut into the ligament by itself alone, so that you can see the joint between the two cartilages. When you have done that, now begin to go upwards on both sides, along the sides, force the thyroid cartilage away from the cricoid, and set free the one from the other till you can see clearly the muscle springing from the side of the cricoid cartilage [*Mm. cricoarytenoidei laterales R. and L.*]. Then begin to bend back each of the two sides of the thyroid cartilage and press them strongly outwards, first the one side [*ala*], then the other. If you do that, you see there two muscles more massive than the muscle which we mentioned earlier, which arise from the lower region of the thyroid cartilage, and ascend obliquely to the third [*arytenoid*] cartilage [*Mm. thyroarytenoidei*]. Should you wish to see these more clearly, then divide the thyroid cartilage in two halves at its median ridge without cutting out with it any part of the structures lying beneath it, shear away the cartilage and clear all those structures away from it. Then you will have the clearest possible view of the whole of the inner space of the larynx. Otherwise, without bisecting the thyroid cartilage, you can *104*
set free the inner lining from it. When you have cut away the cartilage in this manner you can see clearly all the structures found in its interior parts, as well as that which was not previously to be seen. Go to work by starting at the spot of which I said that you see there, entirely by itself alone, the mucous membrane common to the tongue, to the oesophagus and to the larynx, after the muscle has been detached which binds the lower rib [*cornu*] of the hyoid bone to the thyroid cartilage [*M. thyrohyoideus*]. At this spot also you can cut away the whole of the hyoid bone from its contiguous structures and then you can inspect more thoroughly and clearly the mucous covering. As to what concerns the common covering, you see that it connects the epiglottis with the larynx, and binds the two to one another. I have already said that it [*the epiglottis*] is also connected with the hyoid bone to which it is

joined by means of a small muscle [*M. levator epiglottidis*]. In this region there are also fasciae which clothe these structures. As they clothe the epiglottis, the larynx and the hyoid bone, these latter are connected one to the other. Still, these fasciae are very delicate indeed, and the whole strength of the position which these organs occupy is derived from their enclosure by muscles and by that fascial covering which they share. Meanwhile it is really the larynx only with which we are dealing. When you have removed the first [*thyroid*] cartilage from it you then see clearly how it is constructed within. There arise from that common covering certain fasciae in relation with structures of a certain elasticity on the side adjoining the oesophagus and the mouth. The glottis comes
105 from this elastic tissue and from the fasciae. You may call the glottis also a tongue, since it resembles the tongue of a flute in the highest degree, and its position in the larynx is that of the tongue in a flute. But the elastic tissue and the fascial structures of which the glottis is composed, coalesce with the muscle inside the larynx, that of which we said that it arises at the base of the thyroid cartilage [*M. thyroarytenoideus*]. This muscle goes obliquely upwards to the third cartilage [*right and left arytenoids*], and its commencement, its origin and its outgrowth, is underneath at the middle part of the base of the thyroid cartilage, at the spot where the ridge of this cartilage ends. And at this place these muscles meet and connect with one another until, as they slant upwards, they split and part the one from the other, and the one takes the direction of the right joint of the third cartilage and the other that of the left. And now, after each of the two has passed beyond this joint, it joins itself to the arytenoid cartilage. These two muscles [*Mm. thyroarytenoidei*] close the glottis, a task in which they are assisted to some extent by the two-fold muscle of which I said that it, a very small muscle, clothes the base[s] of the third [*arytenoid*] cartilage[s].

This, as I have described it, is the function of the muscles mentioned. But the function of those muscles which lie on each of the two sides of the cricoid cartilage [*Mm. cricoarytenoidei laterales*] is to enlarge the larynx sideways. And when they do that to the larynx, it is to be understood that they do it likewise to the glottis. Similarly, the activity of those muscles which lie behind the second [*cricoid*] cartilage [*Mm. cricoarytenoidei postici*] consists in this, that they draw backwards the parts

of the larynx found in that place, and for that reason they widen it. Thus these four muscles open the larynx and the great muscles which 106
lie within [*Mm. thyroarytenoidei*] and the two small muscles which embrace the base[s] of the arytenoid cartilage[s] close it. You can get a satisfactory view of their working by dissecting away all their parts up to the joints by which they are moved after you have secured their attachments to the third cartilage. Then, when you draw upon the muscle through its origin, towards the head, at the same time you move the whole joint.

In the whole of this musculature, the pair of recurrent nerves distributes itself, and consequently as soon as one cuts these nerves, or bruises them, or compresses them with the fingers or by a ligature, the voice of the animal is damaged, and its resonance lost. As for the other muscles of the larynx, you see that nerve-shoots go to them from the sixth pair itself [*vagus*] during its course along the first [upper] portion of the neck. You see one pair of those twigs reaching as far as the upper laryngeal region, and another [nerve or twig] comes to that muscle of the larynx which goes transversely [*M. thyropharyngeus*] and to the muscle [*M. cricothyroideus*] which fastens the second cartilage to the first and binds the two together. In such a work of dissection as this, you can test the activity of this nerve sometimes by dividing it, or by ligaturing it with a thread, or by compressing it with the fingers. For it is all one which of these you do, nor does it make any difference, except that the nerve which has been cut or contused or crushed does not return or revert to its natural state of activity; but the nerve which has only been compressed by the fingers or by the ligature recovers its activity after a short time if it has not been crushed hard by the fingers or by its ligature, or completely disabled by a slender and strong thread, with which it has been bound tightly. If now you have learned to
recognise, in the body of a dead animal, the position of each one of 107
the nerves which are joined and connected to the larynx, then it will not be difficult for you to recognise and find each one of them as they are exposed in the body of a living animal. It is best if you do this on the body of a pig. For in all animals which have a larynx, the activity of the nerves and the muscles is one and the same, but the loathsomeness of the expression in vivisection is not the same for all animals. Because

of that for my own part, as you know already, I illustrate such vivisections on the bodies of swine or of goats, without employing apes. But it is necessary that you should extend your studies and examine the larynx. This is constructed in the same way in the bodies of apes and men, a construction which is shared by the other animals which have a voice. You must, then, dissect a dead man and an ape and other animals furnished with a voice which have, besides the voice, the vocal apparatus, the larynx. For the animals which possess no voice have no larynx either. He who is not versed in anatomy thinks that in regard to the plan of the larynx great contrasts exist among the six Animal Classes, to which this our discussion refers. That is because neither the absolute dimensions nor the shapes of the parts of the larynx are precisely the same amongst all of them, a point which applies also to the number of the muscles which they have here. But as regards the activity of each one of the parts of the larynx, and the service which they perform, these are one and the same in all animals provided with a voice. That is because in the bodies of these animals the intention of the Creator was uniform with regard to the plan of the vocal apparatus, just as his intention was uniform also with regard to the plan of the
108 respiratory organs in those animals provided with respiration. For the contrasts between these organs in the bodies of these animals consists solely in their absolute dimensions and their shapes. Thus it occurred to me during the time when I applied myself to the study of these recurrent nerves, and was seeking out the origin of the voice, that I should investigate the design of this nerve in the bodies of flying animals, especially in such as have long necks, as for example the crane, the white waterfowl with a long neck, and the large bird which all the Greeks normally call by the general name of 'strouthos', that is, the ostrich. And now as I came to the dissection of these animals, and observed the design of these upwardly recurrent nerves, and found that their design was exactly one and the same, I marvelled much at the lack of any trace of slackness or remissness to be found in Creation. Already in the work 'On the Uses of the Parts of the Body', and in the work 'On the Voice', I had established that the nerve which activates the musculature which opens the larynx, and that which closes it, must ascend from the lower region upwards to the larynx, and that this

nerve after it has descended from the brain, must necessarily move in a circle round some organic part which takes for it the place of a trochlea, round which a cord passes in order to turn round it and to return in an upwards direction; and that in the neck no organ of such a description exists. But as I saw the necks of these animals which I mentioned to be very long, I thought that it would not be possible in a slender nerve which has its origin on the brain, that it should first descend as far as the thorax, and that from there a portion of it should return, which would have to traverse the whole length of the neck. But in that point there is in Creation no slackness or remissness, as, in fact, there is none in any other instance. For the sixth pair of the nerves that descend from the brain goes downwards till it reaches the thorax, passing through the lowest part of the neck, through which it passes in *109*
the other animals also. Here in this region a nerve branches off from it, which climbs up to the larynx in the bodies of these long-necked animals, just as it branches off and climbs up in the bodies of the other animals.

Now since this is as I have described it, then you can convince yourself as to what damage and destruction affects the voice as soon as this nerve meets with injury, not only in swine, but also, as a whole, in all other animals provided with a voice. However, in order that, when you turn your hand to that in any one of the animal classes, you may be in a position to find quickly and to recognise this nerve, you must examine and dissect the animal [first of all in the defunct state] which you wish to vivisect. The matter is as I have already explained it to you, that is to say there is no need for you to dissect[1] a living animal, whether this be a pig or a goat. Thus you will get what you want. But leave the live apes alone, and turn to these animals. First inform yourself by means of diligent study of the structure of all parts of the larynx in the dead animal. Now I will describe to you the structure of the larynx in the pig, which is as follows.

[1] The text here must be corrupt. The emendation suggested by the apparatus criticus would read: 'there is no need for you to dissect any living animal except pigs or goats. Thus you will....' M.C.L.

CHAPTER 5. THE DISSECTION PERFORMED IN THE PIG: (1) THE LARYNGEAL APPARATUS.

I say that it is compounded of three cartilages which are articulated one with another through four joints, as I have described it in the ape. And similarly the number of the laryngeal muscles is the same as that of the laryngeal muscles of the apes, and the positions of the muscles on the
110 larynx are exactly the same as there, and their growth upon and their connection with that apparatus are precisely like those in apes. One can say conjecturally that the gross dimensions of the laryngeal muscles of a pig are twice those of the laryngeal muscles of an ape in instances where these two animals are equal in respect of the remainder of the body, since the larynx of the pig taken as a whole is twice as large as the whole larynx of the ape, provided that the two animals, I mean the ape and the pig, are of the same size. And as for that nerve which connects and grows into the muscles of a pig, it is more than twice as thick as the nerve which in an ape is found on a muscle of the same size. But the muscles of the pig not only exceed those of the ape by far in regard to their gross dimensions, but further they exceed by a great deal in respect of power and importance. Thus the voice of the apes is thin, weak, and small, whereas that of the pig is loud and strong. And since that is so in them, then of necessity not only must the special laryngeal muscles be powerful, but so must be those [other] muscles also which are common to it and to the neighbouring organic structures. When I say 'the special muscles' I mean the muscles which open and close it [*the larynx*] and by 'the muscles which are common to it and to the neighbouring structures' [I mean] the musculature which fastens it [*the larynx*] to the sternum and binds the two together, and the musculature which connects it with the hyoid bone and binds the two together. These latter also contribute some assistance to the peculiar activities of the larynx, since those of them that mount upwards to the hyoid bone connect in their grasp the whole upper part of the thyroid cartilage, and those of them which pass downwards to the sternum connect in
111 their grasp the whole of its lower parts. This, however, is something in the nature of an extra or superfluous advantage for the larynx, as even without possessing these muscles it would be capable of dis-

charging fully its necessary activities. As to what concerns that muscle which attaches the larynx to the oesophagus and binds the two together [*M. thyropharyngeus*], it grasps both the sides of the larynx, and brings them together more forcibly than these. Nevertheless, even when it lacks this muscle also, the larynx is able to effect its purpose of partaking in the formation of the different varieties of tone, provided that there remain in it undamaged the six muscles of which I said that they are joined and grow on to the third cartilage [*arytenoids; Mm. crico-arytenoidei post. et lat.; thyroarytenoidei*]. For the power and the importance of these muscles for the production of the voice is extremely great. Next to them, in power and importance, comes the two-fold muscle [*Mm. interarytenoidei transv. et obliq.*] which passes round the base of the third cartilage, and after this, in power and importance, [come] those muscles which fasten the lower borders of the thyroid cartilage to the cricoid cartilage [*Mm. cricothyroidei*], and the muscles which fasten its [*the thyroid cartilage's*] upper border to the hyoid bone, as well as the muscles which fasten its two sides to the oesophagus [*Mm. thyro-pharyngei*]. For the muscles [*Mm. thyrohyoidei*] which descend from the hyoid bone to the thyroid cartilage pull upwards that cartilage together with the whole larynx, and they bring the upper border of it [*the thyroid cartilage*] up towards that [*the hyoid bone*]. But the muscles which attach the thyroid cartilage to the cricoid cartilage fasten and draw together the two ends of the lower portions of both cartilages. The muscles which come from the oesophagus to the two sides of the thyroid cartilage [*Mm. thyropharyngei*] grasp the thyroid cartilage in that region and joint it to the cricoid cartilage.

In this section I have brought to light the essential function of the hyoid bone in regard to its co-operation with the muscles that descend to the larynx. For you see that these muscles occupy a not unimportant 112
position in relation to the totality of the vocal organs, in that they draw the thyroid cartilage upwards, and grasp it and connect it there [*to the hyoid bone*]. If the muscles which come to it from the hyoid bone did not draw this cartilage upwards and if, in opposition to that pull, the muscles descending to the sternum did not draw it down, and if the muscles which come to it from the oesophagus did not stretch and draw it to both sides, then it would lack in the highest degree firmness

and stability, and it would be quick to turn and slip in all directions, and withdraw itself from the trachea and the oesophagus. But now it is firmly fixed in position by means of the strong attachment of the muscles which I described, and as the result of their traction upon it from both the two opposite sides in four different directions. For that reason it cannot displace itself far upwards, because of the traction of the lower muscles upon it, and it is not capable of displacing itself far downwards because of the traction of the upper muscles upwards upon it. Similarly it is not able to displace itself far to one or other of the two sides, on account of the tension of the transverse muscles in two opposite directions. As this is so, then the whole of this musculature which I specified must combine to be a single great muscular group, and those muscles which draw it in the direction of the sternum must be counterbalanced. Of these muscles two have their origin on the middle part of the upper region of the thyroid cartilage, and two spring from its lower region near the two lower angles. As for the muscles which go downwards to it from the hyoid bone, they occupy the space that lies between the two points to which those
113 muscles are joined and attached, so that there is no place denuded of muscular tissue upon the thyroid cartilage. And consequently, the sites of the muscles which draw it upwards are disposed more obliquely than they are in the bodies of apes. For when they have arisen from the lower rib [*greater cornu*] of the hyoid bone, they place themselves on both sides along the upper line of the thyroid cartilage, and from here they proceed obliquely to a point lower than the end of its crista. And here, in this place, the two muscles meet one another and come into contact with one another. Close by, on the outer side, are the attachments of the muscles which come from the sternum, so that no single portion of the thyroid cartilage is without a covering here.

CHAPTER 6. THE PIG (CONTINUED): (2) DISSECTION OF THE NECK.

Now just as in the apes, after the investing muscle, the so-called muscular carpet, has been reflected from the neck, there come to view first of all the muscles which run from hyoid bone downwards to the sternum, even so you find the arrangement in pigs. And since this is so,

then it is clear that first of all you must dissect away those muscles which are seen in the second place, that is, those muscles which go in the direction of the sternum from the thyroid cartilage, two muscles on each side, since there are four of them in all. And in order that the whole of the front region of the neck may be revealed for you and laid bare, cut away and eradicate the muscle [*M. sternomastoideus*] which comes from the skull to the sternum, a bilateral muscle which lies in this region in the bodies of swine because they do not possess clavicles. But in the bodies of apes this muscle joins up with the one which reaches and grows firmly on to the clavicle [*clavicular head of sternomastoid*], one muscle on each of the two sides [of the neck]. Should you wish 114
immediately to uncover the whole anterior cervical area at the same time as your dissection of the laryngeal region, and to obtain a full view of the 'artery of stupor', you must cut away freely, on both sides, the muscles which come to the sternum, those which arise from exactly those parts of the skull. The incision starts at the root of the ear, at the origin of each of the two muscles, as you have already learned in the body of the ape. When you reflect and remove the sheaths which envelop the vessels and the nerves lying on the neck, then you see very clearly indeed the jugular vein, the artery of stupor [*A. carotis*] and the nerve which descends on the neck [*vagus*] and, besides these things, the branches of this nerve which go to the muscles of which we have already spoken. Should you desire to examine the last stage of this nerve at the skull itself, then dissect away the musculature lying there. When you do that you then have an adequate view of the seventh nerve pair [*hypoglossal*]. And when you turn to these two nerves and compress them with the fingers, or ligature them with a cord, or cut them through, or when bruising or crushing has been inflicted upon them, then you deprive the tongue of the animal of its voluntary activities. And similarly you deprive the muscles of the larynx of their activity when you injure the nerves which join the larynx and grow in it, especially the recurrent nerve. The nerve joins and connects with the larynx in exactly the same places as those where we said that it joins and connects with the larynx in the bodies of apes.

After these preliminary [remarks] I will now describe to you the procedure that you must follow in the dissection of the bodies of

swine in order to expose freely all those structures which lie above
the larynx, and by means of which it enters into connection and con-
115 junction with the hyoid bone...[1] only so far forward that it reaches to
the mandible. Then hereupon they both sink into and are lost to view
in the depth of the tongue beneath the muscle which goes transversely and
extends itself beneath the whole of the tongue [*M. mylohyoideus*]. Now
when the animal is placed on its back in an operation like this, then it
is understood that the part which previously, when it was unaffected
and in its natural state, lay underneath, now comes to be seen superficially.
And here, in such a mode of proceeding as this, you must necessarily
remove this part first. Over this muscle there applies itself to those of
its parts which lie on the mandible another muscle, one on each side,
that is the muscle which opens the jaws [*M. digastricus*]. It begins to
connect and join with the jaw in the place that constitutes for it a sort
of angle, and its connection and junction is at the end of the broad part
of the mandible, so that it meets and touches the muscle found in this
region, that is the muscle which draws the mandible upwards [*M. masseter*], a muscle other than the M. temporalis. But this one of which
we are speaking, the mandibular muscle [*M. digastricus*], extends itself
further. It arises first of all from a hard band on the styloid process, and
it does not extend to the anterior end of the mandible as it does in apes.
When you have dissected the whole of this muscle also and separated
it from the tongue-muscle which runs transversely and lies beneath it—
though where the animal has been placed upon its back, you see it
superficially placed, and thus it is the first of all these muscles to be
dissected—you will be in a position to see satisfactorily its endings, how
they are connected and made fast to the jaw-bones in the places where
the tongue is free from the muscles surrounding it, and laid bare, and
concealed behind nothing except beneath the enveloping fasciae. As for
116 the place on the mandible where this transversely directed muscle
[*M. mylohyoideus*] ends and vanishes, it is there that the wide part of
the mandible is found, and there also lies the muscle [*M. pterygoideus
medialis*] which, from within, clothes the deep aspect [of the mandible]
and attaches itself to it. This is a muscle of considerable size, and its

[1] The missing words are referred by Simon to the hypoglossal nerve because the remnant of the sentence as well as the following sentence are evidently applicable to that nerve and its relations.

function is to raise the mandible upwards. You can also see that it comes from the upper jaw. There emerges that soft nerve [*lingual*] peculiar to the tongue from the place between the thick muscle which occupies the wide part of the mandible, and the muscle which was previously mentioned, that which has transversely directed fibres [*M. mylohyoideus*].

CHAPTER 7. THE PIG (CONTINUED): (3) THE TONGUE.

After these things which we have described here, you must dissect the whole of the muscle of the tongue, which springs from the two lower cornua of the hyoid bone along the whole of their upper borders, in the same way that there springs from the lower border the muscle which descends downwards to the larynx [*M. thyrohyoideus*], as we described previously. Between the two, on the curved portion [of the hyoid bone] lies the muscle [*M. stylohyoideus*] which attaches the hyoid bone to the skull, and binds them together, the one with the other. As for the end of its two lower cornua, that is the one which in the body of the ape connects with the thyroid cartilage, this is connected with the cranial bones in the place from which there springs the origin of the muscular component of the coverings of the oesophagus. In their course, the two meet and come into contact with the pharynx on both sides, in a place not far from the common nerve [*N. glossopharyngeus*] which goes to the pharynx and to the root of the tongue. This nerve also is uncovered and can be seen by you in the course of this procedure with which we are here dealing. As for what concerns it, you can see that first a part of it is directed to the pharynx, and thereafter the remainder curves down towards the root of the tongue, and joins it
and implants itself in it. But now, if you have dissected the transverse *117*
muscle of the tongue [*M. mylohyoideus*], you then see clearly its hard and also its soft nerve [*N. hypoglossus and N. lingualis*]. Of the two, the hard one sets itself about to break up and to ramify in its muscles, and the soft one ramifies in its covering [*mucous membrane*]. And between these two nerves lies the spongy flesh peculiar to the tongue [*sublingual and submandibular salivary glands*]. At its first beginning this gland is visible, but then immediately, as it goes on, it covers itself and hides itself beneath the soft nerve [*N. lingualis*] which breaks up into its branches in this place. Then, when the gland has travelled onwards

beneath the nerve, it becomes again exposed and uncovered, visible to inspection, especially after you have completely dissected out the nerve right up to the place of its junction with, and its implantation in, the tongue. Thus too this gland continues as far as the front end of the mandible, to the place at which the right side of this is attached to the left. When it reaches this place it cannot be seen unless the animal's mouth is opened. When the mouth is open and the membrane ensheathing the tongue has been scraped off from the bone, then this gland becomes plainly visible to inspection, after the whole tongue has been drawn towards the inner parts of the cavity of the mouth. At the terminal point of this gland is the origin of the vessel which one calls the salivary spout, and this vessel opens into the mouth at the side of that part [*frenulum*] of the tongue which is fastened to the mandible. You should prepare by dissection all these three organic structures of which we spoke, and remove them, that is to say the hard nerve, the soft nerve, and the gland related to the tongue, lying between those
118 structures mentioned. You first see, then, on the line which divides the [intact] body into two halves, those lingual muscles which take their origin from the upper border of the hyoid bone. These muscles extend as far as the front end of the mandible, and that is the place at which they are attached and firmly implanted. They are muscles united together, and one could well say that they may be a single duplicated muscle [*Mm. geniohyoidei*]. If you dissect the whole of this double muscle away you can then see clearly beneath it the remaining lingual muscles, I mean those muscles which mount upwards obliquely from the lower region, and they are the muscles which spring from both the lower cornua of the hyoid bone and go to the sides of the tongue. Moreover these muscles [*Mm. hyoglossus and chondroglossus*] are duplicated, one on each of the two sides. And if you take them away, the spot appears where the artery grows into the tongue, an artery of very great size in comparison with the mass of the tongue [*A. lingualis*]. This artery goes to the tongue, taking its course upon the cartilaginous portion of the structure which connects the skull with the upper cornu of the hyoid bone, and thus binds the two with one another.

119 [Ḥunain says: In three Greek MSS. which we have so far met in addition to the Syriac MS. we found that, confirming what Galen says shortly after this point, this intermediate piece is not cartilaginous but ossified. And if this is so, then one cannot escape from one of two conclusions, either that there is an oversight of the scribe, or that he was a person who thought he would improve the text, and consequently altered and corrupted it].

From each one of these two double muscles, whose description we are here discussing, one portion springs from the lower cornu of the hyoid bone [*M. hyoglossus*] and the other portion springs from its cartilaginous cornu, extending itself straight upwards [*M. chondroglossus*]. Both portions of the divided muscle, of which there is, as I have described, one on each side, after they have advanced slantingly forwards, connect and unite with the tongue in an uninterrupted and unbroken junction. The attachment and implantation of both of them take place at the particular spot where the muscle which comes away from the skull and mounts up from below towards the tongue, passing by the tonsils, goes to the side of the tongue and attaches itself there [*M. styloglossus*]. This muscle extends itself over so elongated a course that it almost reaches to the tip of the tongue. But the double muscle [*M. hyoglossus with M. chondroglossus*] goes obliquely, meets, and coalesces at its end with the side of the mid-part of the tongue and *120*
makes contact with that muscle which I have just mentioned [*M. styloglossus*].[1] You see further, how the two remaining muscles extend themselves lengthwise in the middle of the tongue, and for their part they both attach themselves by their extreme ends to the front end of the mandible, and embed themselves there. They both start from the root of the tongue, so that one might well say that all these muscles are a part of the tongue, if it were not clearly to be seen that there is a difference between their substance and its. For in [regard to] the formation of their flesh they are similar to all other muscles, but the peculiar substance of the tongue is not like that. On the contrary, it is whiter, more spongy and more porous.

[1] This sentence seems to describe the decussation between M. styloglossus coming from behind downwards and forwards, and on the other hand the M. hyoglossus (main fibres) directed backwards and upwards.

CHAPTER 8. THE PIG (CONTINUED): (4) THE HYOID APPARATUS.

We wish now to describe the state of affairs at the root of the tongue. But in order that you may derive benefit from the acquaintance with the nature and the form of the hyoid bone, not only for the clear understanding of what we have already said in this Book, but also of that which is about to follow, because the form and the structure of the hyoid bone in swine differ from those described in the apes, I will first explain how the matter stands with regard to the form and the structure of this bone [in swine]. I say that the two lower cornua of the hyoid bone come as far as its middle part, that is a part which possesses a greater width than in apes. And from this part also there pass two upper cornua which run parallel, the one not far distant from the other. In the intermediate space, between the two, is a ligament of the class of fascial sheaths which connects them. The rest of the body of the hyoid bone is ossified. But its two upper cornua which we have mentioned here, are two cartilages. At their endings you see two ligaments [*stylohyoid*] springing from them. These do not go straight
121 upwards for their whole length, but you see both of them, in the same manner as the lower cornua which make their way downwards and sideways, making their way obliquely forwards each towards one of the two sides of the skull, like the two ligaments in the bodies of apes, of which I said that they attach the ends of the two upper cornua of the hyoid bone to the ends of the two needle-like [*styloid*] processes. Only, in the bodies of swine, these ligaments do not remain uniform in their substance, and they do not attach themselves to the ends of the styloid processes, but first they change over into cartilaginous substance, then into osseous substance, then again into cartilaginous substance, then back again into ligamentous substance, and afterwards they attach themselves to the skull and embed themselves beside the two styloid processes. For that reason it happens that the whole mass of this structure which connects the hyoid bone with the skull is not homogeneous as it is in apes, but on the contrary it is put together from three components, unlike one another in regard to their substance. Thus the middle piece is bone, the two parts, lying one on each side of this middle piece, are

cartilage, one resembling the other, and then, after the cartilage, come two strong ligaments. The whole mass of this structure stretches out in circular form after the fashion of a nerve. In fully matured swine, its intermediate part is hard and osseous, but in young farrows it is flexible and cartilaginous and in senile swine it is actually bone. In the apes the whole mass of this structure, put together from the five components described, is a single homogeneous structure and, in fact, it is a round ligament as I have already described. Among the 'creeping' animals on the other hand [*Virenidae*] the chief mass of its substance is
a bone, not rounded bone, but rather flattened, and for the hyoid bone 122
it fulfils the offices of support and of a prop. And as for the remaining four animal classes—they stand between the apes and the 'creeping' animals—the nature of these two structures is in some kinds more nearly related to that in the apes, in other kinds further removed from these. As for the state of affairs among the remaining classes, this I will describe later on. But the genus of the swine is not far removed from that of the apes. So also is it in the class of 'animals with interlocking teeth' [*carnivora*], though they do not resemble one another in all respects. For in regard to the extremities of the lower cornua of the hyoid bone, there exists a certain contrast between them and what we described in the apes. The special mandibular muscle which opens it [the mandible] has in swine its origin on the styloid process.[1] And the contrast between them does not lie here alone. For a further point is that this muscle does not become tendinous in its middle part, as is the case in apes; on the contrary, it possesses a strong tendon which connects it with the hyoid bone, and the whole of the rest of its substance consists of flesh. And the bone[2] which attaches the upper cornu of the hyoid bone to the skull of the animal and binds the two with one
another has, as described, three parts. The mid-portion is osseous, and 123
there courses upon it the branch springing off from the artery of stupor

[1] The styloid process, so-called, of swine is not the same as the styloid process of Primates including Man.

[2] Ḥunain says: 'We have found, in all the Greek MSS, what we have translated. However he [Galen] should not say "bone", but "body" since most of it is not bone, but cartilage. For this thing is compounded of three parts, and in fact, two parts thereof are bony and one cartilaginous; yet he says it is a bone. He calls it "bone" because there is more bone than cartilage, or because the bone is more rigid. He has, then, judged that it should be called bone because this is more important than the cartilage'.

[*A. carotis*] and [this branch] mounts upwards to the tongue [*A. lingualis*].

It is best and most expedient for you to remove the whole of this hyoid bone, together with its offshoots of which we spoke so that you may examine it closely. You will thus understand the anatomy of the laryngeal structures as previously described, as also the anatomy of the parts [composing] the root of the tongue, which we have still to describe, should you at any time have wished to make clear to yourself the state of affairs at the root of the tongue, and that the remaining structures with which it [the tongue root] is united should also become visible to you.[1]

Accordingly make your dissection from the start as I will describe it. First cut away all the muscles springing from the hyoid bone. Even though I have already described these muscles earlier, that will not prevent me from mentioning them here also. I say, then, that two of the muscles proceed from its lower border to the sternum [*Mm. sterno-hyoidei*] and two other muscles proceed from its upper border to the end of the mandible [*Mm. geniohyoidei*]. In the apes, other muscles on both sides of its lower border proceed to the scapulae [*Mm. omohyoidei*] and in swine they commence in such a way as though they would pass towards the scapulae, yet they do not join or attach themselves to these,
124 but go to the muscle in the cavity of the scapula, and between them there is found a tendon of the nature of the fascial tissue. In the apes, other muscles have their origin on the lower border of the hyoid bone, and those muscles are very slender and they go to the skull-bone where the root of the awl-like [*styloid*] process is [*M. stylohyoideus*]. Analogous to these, in the bodies of swine, are muscles which go to just the same place, but they have their origins on either side on the convex parts of the whole of the lower cornu of the hyoid bone. And these muscles are strong. You must now detach and remove the whole of this musculature, and together with it the muscles of which we said that they go from the hyoid bone to the jaw and to the tongue [*Mm. genio-hyoidei, hyoglossi, chondroglossi*] and with these also, the muscles which from the skull onwards go obliquely towards the pharynx, and reach as far as the two sides of the tongue [*Mm. styloglossi*]. When you have

[1] Scribal addition to text: At this point, he speaks of the role of the root of the tongue.

detached and displaced all these muscles, you can see the root of the tongue combined with all the structures near to it, except for a small section. The connection is made by the covering [*mucous membrane*] common to the tongue and to the whole mouth, with which the tongue is joined and connected to all the other structures associated with it. By means of this [covering] it [the tongue] is connected with the oesophagus and the larynx. If you take out all these parts, so that the tongue is denuded and uncovered, then you see its root with the following construction in swine.

I say that at the spot at which there is the commencing outgrowth of the two upper cornua of the hyoid bone, in the centre not only of the place of origin of the two cornua, but also of the whole of the two upper cornua, you will find a ligament of the nature of fascial tissue. And this ligament has likewise a root, that springs from that very spot at which the roots of the cornua originate, and from the interval between the two of them. For you see that the roots of these two upper
cornua do not touch each other, but they remain separated from one *125*
another, corresponding to the distance of the one of the two cornua from the other. And here, in the place between the two origins, there is found a ligament which goes to the head of the epiglottis, and two small muscles so united together that you can say because of this union that they are not two muscles, but a double one. They attach themselves at the extreme end of the epiglottis, and coalesce with it [*Lig. hyo-epiglottica*]. It is best that you do not say that this is the extreme end of the epiglottis, but on the contrary that it is its first part, the point of its commencement. It is also rounded off. If now, from this point of which we said that it is the commencement of the epiglottis, you follow the dorsal surface or ridge of the epiglottis, you then see forthwith the root of the tongue, because in this place alone the tongue unites itself with the epiglottis by means of a fleshy sort of bridle. But as for all its other extremities found there, their union with the adjacent parts of the epiglottis comes about through [the medium of] the covering which ensheathes the tongue.

CHAPTER 9. DIGRESSION ON THE NOMENCLATURE OF GROWTH-PROCESSES.

And since the affair is as I have described it, then you should not seek where either the tongue or any other organ originates. For only nerves, veins, arteries and tendons have genuine origins. And one can say with truth that they spring out from such and such a place. The smaller ones branch off from the larger, in the manner in which its branches grow out from the trunk of a tree. Then they ramify in the same kind of way as the larger branches break up into smaller ones and these smaller ones into still smaller ones; then, from these last, others branch off again, and that goes on unendingly, so that the arrangement becomes at last the same as in that sort of tree of which the ultimate twigs continue to the fissured endings. And thus each single vein, artery and nerve reaches its ending, its furthest extremity, calls a halt, and divides up no more. But as for what relates to the remaining organs, among these
126 there is not even a single one that develops out from another. Nevertheless, a person who strives for a clear mode of expression in the demonstration of that which is to be seen in a dissection is often compelled to say that one structure grows out from another, and yet again that the one attaches itself to and joins the other. It is best that you should describe all these things in the way which is common to and comprehensive of them, that is to say thus, that 'this comes into connection with that and unites itself to it', just as in regard to the eyelids, when a wound occurs, it happens as a result that one eyelid becomes partially united with the other. Similarly we have seen wounded fingers that have joined one with the other. Furthermore I say that in the creation of the embryo, were it to happen that one of its organic parts was created first, then secondly and successively another, then in succession a third, fourth and fifth part, you would not need on that account to conclude that the secondary organs grew out of the primary, since it is possible that that affair resembles the process of building, and that just as the builder merely lays one object upon another, and binds one thing with another, so also it is with regard to the formation of an animal. This is the way in which the bedstead, the chair, the chest and the ship are put together, that is to say that in these objects one lays

down one portion before the others, and then piles up the remaining parts upon and after that portion, so that the parts are firmly joined to one another, some being fastened and fixed in others, some being welded and some tied to others. And of the construction of a ship, you cannot say that its keel might be the root out from which its remaining parts grew, nor yet of the construction of a house that its foundations are the root of its remaining parts, since the remaining parts of the ship and the house are simply built and combined on top of these founda- *127*
tions, and their formation and creation do not proceed from the substructure, but are merely laid down upon it and after it. But this is not a place in which we need say more on this subject since our object here is simply to describe the procedure in the exposure of the bodily organs, not in the dead animal only, but also in the living. So I return once more to that with which I was dealing, an account of the tongue.

CHAPTER 10. STRUCTURE AND FUNCTION OF THE TONGUE, PHARYNX AND LARYNX, ILLUSTRATED BY EXPERIMENTS.

I say that everyone knows that men are served by the tongue in their need for speech and for the distinction and the recognition of the various kinds of food and of taste, of which they are in need. And further we find, by observing it, that in chewing it moves the food about in the mouth, turns it over for us and pushes it hither and thither for us as we wish. Some believe that it also confers great advantage in swallowing, since it first carries, on its back, the food which has reached the mouth, and then thrusts it, travelling along in the pharynx, towards the oesophagus; and they conclude that these actions which are performed by its muscles are followed by a very important natural activity as soon as the muscle which goes to the thyroid cartilage [*M. thyrohyoideus*] moves upwards. It displaces itself upwards, so they believe, towards the root of the tongue, whenever the tongue is stretched in those actions mentioned. And as soon as this muscle displaces itself upwards, the larynx, they believe, displaces itself at the same time, and consequently approaches nearer to the epiglottis, and connects with it so as to be overlapped and closed up by it, so that no portion of food or drink becomes deflected and invades the lungs

through the larynx. Of the absurdities which are inherent in the views
128 of these persons I will speak in another book, that is, the one in which I examine the obscure movements which the anatomists do not know. But as for those details which one finds in a dissection, and which reveal themselves to the eye, and ensure the refutation of those persons and the invalidation of their assertions, these are things which I will describe here. I say that when you have learned previously from the dissection of the body of a dead animal the position of each of the two nerves of the tongue [*N. hypoglossus and N. lingualis*] you must then accustom and train yourself to make the incision in the skin of the neck, exactly where the 'hard' nerve [*N. hypoglossus*] lies beneath it. This is something which you, who have already seen how I made it, will be in a position to perform with the slightest of efforts. Moreover I am acquainted with a large number of you who have already performed that excellently. But as for those who have not seen how I performed it, I have reason to think that the reward of perseverance should benefit them also. Such a man must first of all accustom himself by practice on the body of a dead animal, so as to be competent to divide, at one stroke, the whole of the skin, and the underlying muscle, which one calls the muscular carpet [*M. platysma myoides*]. Next, let him draw apart the two margins of the incision with hooks and expose the organs lying beneath the muscular carpet. But there is one thing against which he must be on his guard, and that is the cutting through of a vein or artery. He who has already trained himself by practice will perform that with the least effort, without blood spurting over him, and the 'hard' nerve [*N. hypoglossus*] will soon be laid open for him. As I have said, there is one on each of the two sides of the body. And since, in regard to the distribution of veins, of arteries, and of nerves, the arrangement here is the same as in all organic structures, that is, a
129 symmetrical dichotomy, so here, one half of the tongue immediately loses its mobility when one cuts through one of these nerves; and if we divide both nerves, then the whole tongue will be deprived of voluntary movement on the spot. I have already said, many times, that when you ligature this nerve with a thread, or pinch it with your fingers, or crush it or bruise it, you inflict upon it damage equal to that produced by cutting it through. Of that I now remind you here once again, and

moreover of this also, that it is best and most expedient, if you intend that when you relax the ligature the animal should return again to the state of being able to perform its natural function with that organ, that you should not sever the nerve, crush it, or bruise it, or constrict it tightly and very strongly with a ligature, nor again that the thread with which it is ligatured should be very tense and slender, since if the ligature is like that, then it cuts into the depth of the nerve, and produces in it an injury comparable with that which results from section or bruising. Now after you have injured the nerve, by whatever sort or kind of injury you like, and you have deprived the tongue of voluntary movement, you can now, if you wish it, stitch up that incision [i.e. the incision in the neck]. Otherwise if you do not stitch it together, you can bind a soft sponge firmly on it, and leave the animal until its consciousness returns, and it becomes strong again and recovers from the transient agony in which it was plunged at the time at which the incision was made into it. The animal when it is in this state may be assumed to be thirsty. In that case you will see that it soon drinks when it sees water in a vessel from which it can drink. Then, when it swallows down the water which it is drinking, you will see how the larynx moves upwards, in exactly the same way as it raised itself
up when the animal was uninjured and in its natural condition. This is *130*
one of the proofs that the constriction of the tongue has no part to play in the movement of the larynx, since we find that the larynx is drawn and moved upwards while the tongue is doing absolutely nothing. If you like to take a vessel with a narrow outlet, and you place it on the dome [*dorsum*] of the tongue, and pour the water out from it into the pharynx, then you will see that the animal swallows the water, and that the larynx hastens to rise upwards. This is also a procedure which we have often carried out in men who are found in deep heavy stupor. And it is carried out in the same way with other animals when they are gagged for drenching; for one then takes hold of the tongue of such an animal and packs it securely down, and next pours down what fluid potable medicaments one wants. Now, however, leave this and similar matters aside. For here we intend to deal only with those details which appear visibly in a dissection. So pass on with us to the discussion of another point.

When you cut away and extirpate completely the 'transverse' muscles, I mean the muscles which come to the thyroid cartilage [*Mm. thyropharyngei*], now detach the larynx from its connection with the tongue, and you will see that in that condition the animal swallows just as before, and you will see that the larynx displaces itself upwards in precisely the same way as it did before. And I should only like to know whether these facts alone, which emerge visibly in the vivisection, do not invalidate the opinion of those persons who believe that the larynx moves itself together with the muscles of the tongue. One circumstance that ought likewise to invalidate it is something you can see before the vivisection of the live animal. It is the fact in regard to
131 which some [anatomists] go profoundly astray and err most seriously since they do not know that from the two lower cornua of the hyoid bone that muscle [*M. thyrohyoideus*] is attached and implanted upon the larynx which comes from their lower border, and that the muscle which comes from their upper border is connected with the tongue [*M. hyoglossus*]. But they believe that the whole hyoid bone, when it is raised up by the muscle which goes to the tongue, raises the whole larynx with it. And if they say that, it is clear here also that they do not in the least understand the activity of the larynx, that actually it is the organic structure alone which displaces itself upwards and contracts towards its head, that draws up with itself the organic parts to which it extends. However, leave aside this and like matters. For, as I have already told you, I have summarised all that can be said about that in another place. Let us now describe the condition of the nerve of the neck [*N. vagus*], and begin our discussion from another point, as follows.[1]

CHAPTER II. FURTHER EXPERIMENTS ON NERVES IN THE NECK.

I say that to one who through practice has acquired dexterity in exposing the vagus nerve it will become so easy that he will be able to complete the task with a single stroke of the knife. And this is not something which I alone can accomplish, for it is performed by many of my colleagues also. To do the same in his turn is easy indeed for anyone

[1] [Scribal addition:] In this place he speaks of the state of the nerve which one sees in the neck in the living animal.

who is present when one performs it, and who sees it with his own eyes. But to describe it in words is very difficult. However, as I have thought it right in this book to try to serve the advantage of those who have never been present or seen me when I was performing a dissection, I must describe this operation also in the clearest possible way. And so I say that it is best that you extend the animal on its back on a board
that is perforated by holes through which run the cords with which its 132
limbs are tethered, so that they [the cords] come through and out on the undersurface of the board, and are so knotted together that they completely prevent the animal from moving about. Previously I have also said that it is best if the animal be a pig. The bristles should be shaved off from those parts which the incision encounters. Now divide them [those parts] with a single incision that runs in a straight line, one on each of the two sides of the trachea throughout the length of the neck. Commence at the trachea, and continue from above downwards for a considerable distance. When you do that, then in this region portions of 'spongy flesh' [*lymph glands*] reveal themselves to you, which you can easily tear out and clear away with the finger-tips without using a knife. Next you can see the artery which is known as 'the artery of stupor' [*A. carotis*], one on each side. With it you can also see the deep jugular vein, and the 'nerve of the sixth pair' [*vagus*], enclosed in a common sheath. Dissect away this sheath from them. Then introduce, between the artery and the nerve, a bluntly pointed hook with an eye, of which the end is moderately sharp, so that it enters easily into the fasciae without any perforation being made in the veins or arteries. And attached to this hook there should be a thread folded into two strands—either a stout thread, such as is suitable for sewing, or a thread such as is used for ligatures. This should run through the eye of the hook in order that when you draw out the nerve with the hook, you can grasp with your fingers one of the two strands of the thread, and withdraw the hook backwards together with the other strand of the thread. If you do that well, then the thread falls beneath the nerve, and when you draw both its ends outwards, the nerve will be drawn up with it, so that it can be ligatured by itself alone, without the
artery. And now, when you ligature each one of the two nerves by 133
itself, then you will see what it is that the animal experiences as a result.

What happens is that when the thread has been tightened round one of these two nerves, the animal retains only one-half of its normal voice. And when both of these nerves are tightly constricted with the thread, the result is that the animal remains without any voice whatsoever, except that it then has a kind of respiration which resembles hoarseness of the voice. But should both the [carotid] arteries be ligatured, that does not harm the animal at all.[1]

This is one of the things which can be seen by the naked eye and recognised as a result of this kind of dissection which I have described for you. But here is yet another point that you learn to understand through this, namely the nature of the recurrent nerve [*N. laryngeus recurrens*]. Should you wish to inspect this nerve and investigate it, then draw with a hook upon the two margins of the whole incision. Moreover, on both sides you can extend the incision upwards in the direction of the larynx, incising the skin and reflecting it in its entirety together with the muscle which is called the muscular carpet [*M. platysma myoides*]. When you do that, then, in addition to the recurrent laryngeal nerve (which you see entering into the larynx at its lower border at the spot which you have learned from me to recognise), there also reveal themselves to you all the other nerves which branch off from the sixth pair [*glossopharyngeal*, *vagus* and *accessory*] and the nerve springing from the brain itself. Grasp this nerve also with an eyed hook bluntly pointed. After it there will also appear, as I described to you, the special nerve of the pharynx, that is, the nerve of which the pathway and the course lie deeply embedded and of which the exit from the skull passes between the two foramina of the sixth pair of nerves. But the first of all these in respect of position are the nerves of the seventh pair, which is distributed to the muscles of the
134 tongue. You can very easily constrict this nerve with a ligature, and it will then be shown that the tongue remains flaccid as though paralysed and impotent. By means of the constriction of the nerve of the pharynx with the thread, the hoarse voice, as one hears it in the phase of exhalation, is completely destroyed. Now the nerve of the tongue

[1] The ligature of the carotid arteries seems here to describe an alternative experiment, leaving the vagus nerves untied. The effect of ligature is not noticeable in those species in which the blood-supply to the brain is derived mostly from the external carotid and vertebral arteries.

[*N. hypoglossus*] courses over the osseous portions of the structures which attach the hyoid bone to the skull. And below this nerve there lies in the depth the nerve [*N. glossopharyngeus*] common to the pharynx and the tongue, which is not easy to see and which cannot be secured by hooks unless you first of all displace the artery which goes to the tongue, drawing it outwards by means of a blunt hook. Should you have progressed so far that you have been able to discover this nerve, then draw it upwards far enough to enable you to ligature it, if you want, or to damage it in some other manner. If you do that, you see that the tone of the exhalation of the animal, which still persisted after the damage to the recurrent laryngeal nerve, becomes lost. These are things which you observe and distinguish by means of this procedure which I have mentioned to you. And you observe also that as a result of the damage which has involved the muscles and the remaining nerves of the larynx, only a very slight change comes over the voice in respect of its weakness, power, sharpness and depth. Of that, however, I have already spoken exhaustively in the work 'On the Voice'. Similarly I spoke of the muscles and nerves which lie between the ribs [*Mm. and Nn. intercostales*], from whose slackening or motor paralysis it comes about that the animal is deprived of its voice. Moreover in Book VIII of this [present] work I have described how you should lay hold of these nerves with hooks.

CHAPTER 12. CONCLUSION, AND ACCOUNT OF THE LOSS OF SOME OF THE AUTHOR'S EARLIER WRITINGS.

There still remain numerous other features which can be seen in the neighbourhood of the larynx and of the trachea, and which the earlier [anatomists] have not recognised. These are matters that belong appro- *135*
priately to the investigation of those concealed movements that have not been recognised. I do not think that I should add them here, because I wish to write a single volume on the concealed unobserved movements, and because in addition to my previous burden another great burden has been laid upon me. For after I had written out the books of the work 'On Anatomical Dissections', as I was very nearly at the end of them, it so happened that there broke out that great fire in which the Temple of Peace was burnt down together with many

warehouses and storehouses in the Via Maxima, in which were stored those books of mine on Anatomical Dissections, together with all my other books. None of my works survived, except what I had already handed over to be transcribed. At that time I had already published eleven Books of the present work also; but as for the Books which will follow these [i.e. Books XII–XV], and which were then burnt, I am returning to compose them for the second time. There were also burnt many other books on anatomy which I had not revised sufficiently to allow me to publish them. For I used to write them and note them down bit by bit in disconnected passages every time I was dissecting an animal, and not only animals belonging to the six classes of which the body and the construction are like the body and the construction of Mankind, but also animals of the kind which crawl, those which move forwards by bringing the abdomen to their aid, water animals, and those which fly.
136 And if I complete this work that I have started, as is my intention here, I want to dissect those animals also and to describe what there is to see in them. I do that, as you know, with the animal placed in front of me, while I am looking at the things about which I am talking, especially when I am describing the method to be followed in their dissection.

End of the Eleventh Book of the work on Anatomical Dissection. Praise to God alone.

BOOK XII

THE GENERATIVE ORGANS AND FOETAL DEVELOPMENT

In the name of God, the compassionate, the merciful. The Twelfth Book contains a summary of the structure of the generative organs. The Twelfth Book of the writing on Anatomical Dissection.

CHAPTER I. THE GONADS. NOMENCLATURE OF GLANDS.

In this Book I describe the structure of the generative organs. The 137
significance of the anatomists' expression 'generative organs' is the organs which are designed for the generation of children. They are the uterus and the testicles [*ovaries*], the penis of the male and the vulva of the female, together with the seminal ducts [*uterine tubes and vasa deferentia*]. For these are organs which are found in males and in females, though some say that the female possesses no testicles. This, then, is the first matter of which we must speak. For this is not one of those theories which are substantiated only by cogent argument, but it can be proved sound by visual inspection. This is something done by those peoples amongst the Greeks who practice witchcraft, and it also occurs among us in many districts, such as Cappadocia and elsewhere. Thus the village folk take sows, and tie them upon ladders. Then upon both sides, I mean on the right and left side, in the situation of the flanks, they make an incision in the longitudinal direction of these, of an extent which renders it possible to pull out the ovaries, of which they must know the situation, so that the incision is not made too long. For if anyone tries to do this without having trained himself in the task, he
is not certain that he is not cutting in above or below the right place, 138
and he is then compelled to enlarge the cleft of the incision in order that the ovaries also may become recognisable and clearly visible. And when he does that, then the wound becomes wide and gaping, and because of the inflammation which results, its edges do not grow

together. But if preparations are made for the wound to heal as soon as all requisite care has been correctly applied, the pig which previously was a female does not remain a female, any more than does the male pig remain male when its testicles have been cut out; and in the Greek language one calls the animal 'oudeteron', which is to be explained as meaning 'neither male nor female'. But that to which the name should in fact apply is not an animal whose testicles have been cut out, since the male or female sex must necessarily have been present before the testicles in the animal.[1]

Between testicles [*ovaries*] and testicles a not inconsiderable contrast exists in regard to the distinctive nature of their substance. For the testicles of the female animal resemble the spongy flesh which supports and holds the veins and arteries at their places of subdivision [*lymph glands*], since they are distinguished by their density and solidity; but the testicles of the male animals are of a contrary type. That is to say they are spongy and porous, and distended with a white fluid, just as are the mammary glands. This variety of bodies the anatomists designate in the Greek language 'adenes', that is, 'spongy flesh'. For they [the anatomists] have in mind those portions of the body in which there is very little blood or which are almost completely bloodless. And when one observes them, then one sees that they are contracted in a space peculiar to them. Their aspect is the same as that of the fleshy bodies, except that the blood in them is more scanty than in flesh. And one calls them 'adenes', although that substance in the body which truly
139 lacks blood is the fat, which, however, because of its moisture, its softness and its whiteness is widely distinguished from spongy flesh [*glandular tissue*] as it is also by its substance; for you see that it [fat] resembles oil that has become firmly clotted. But the spongy flesh lacks elasticity and greasiness, and contains firmness and adhesiveness, particularly where it supports the veins and arteries at their places of subdivision [*lymph glands*]. In the other variety which is still more spongy and more permeated with fluid matter, you see a greasy fluid when the body of the animal is fat and well-nourished. Also you can well see that with this variety of spongy flesh [*glands*] veins and arteries combine themselves, and they grow into it quite recognisably. In specimens of

[1] I.e. before the testes were developed in the foetus.

larger size you find that, besides these, nerves join and attach themselves to the spongy flesh. Furthermore there affix themselves to it, in many places, canals whose substance is like that of veins and arteries, and other canals which originate from the spongy flesh itself [*secretory glands*]. These are the ones in which proceeds the outflow of the fluid which accumulates itself in that [spongy] flesh. These excretory channels have in their substance a peculiar property, namely this, that their substance stands between that of the veins and arteries.

Now the testicles are just such spongy flesh as this.[1] For there adhere to them very large veins and arteries, and from each of them [*the testicles*] there grows out yet another duct in which flows the fluid which is produced in them. And in fact that which is produced by all animals in the testicles is a thick white fluid, though this is not uniform in them all, but is capable of varying considerably in respect of its increase or its decrease. For the most part, with the exception of Lycus, all anatomists agree fully on the point that the female animals have *140*
testicles. And they agree also that the veins and arteries which come to them sprout out of and spring off from precisely the same places in the females as in the males, except that these veins and arteries in the female animals are very much less elongated than in the males. That is because in them the uterus lies internally upon the membrane applied inwardly to the abdominal muscles, the so-called peritoneum, but their testicles [*ovaries*] are fixed in a much higher place than the neck of the uterus.

CHAPTER 2. THE UTERUS AND ITS PERITONEAL RELATIONSHIPS.

Whoever now wishes to study adequately all that is to be found in the uterus should first separate, as I have already previously described, the two so-called pubic bones from one another and, in addition, bend and press both [of them] backwards in the direction in which they lie, the one which lies on the right side towards the right, and that which lies on the left side towards the left. When he does that, he will then see clearly enough the community of relation of the uterus with the organs bordering upon it. You commence with the study of the urinary

[1] 'As this', i.e. 'the *other variety*' of spongy flesh, contrasted with the variety of spongy flesh considered to be lymph gland tissue.

bladder. For the urinary bladder is the first thing which is to be seen after the operation which we have already mentioned. You must now make it free and separate it from the places by means of which it is bound up together with the uterus, and lay open to view the uterus in all directions, so that you leave it denuded. Next, you examine its neck [*cervix uteri*] in order to ascertain how this runs and how it ends in the sheath [*vagina*], the female pudenda. When you do this so that the urinary bladder conceals nothing more of what you require in the dissection of the uterus, then you can examine its relation with the so-called straight intestine, that is the rectum. That is because, just as the urinary bladder lies upon the uterus, so the uterus lies upon the
141 straight intestine. When the uterus has revealed itself to you from all sides, you are thus able to examine exhaustively, by themselves alone, those veins and arteries which go to the testicles [*ovaries*], and you can see from where they come, and how some of them attach themselves to the testicle itself, and grow into it, while others split and break up on the uterus itself, after they have divided themselves into numerous parts. But you see also beside them those veins and arteries which, below these, beyond their association with the testicles, join and connect with the body of the uterus itself, and grow within it, and distribute themselves clearly to the whole of the lower part of it onwards as far as to its neck. You may name this organic part which lies between the vagina, the female pudenda, and the uterine cavity, the neck and cervix of the uterus.

If you examine this by itself then it appears to you that the uterus must be a single cavity organ just as is the cavity of the two vessels which are both called 'bladder', I mean that bladder which is connected to the liver, that is the gall-bladder, and that bladder in which the urine is collected. But if you detach and remove from it the membrane enveloping it from all sides, there show themselves to you two cavities, of which the one allows itself to be separated from the other with the minimum of effort without the knife, by means of the process which Herophilus calls 'flaying, excoriating', in the way in which the skin that envelops the whole body comes to be separated from that which lies beneath it. For the bodies which one frees from one another by means of 'flaying, excoriating', are bound together only by means of

arachnoid-like ligaments. Possibly, many of those who concern themselves with nomenclature and the drawing of deductions from names do not agree with us in calling these things ligaments. However, neither should we call them suspensory ligaments, since it is preferable to refer to the 'suspensory ligaments' of the uterus, following the usage of the anatomists with regard to what has both length and strength together. These [*suspensory ligaments*] we find stretching out from the muscles in the lower region of the abdomen as ligaments which reach the uterus [*round ligaments*]. They are wholly analogous to the muscles which in the male body go as far as the testicles [*M. cremaster*]. I referred already to this muscle where I dealt with the anatomy of the muscles. *142*
And I refer to it again in the place where I discuss the anatomy of the male genital organs. Now as the state of what is revealed by dissection is as I have described it, then you can name each one of these organs as you will. But even as I made my mode of expression in each single one of the other objects clear and explicit, so also I will set out succinctly and clearly what I say about the uterus. I say, then, that after you have removed from it and excoriated the outer membrane which combines and unites from all sides with the peritoneum, being, in fact, only a sub-division with the same membranous nature, you can separate the two uteri from one another and free the one from the other easily, up to the point where they come to a neck common to both, situated in their lower extremity. It is for this reason that the uterus is named in two ways. One of these follows the number which the grammarians call the 'singular', and the organ is called 'the uterus'. The other follows the number which they call 'plural', and it is then called 'the uteri'. Among the anatomists known to me, I know no one who preceded Hippocrates in designating the uterus in two ways, 'uteri' in the plural, and 'uterus' in the singular. And Plato follows Hippocrates in that, since in his work entitled Timaeus he says: 'And in women, from the same causes, whenever the so-called matrices or uteri, which is an internal organism with a desire to bear young, remains long without fruit beyond the proper time, that is difficult and hard for it to bear, so it becomes unruly and bad-tempered.' Thus you see, my friend, that this man also at one and the same time refers to the uterus in the plural and says 'uteri', and then employs it in the singular and says 'organism'.

143 And also he calls it at the end of his account once again 'uterus', since he says with reference to it: 'When the harvest comes, culling as it were the fruit from the trees, they cast the seed in the uterus, as one casts it on the ploughed land'. Now since this is the position with regard to the uterus, you can give it a name which denotes one, in the singular, and say 'uterus', on account of its neck, and of its external membranous covering—it is because of this membranous covering that many people do not know that it consists of two uteri—and, you may also give it a name referring to the plural and say 'the uteri', because in fact there are two uteri, which a single mantle, a protective covering, envelops in common, and that is the membranous covering growing out from the peritoneum. The two [*uteri*] have a neck common to both, that is, the part from out of which there emerges and comes to birth the foetus which will have been developed in one of the two.

Now when you reflect their common protective covering, you will see the substance peculiar to them as a body which has fibres varying in position. When I say it has fibres varying in position, I mean that on it you find fibres which run obliquely (and in fact these are the majority), and other fibres which go partly as it were transversely, partly straight and erect in an upright direction. This is also to be found in the body of the urinary bladder, when you remove the peritoneum from it in its turn. You must understand that the unity of the uterus, which comes about in consequence of the membranous covering surrounding both uteri outwardly, is not something which is to be found in all animals. What is found in the apes and in animals resembling apes, I mean the animals which are called satyr, lynx and cynocephali, and likewise amongst sheep, goats and cattle, before you remove the protective covering which invests the uteri outwardly, is that the uterus appears as a single unit, as is the case in mankind. But in pigs, dogs, and in
144 general in all animals with forwardly springing teeth, which give birth to many young, the uterus is seen as two-fold. So much so is this, that the two uteri immediately separate off from the neck and go, one in the direction towards the right flank, and one in the direction towards the left.

I do not comprehend how the anatomists have accustomed themselves to call 'coverings' the bodies of these organs which nevertheless are themselves organs. For they have said that the stomach and the intestine are both of them composed of two 'coverings'. And since they have given them this name, of necessity we must employ the terms which have become customary, even if they have not been applied in keeping with the true conditions. For this is not something which goes on among people with regard to these organs only, but one finds it very often indeed in all details affecting men's daily lives. They employ such names as these, without its entering into their minds whether these are names which are being employed rightly or not. But do you follow me, and follow also what Plato says, and the slender regard which Hippocrates accords to concern with the investigation of names, in the use of which Herodicus and others who copied him went to excess. Direct your efforts to satisfy one requirement only, that is, to acquire for yourself a thorough knowledge of the objects themselves, in the manner in which, as you see, I also have exerted my painstaking efforts in all my earlier writings and in this work here also.

CHAPTER 3. DISSECTION OF THE PREGNANT UTERUS IN A DEAD ANIMAL.

After you have established clearly for yourself and investigated the complete substance of the uterus in which there is no foetus, and when you have understood this, then pass on to the examination of the uterus in which is a foetus, and to the investigation of how the foetus lies in it, and how the membranes which enclose it are composed. It is well known that from the body of the animal you must turn out and evacuate *145*
the uterus in which a foetus is contained, employing the current usage of anatomists. Afterwards go on to the dissection of what I have specified to you. In both dissections you can see something common to both, namely how the matter stands with the seminal ducts and the seminal vessels which connect themselves with two clearly distinguishable orifices at the two cornua of the uterus, and coalesce with them. However, in female animals one finds them not, as in males, wide immediately from the testicles onwards. On the contrary, at their outgrowth and origin from the testicles [*ovaries*] they are in the female animals as it were nearer to the nature of membranes. And consequently they are quickly torn and rent when the fine sound enters

into the lumen of the seminal duct [*Fallopian tube*]. This vessel at the point of its junction and union with the cornu of the uterus possesses internally a considerable width, and the further it travels in the direction of the testicle, continually and gradually it gets narrower and narrower. But that part which belongs to the species of membranes, and lies next to the testicle, splits quickly, so that the fluid present in that vessel, which is just the same as the fluid secreted in the seminal vessel, flows out from this membrane-like body when anyone compresses it.

As for the body of the uterus itself, it becomes steadily thinner and more attenuated than before, while the embryo grows and becomes larger, since it extends and expands in all directions. But after parturition its cavity diminishes and becomes smaller than it was in the period of pregnancy, and the measure of the thickness and stoutness of its body increases in the same proportion as the dimension of its cavity is reduced. Now this is again something which commands a man to admire the work of Creation, namely how the mouth of the uterus becomes so narrow that the point of a sound enters into it only with difficulty. And did we not know for certain that the foetus comes out through it, then we should certainly not believe that the mouth of the
146 uterus, which is constricted and occluded, should reach such an expansion that a fully formed animal could come out through it.

CHAPTER 4. THE ARRANGEMENT OF THE FOETAL MEMBRANES IN THE GOAT.

Now, if you wish to dissect a uterus in which there is a foetus, a dissection which we usually make on goats, then you must prepare a small reed, one foot in length, whose end is pared down so that at one time you can introduce it into the mouth of the neck of the uterus, if you wish, and at another time into one of its two cornua as soon as you have freely exposed its end. Should you wish to blow into it, just as the goldsmith blows up his fire by means of an instrument similar to this, the blow-pipe, and you do that at the neck of the uterus, then there is distended the space between the ovarian cuticle [*chorion*] and the uterus. And if you do that at the two cornua of the uterus, then the membrane is distended which one calls the sausage-like one [*allantois*].

When that happens, then the performance of the dissection becomes easier and more convenient, because the inflated organic parts give you clear guidance to their disengagement from the organic parts in contact with them. But if, after you have made the dissections in such a manner two or three times, you want to dissect immediately, without inflating, then you will find no difference in the affair, if you follow it carefully. You should first begin the dissection by incising the uterus by itself alone, cutting it with a knife, without interfering with the chorion, since it is free from it and separated on all sides. For its attachment and adhesion to the uterus exists only through the cotyledons. In some animals the cotyledons resemble the indurated outgrowths which arise at the orifices of the veins distending themselves at the anus, and at the vulva of the female [*haemorrhoids, varicosities*], but in other animals these cotyledons are glandular structures of considerable size. When you have thus incised the uterus and cut it at a place between cotyledons
—it is most easily done when you inflate it, though it is by no means 147
difficult even when you do not—you must then make free the cotyledons and peel them off from the uterus with the fingers, so that they remain adhering to the chorion. Next you set loose the so-called sausage-like covering [*allantois*] from the covering called the amnion, that is, the covering which envelops and contains the embryo.[1]

The so-called sausage-like covering [*allantois*] is that which envelops this [*the amnion*] from without, on its underlying convex segments. Again, it is much thinner than that called the amnion, as well as more elongated than it, and its extreme terminations reach as far as to the two uterine cornua. And if it happens that on each of the two sides [*right and left cornua*] a foetus is present, then one of the two endings of the allantois reaches as far as that uterine cornu which lies on its side, and its other end enters into contact with the extremity of the allantois which belongs to the other foetus and which extends towards that side.

Thus the two ends of this membrane [*allantois*] reach as far as to the place described. Their middle portion, however, is interrupted by an
easily recognised aperture which opens into the urinary bladder of the 148
foetus. The affair is as I have described it, namely that its liberation from

[1] Ḥunain here interpolates a note relating to a sacrificial animal offering its blood into the bowl, or 'amnion'. A foetus in its amniotic sac looks very like this. B.T.

the membrane named the amnion proceeds more easily and smoothly if one inflates it, that is, if its end where it is joined on to the seminal duct is inflated. That is because outwardly it is encompassed and narrowly enclosed around in the interior of the chorion, while it [*the allantois*] encompasses and narrowly surrounds the membrane called the amnion in the place which I specified. Since that is so, then the remaining parts of the membrane called amnion encounter the chorion and place themselves closely in contact with it. Consequently they require just such disengagement as does the sausage-like membrane while it is becoming freed from this.

CHAPTER 5. THE MAIN BLOOD-VESSELS OF THE FOETUS, AND THE CHANGES THEY UNDERGO AT BIRTH.

Now, as this passage in the middle of the sausage-like membrane discharges thus into the urinary bladder of the foetus, so also the whole of the arteries and veins in the chorion are attached in one and the same place to the foetus. In all they amount to four. These four are like the trunks of trees which are composed of numerous roots. Two of them are arteries and two are veins, like the arteries and the veins in the mesenteries around the intestines. That is to say, if you consider the chorion alone by itself without the cotyledons you find that it resembles the mesentery around the intestines, and similarly it has veins and arteries bound down by delicate membranes. And now, since from all the veins and arteries in the chorion there arise two great veins and two arteries, these then make up four in all. They encircle the duct [*urachus*] which leads through between the sausage-like membrane and the urinary bladder; and this duct comes to lie in the middle of them. And the thing formed from the five structures associated together is what is called the umbilicus [*umbilical cord*]. Some maintain that this is not really the umbilicus, which, in their opinion, is the place where these five ducts are attached and connected beneath the skin of the foetus.
149 But do you, for your part, leave others to dispute and argue about names, and begin to dissect the skin which encircles the attachment and ingrowth of these five vessels. Next, dissect away the muscles underlying it until you reach the peritoneum. When you do that, you will see that the two arteries encounter the urinary bladder and encircle it,

one on each of its two sides, until they unite themselves with the two arteries going to the lower limbs [*Aa. iliacae*] at the place where the artery lying inwardly upon the vertebral column [*aorta*] first divides, and out of its two subdivisions the two arteries going to the lower limbs arise. But before those two arteries [*Aa. umbilicales*] connect themselves with these two, branches spring off from them which go to the urinary bladder and to the testicles [*ovaries*]. The two veins [*Vv. umbilicales*] you see uniting with one another and combining so that they become a single vein. And that single vein reaches to and joins the liver at a place slightly above the vein which in fully formed animals is called the hepatic portal vein.

Should you desire to follow this vein and to learn to understand its division in the liver, you will find that it resembles a vein conjoined to the vena cava, as well as to that vein which in an animal after it has been born one calls the hepatic portal. The reason is that those veins in which, in fully formed animals, nutriment is transmitted and passes from the stomach and the intestines, have also to serve for the transmission of blood which goes to the body of the embryo. But as for the flow of nourishment through the vena cava and how it reaches the body as a whole, that takes place exactly in the same way in the fully developed animal and in the foetus.

Now just as this state of affairs which I have described to you occurs exclusively in the bodies of foetuses, so also one finds in the heart something exceptional in the connection of the vena cava and the chief artery [*aorta*]: it is that the vena cava is drilled right through into the
venous artery [*pulmonary vein*] whose origin springs from the left one *150*
of the two cavities of the heart, and the chief artery [*aorta*] is drilled into the so-called arterial vein [*pulmonary artery*], which sprouts out from the right one of the two cavities of the heart. However, of all these things which we have mentioned nothing remains except indications. But their distinctive signs remain preserved, and exist during the whole lifetime. The following two things only are to be seen during the whole of the remaining span of life. One is an indication of the vein which goes from the umbilicus to the liver [*ligamentum teres*], and the other is an indication [*ligamentum arteriosum*] of the thoroughfare between the chief artery [*aorta*] and the arterial vein [*A. pulmonalis*].

But of the thoroughfare or channel [*foramen ovale*] between the vena cava and the venous artery [*pulmonary vein*] there remains, during the whole span of life, no remnant of any noteworthy dilation, in spite of the fact that this opening does not disappear and is not obliterated as soon as the foetus is born. For you find that the opening and the thoroughfare closes up only gradually in the first days. It does so because the membrane in which was the opening and the thoroughfare comes into close contact with the substance of the heart and unites with it. But as for the opening which is the thoroughfare between the chief artery and the arterial vein, this is situated in the substance of the vein and of the artery itself, and in foetuses is large [*ductus arteriosus*], until, when the foetus is born, it becomes progressively blocked, contracts and becomes desiccated, the longer it exists, just as do the vein which goes from the chorion to the liver, and the two arteries which encircle and surround the urinary bladder. Now when these arteries and veins become very desiccated, then they come to resemble the structure of nerves. Similar to this is what happens to the duct which discharges the urine [*urachus*]. For this also dries up, becomes hardened, closes up, shrinks and contracts after it has become incorporated in the foetus with the cavity of the urinary bladder, and has inosculated itself there with a clearly recognisable permeable
151 opening so that the fluid stored in the hollow of the urinary bladder encircling it, when it becomes compressed, streams out in the effluent duct of the urinary bladder, and then, when it is compressed by the urinary bladder again, for a second time, by pressure exerted upwards by this bladder on the duct discharging the urine, it arrives in the so-called sausage-like covering [*allantois*].

CHAPTER 6. EXPOSURE OF THE LIVING GOAT FOETUS *IN UTERO*, WITH OBSERVATIONS ON FOETAL MOVEMENTS.

I have now described to you, for the most part, all that is accessible to inspection in the dead foetus, and to it I must subjoin and add an account of what there is to see in the living foetus. Accordingly I say, the goat—since we are accustomed to undertake this dissection specially in this animal—must be prepared in the following manner. You should bind it and secure it, stretching it on its back with its head raised a little. The hairs on the lower parts of the abdomen are shaved off, so that when you subsequently incise the abdomen, the cut may travel along the whole abdomen at a single stroke so that it pierces through to the peritoneum. And the cut should be carried out at the place between the veins and the arteries which descend down from the sternum [*superior epigastric branches of internal mammary vessels*] and the veins and the arteries which ascend from below [*inferior epigastric vessels*] and belong to the mammary glands and to the uterus in common. For these associated veins and arteries stretch out alongside the rectilinear abdominal muscles [*Mm. recti abdominales*] of which the line of encounter is a boundary which separates the right and left sides. Accordingly the incision should now be made here in the section in which lie the fundus of the uterus and its lowest portion in which the foetus is found. It is clear that in incising you must take good care that the knife does not penetrate too deeply, otherwise it cuts into the uterus together with the peritoneum. For at the time of pregnancy the uterus, in consequence of the swelling that it undergoes, approaches the membrane which one calls peritoneum, and becomes attached to it.

But you must in any case soon cut into the uterus, and you may then *152*
think for this reason that it is useless and superfluous for you to guard against cutting into it [*the uterus*] with the first stroke. But reflect that you do not know if the incision will encounter one of the cotyledons. Consequently it is best if you first set free the uterus, and then incise it carefully in the region between the cotyledons. For if the incision encounters the cotyledons, the result will be that the blood gushes out. As for the fundus of the uterus and its lowest portion, over which you should carry the incision, this is indicated to you by the inflation and the swelling-up of the abdomen. The length of the incision should be great enough to enable you to introduce your hand and to turn over the foetus. For its back lies upwards, and its umbilicus downwards. You must set free the umbilical cord in order to acquaint yourself with the state of the pulsations of the arteries found within it. For what you need to know most at this time and by that operation is whether the rhythm of the arterial pulsations in the foetus and in the pregnant mother is one and the same, or whether there is any contrast between them.

Now as you have laid bare that part of the uterus in which the foetus

is, proceed here likewise to compress with the fingers the roots of the cotyledons where they adjoin the uterus and, at the same time, press together with them on the whole chorion. Then add to that action and proceed further by incising the body of the uterus itself, between the cotyledons, in order that no bleeding may result since the veins and the arteries in the chorion take their origins from that place. But if you strip away and peel off that part of the uterus which is found in the region of the umbilical cord, then you can feel with the fingers of one hand the arteries in the umbilical cord, and with the fingers of your other hand you can feel the arteries of the pregnant animal in one of two ways, either by feeling the artery lying inwardly upon the vertebral
153 column [*aorta abdominalis*] or by exposing the artery in the axilla, or the artery in the inguinal region [*A. femoralis*]. And if you find that the arteries in the umbilical cord of the foetus pulsate in another fashion than the arteries of the pregnant animal, you can easily deduce by analogy how the progress of the foetus is being controlled. This is a subject which the Sophists investigate. They ask whether the child be a part of the pregnant animal, or whether this latter only carries it in the way in which the tree carries the fruit, or whether the foetus exists in its parent, being itself an animal.

Now when you have seen what is visible of that, you can as soon as you wish set the foetus in movement, and so stimulate it that it jerks and raises itself upwards. And when you stimulate it to do that, then the membranes which lie upon it and envelope it tear, and within them you see that at one time it moves one of its feet, and again another time it moves the thorax also, although it does not breathe through the mouth at all. For that one can well see. And the movement of the thorax is not like the movement which we make when we inspire air, or expel it in expiration, when the thorax expands in the phase of inspiration, or contracts in its expulsion of air through expiration. It is in fact simply like a movement of the thorax when we change it from one attitude or pose to another without drawing breath. You see with your own eyes that its thorax clearly shifts and changes from one attitude and pose to another, and you can also see no less clearly that it does so without breathing through the mouth or the larynx. For you find on inspection that the foetus is restricted to changing its position

in the uterus, as its veins and arteries are conjoined with the veins and arteries of the pregnant animal through their connection with the veins and arteries in the chorion. When you have first examined all these 154
things as often as you like, and have observed thoroughly the movements which the foetus makes with the lower limbs or with the thorax, then you can, as I have told you, stimulate the foetus whenever you wish and set it in motion until it jerks. That is done by ligaturing the veins and arteries in the umbilical cord. The same effect would occur were you to take hold of these veins and arteries with the fingers and to compress them so that nothing reached the embryo of that which comes to it from the chorion [*placenta*]. Occasionally that will also happen when with the fingers you grasp the arteries alone by themselves without the veins.

CHAPTER 7. THE SPERMATIC CORD AND SCROTUM; THEIR COVERINGS AND CONTENTS

This, then, is what you can observe by ocular inspection in regard both to the uterus and to the foetus in pregnant or non-pregnant animals. But as for the 'spongy flesh' [*gland tissue*] which you find in male animals at the region about the root of the penis, on both sides of it [*prostate gland*], and the ducts which have their origin from this 'flesh', that is, those which some call 'parastateis' and which resemble spongy flesh, this is something which I have not found in female animals. But in male animals, and especially in those which leap about very much, I have found the ducts very clearly recognisable, and the 'spongy flesh' [*prostate gland*] large.

Let us now describe how to dissect the reproductive organs of male animals.[1] We say that in order for you to secure that the animal which you are dissecting resembles a man, you must take for that dissection an ape. But in order to achieve the effect of clarity in the appearance of such of those organs as are small and hard to see, then you must take
a he-goat, a ram, a bull, a horse or a male donkey for your dissection, 155
because that animal must necessarily possess a scrotum. By scrotum, I mean the suspensory skin which surrounds the two testicles. But as

[1] The translation of the following two sentences is based on a simple emendation of the Arabic text, which is corrupt. M.C.L.

for what concerns those animals which have testicles attached at the root of the thigh or not visible at all, these have no scrotum at all. I have heard it said of Quintus that he was accustomed to carry out this dissection on a living he-goat, which he supported upright [erect] so that in this position it was similar to a man. But for my personal opinion I am of the view that it is superfluous to dissect the testicle of a living animal, since that is of no use either for the study of the constitution of the organs which become visible by means of this dissection, or for the investigation of any particular functions. On the contrary, it makes the affair harder, more difficult and more troublesome as regards the comprehension of the organs upon which you can quickly and thoroughly instruct yourself. That is because blood must then necessarily burst out. And since that is so, it is best and most preferable if we conduct this dissection in the body of a dead animal. We carry it out in the following manner.

You must cut through the skin by itself alone, without severing the membrane which is applied to it inwardly and lies beneath it and adheres to it just as in the other bodily parts. And this skin should be set free from the organic parts lying beneath it by means of flaying and excoriating. Amongst the things which serve you as guidance is the fact that this, the membrane investing the testicle, is attached as an inwardly lying layer to the skin clothing the abdomen. In well-nourished animals it is clammy and tough. This membrane is to be set free from the skin with the knife, and it can easily be stripped off and drawn away by the fingers from what underlies it. It can then be seen clearly going down together with the skin clothing the abdomen, and it comes to be one of those membranes which the surgeons call 'able to be stripped or peeled off'. You must now set it free properly from
156 the structures lying beneath it, so that you may make out how many of them there are in all, if you are one of those who take account of this detail. For it must be admitted that research on that point, if one desires to extract any advantage as regards the treatment of hernia, is superfluous and unnecessary.

You should now detach all membranous-like structures which you discover beneath the skin until you come as far as the muscle which lies beneath them [*M. cremaster*] and which, as you see quite clearly, goes to the testicles and spreads around the duct, the channel which many anatomists call 'the conducting canal' [*spermatic cord*]. As for the heads of these muscles, there is no advantage to be gained from their knowledge for one who treats hernia by the employment of the knife. But the anatomist must learn about that also together with other details because of what may be needed, by studying the work 'On the Use of the Bodily Parts'. Actually these muscles are in two pairs, and each two muscles reach as far as each one of the two testicles. Of these two pairs of muscles, the one has its origin from the two pubic bones, the other from the third pair of the muscles clothing the abdomen.[1]

Some have also said that that which goes to each of the two testicles is a single muscle, but they were deceived simply because they dissected other kinds of animals. But in the bodies of apes the position with regard to this muscle is the same as in the human body, that is to say that one finds in it that two muscles go to each one of the testicles, 157
and can be discovered and clearly seen by whoever, in the surgical procedure for performing the operation for rupture, becomes able to distinguish them well. However, you must first of all see them clearly in the bodies of apes, so that you recognise them easily in the bodies of men who are under operation on account of a hernia or for another cause. For as many things have escaped the notice of anatomists in dissections undertaken for a predetermined purpose, how much the more will you fail to perceive everything that you need to know fully, through dissections undertaken without definite purpose. But now I will describe to you the procedure by the application of which one comes to perceive adequately the substance and the nature of the reproductive organs, provided that previously one has trained oneself on the bodies of apes, and has not always restricted oneself to studies upon goats or rams, as many are accustomed to do, in order to get a good view of all that they desire in large animals. What one should do is to train oneself on the bodies of these animals in order to see the fine veins, arteries and nerves. But one should also train oneself no less thoroughly on the bodies of apes, in order to see what is exactly the same in both classes and what is different. For example, there is a

[1] Galen here is in error: see below, p. 126, where his description is correct. This error is noted by Ḥunain as being present in the Greek MSS. B.T.

distinction in regard to that muscle [*cremaster*] which you see in the human body and in apes consisting of two muscles on each of the two testicles, but in the body of the he-goat, on each of the two testicles you see it as a single muscle which arises from precisely the same muscle as that from which you see it springing in the simian body.

This muscle can be set free by two different surgical methods. At one time you can begin the dissection from above, and at another from
158 below. That is to say, occasionally on beginning to dissect first the muscles on the abdomen, as we described in the place where we dealt with them, when one comes to the second pair of these muscles [see footnote, p. 125], one sees in those regions outside the abdomen a delicate muscle growing out, which goes to the two testicles [but meant as unilateral only], as one also sees on the inner [medial] areas, where the two pubic bones lie, the origin of another second muscle, smaller than the former one, and these two, as soon as they lower themselves, follow the duct [*spermatic cord*] as far as the testicles, and they encircle and enclose it completely. This is the duct which some call 'conducting passage'. Now as to whether this is so do you investigate by means of the dissection.

I said previously that first you must remove the skin and, after it, the membranes that adhere to it. That you can do in one of the following two ways, by beginning either from above or from below, so that you can see the skin which descends from the skin enveloping the abdomen, and which serves as a constant wrapping for the testicles. It sustains no interruption until it reaches its [lower] end, and from it the scrotum which encloses the testicles comes into being. Upon the musculature
159 clothing the abdomen there are found two other bodies of the nature of membranes which are attached to the skin from within and spread out beneath it. These you must likewise examine carefully, to see how they descend together with the skin. For both of these two structures are to be seen time after time in cases of hernia. After all the skin has been cut through they can be peeled off by the use of the fingers. They are named 'membranes allowing themselves to be detached', and 'detachable membranes'. Next, after these two membranes, there appear those two muscles which completely enclose this efferent duct as far as to the testicle, and after these, the efferent duct as far as its attachment to and its conjunction with the testicle. After the efferent duct there

come into view the veins and the arteries in its inner parts; these are the ones which nourish the testicle.

All this is also clearly to be seen in the bodies of apes. But those things of which I will speak to you after this are also to be seen in the bodies of apes, but not clearly. Consequently we are often in need of large-bodied animals. For example, there is found here a small vein, in the place where the seminal duct lies, which is so small that it cannot be seen clearly in large-bodied animals, much less in others. If now the dissector comes upon this and finds it filled with blood, he finds that blood drawn out in it in a straight line and not suffusing the outer wall. Upon this there frequently lies a clot of that blood, which you can neither rinse nor wipe away from it. But when you press on it, you then see that the blood moves, in this direction and that, just as happens in other veins and arteries particularly when you dissect this part of the body immediately after the death of the animal. And therefore you should make this dissection occasionally in a live animal, for in these living animals the small veins are evident. For the same reason it is best and most preferable to repeat frequently the dissection of every single organic part, in order that if in one animal or in two something remains *160*
obscure, and we do not see it clearly, we may observe it in the third, fourth, or following animal which we subsequently dissect.

Also, as for what relates to this vein, we are unable to set it free from the seminal duct [*vas deferens*] and to separate it because it is so small. But everything else besides it which is found on the leading-duct can be clearly separated, one part from another, as soon as you are in a position to cut off with a sharp knife the membranes binding them to one another. These membranes are delicate. As I have said already, you can commence the dissection from above or from below. But in conformity with the description which I give here to you, you must necessarily begin with one thing and end with another, and it can happen that what comes first in the description may come not first but second in the dissection. And now, since I have already described to you, from above and downwards, the structures which reach the testicle, so you also must investigate, and by means of dissection examine with your own eyes, how they all fasten upon and grow on to the testicle at its lower hinder part, where the seminal duct [*vas deferens*] originates.

The 'leading-duct' [*spermatic cord*] is united with the testicle and combines with it at this place only. But its remaining parts are free from the testicle, standing well away from it. That is, after it has widened out, it encloses the testicle, just as the membrane surrounding the heart (its sheath, if we may be permitted thus to name it here)[1] encloses the heart. Nevertheless, since many medical men have in the past called it, in Greek, 'erythroides', we too must call it by this name, since out of strife and disputes over names no advantage accrues to the practice of
161 the healing art, and it also results in man's life being wasted in trifling and vanity. But as for the knowledge of whether the membrane from which there arises this duct, this through-passage of which I said that some anatomists call it the 'leading-duct' [*spermatic cord*], is so connected with the peritoneum that these two, in conjunction, constitute a single structure, or whether it is something else, this is useful to whoever knows it. It is also useful to know that in this duct, this through-passage, until it reaches the head of the testicle, the veins can be seen travelling which nourish the testicle and that other organ named epididymis. So also can one profit by the knowledge that the seminal vessel and its duct [*vas deferens*] originate from this organ named epididymis.

You will also find that the veins which nourish the testicle and the organ named epididymis, before their attachment and coalescence with it, entwine themselves in many coils, which lie upon one another [*pampiniform plexus*]. And you see that the tint of the blood alters, so that it becomes whiter. For it is being prepared for semen to be formed from it. If you free those nutritive veins, then you can observe and see that their principal fastening and connection takes place at the head of the testicle, and that they have a secondary connection with the organ called the epididymis. You can also see clearly the membrane [*scrotal septum*] which separates the right testicle from the left, and in addition you can cut into the testicle itself, and see that in its middle [interior] it has a condensation like that of the membranes [*mediastinum testis*]. Some think that that is peculiar to the testicle. Behind the testis you see the organ named epididymis attached to the lower portion of the testicle. You must set it free from the testicle so far that you can see

[1] The Arabic text for this phrase is corrupt, and the English version is based on an emendation. M.C.L.

that on each of its two sides something hard is concentrated, which indicates that the two are so conjoined to one another that they easily allow of their being drawn apart, and they are not united in a single structure. The arrangement is this, that each single one of the nerves of the brain and of the spinal marrow is just an offshoot which sprouts *162*
from the actual substance of the brain and of the spinal marrow. The matter there is clear. Since every nerve originates from one of the two of these, it must sprout from its source as do branches from the trunk of a tree and the twigs and the leaves from the small branches. But the connection of the epididymis with the testicles is merely such that if one separates them, neither of the two is damaged in the process, but each of the two remains after the separation self-contained and distinct.

Now around all these parts which we have mentioned there enrolls itself, on their path during their passage through the duct or thoroughfare that we have described, a delicate membrane which encloses all of them as a whole, and every single one by itself. This membrane takes origin from the peritoneum, from the region of the loins. Its site of origin and commencement you will clearly see, when you come to the dissection of the parts lying above the leading-passage [*spermatic cord*] where there applies itself to the seminal duct and vessel [*vas deferens*] that small vein which the surgeons name 'the capillary vein'. And as for this vein, one has occasion to marvel how it comes about that dense blood streams out from it, as it does from the vessel, the venous channel, which lies at the place known as the hinder junction. There is nothing connected to the skin in this place which joins it to the underlying parts in the way in which it is connected to what underlies the rest of the skin of the testicles. But because of this duct, and of the venous container out of which the blood frequently streams, the skin here, my friends, is free from that which lies beneath it. And its connection there with what lies beneath it is called the hinder junction. Some anatomists name 'capillary-like vessel' the artery which we mentioned earlier and which in the body of the foetus goes to the testicle,[1] and in the body of the fully formed animal, dries up.

[1] This is presumably a mistake for 'chorion', since the vessel referred to is the umbilical artery. The word for 'testicle' occurs in the Arabic two lines lower down, and may have become misplaced. B.T., M.C.L.

CHAPTER 8. THE VAS DEFERENS, SEMINAL VESICLES AND PROSTATE

Now, if you have examined everything in the testicle, and in the thoroughfare or duct which leads to it, then go upwards to the
163 peritoneum, and introduce a sound through the aperture there [*deep inguinal ring*], either the sound which one calls 'spathomele' ['flat broad probe'] or the so-called 'dipyrene' ['double-knobbed'], in order that, when the head of the sound is being thrust upwards on either side the aperture in the peritoneum becomes more clearly recognisable, and you see that it gradually narrows itself so that a thoroughfare, a passage, is formed in the place where the groins are, and you see how then once again it widens steadily and gradually until it arrives at the testicle.

After you have examined these things you must fully convince yourself how, together with the so-called nourishing veins, delicate membranes descend and go to the testicles. These originate from the peritoneum at the region of the loins, and they serve to ensheathe these vessels and with them the seminal duct and its vessel as it descends. You must also learn how this seminal duct detaches itself from those nourishing vessels immediately, when it has passed beyond the upper end of the thoroughfare [*internal inguinal ring*] and betaken itself to the lower part of the peritoneum. For you will see that the vein and the nerve, which both go to the largest of the testicular muscles [*M. cremaster*] ascend upwards until they reach the kidneys. And you will see how the seminal vessel, the seminal duct [*vas deferens*] descends towards the neck of the urinary bladder, and you will see one on each of the two sides. For you find everything in the reproductive organs on each of the two sides, I mean the right and the left, quite alike. But now, since many structures rest upon the broad bone, that is to say the cross-bone [*sacrum*], consequently their separation from one another becomes difficult. But as for the reproductive organs, the description of which I have as my aim here, you must leave out of account and disregard the rest of what is there to see, and follow the two seminal ducts or vessels, which go to the flesh that lies at the neck of the urinary bladder because of the
164 muscle which enrolls itself around this and encircles it. That is the muscle which one calls 'the stop-gap' [*M. sphincter vesicae*], a name which one

also gives to the one which lies at the end of the straight intestine [*rectum*] since both of them are created for one and the same effective purpose only, that is to say that they relax and shut down the orifices for the excretion of food and drink. For the seminal vessels or ducts join this part of the neck of the bladder after they have dilated and enlarged themselves, in the same way in which the veins dilate on which the disease named 'kirsos' breaks out, and from here [this resemblance] Herophilus has named them 'varix-like prostates' [*ampullae of vasa deferentia*]. We give them the same name, as we follow old custom in the application of names. Herophilus, then, has named 'varix-like' both these two ducts or vessels. He gave them this name, deriving it from what happens to them, that is, the fact that near the place of their attachment and coalescence with the neck of the urinary bladder they dilate and enlarge themselves, just as the veins which are affected by the disease named 'kirsos'.

Bordering upon these two, two other ducts are found, one on each side, and these two ducts Herophilus has called the 'gland-like' —'glands' being that 'spongy flesh' [*vesiculae seminales*]. He gave them that name simply because they originate from the spongy flesh which just at this place joins the neck of the urinary bladder at the very same point as that to which those two vessels or ducts are attached. Whoever dissects these two canals and keenly examines their structure from within will find that their substance possesses a peculiar consistence, closely related to that of the structures from which they spring off. The *165*
same is true of the two varix-like canals [*ampullae*]. We have already said that both the varix-like canals originate from the body named epididymis, and that the place of origin of the two canals which resemble glands [*vesiculae seminales*] is the spongy flesh at the side of the neck of the urinary bladder [*prostate gland*].

CHAPTER 9. STRUCTURE OF THE PENIS.

After you have started here, proceed to the dissection of the penis. The penis grows outwards from both the two pubic bones at their meeting-place. That is to say the male genital organ, the penis, commences where the neck of the urinary bladder ends. Only the actual body of the penis, with the exception of the foreskin, is named penis. But that which encircles the region where the prepuce begins is named the corona glandis, and that is the region where the skin ensheathing the penis is united to and combines with the head of the prepuce. Everyone knows that by the expression 'prepuce' is meant only the portion of skin which surrounds the end of the penis, and that what is surrounded and encircled by this portion of the skin is called the gland [*glans penis*]. And that is the region at which the canal ends which perforates the penis, and lies underneath it throughout its length. Some anatomists have erroneously believed that this canal or duct runs in the centre of the penis, proceeding to the glans. The substance of the penis is something that has no counterpart in the organs of the body. That is because its appearance resembles that of a sinew, as it is white and bloodless, and within it there are hollow spaces for pneuma, which increase its dimensions in all directions, so that it becomes larger than it was before. And whenever those hollow spaces empty themselves, then the whole penis shrinks, becomes pendant and contracts itself.

166 On each of the two sides the penis has a very long slender muscle [*M. ischiocavernosus*] that is difficult to see, and two other large muscles [*M. bulbocavernosus*] in the place where it comes near to the constrictor of the urinary bladder. The whole of the body of the penis is completely hollow. It is called tendinous simply because of its similarity to the substance of tendons, a thing which one finds in many other structures whose substances are tendinous, and these one is accustomed to call 'ligamentous tendons'. Now since this is the substance of the penis, in its intrinsic nature it possesses no sensitiveness, just as other parts also which derive their growth from tendons have no sensitiveness, and they are those which the great majority of anatomists call 'connecting tendons'. To the penis there go nerves, and likewise veins and arteries, to serve for the necessary fulfilment of needs connected with the useful functions performed by each one of these parts in the organs of the animal. So also, when you have commenced with the veins, arteries and nerves which you find connected with the penis, then go gradually upwards and follow them until they lead you to their origins and roots. For to the penis there go out veins, arteries and nerves from the site of the great bone, that is, the cross-bone [*sacrum*]. As for what veins and arteries are there, that I shall describe to you in the place where I describe the anatomy of the veins and arteries, and I shall describe what nerves are there when I present the anatomy of the nerves which spring off from the spinal marrow.

CHAPTER 10. DISCUSSION OF AN ALLEGED EXTRA-UTERINE PREGNANCY.

With the description of the dissection of the reproductive organs which I had set myself as my task I am nearly at the end. But since there has been considerable discussion and widespread reports about the foetus which some claim to have been found in the body of a goat outside
the uterus, I had intended to include in the earlier chapters, preceding *167*
this one, an account of what should be said about that. But since then, Theophrastus the physician has already investigated the cause of the error in the claims of those persons, and he has explained it, and thus he has saved me from having to expose it and has relieved me of a whole long discussion. For those who wish to do so can refer to this work of Theophrastus and can read it. I will only give briefly the sum of what Theophrastus said on this point. He says that the man who cut open and dissected that goat made his dissection and his incision upon the spot where the urinary bladder lies. Some anatomists call this spot the pudenda. There, in the structure which he had split open, urine was found. Now the man who was carrying out the dissection thought that he had not incised the urinary bladder, but on the contrary the uterus, and he brought those who were present to witness his dissection round to the view that he had made a mistake about that goat in believing that it was pregnant. But afterwards, when they split open the belly of the goat, they found her foetus. This is what Theophrastus says on this head. Moreover in his book he maintains positively that it is not possible for any animal to carry a weighty foetus outside the uterus, without however bringing forward any evidence at all for that conclusion. Others have tried to establish by proof that this is something impossible. But there is no need for me to speak about the statements of these two groups, for the investigation of these matters is suited to the processes of reasoning by analogy and logic, but not to the demonstration of anatomy. And in this work I have here set myself
as my task only to describe the method of dissection to those who wish *168*

to instruct themselves about each one of the composite parts in the body, that is, the organs, and about the single, simple non-compounded parts, which they are and what sort of objects they resemble.

End of the Twelfth Book of the writing of Galen On Anatomical Dissection. Hunain ibn Ishāq has translated it. Praise be to God, the Lord of the worlds, and blessing rest in Muhammed the Prophet, his family and all his companions.

BOOK XIII

ON THE VEINS AND ARTERIES

In the name of God, the compassionate, the merciful. The Thirteenth section of Galen's work on Anatomy, translated by Ḥunain ibn Isḥāq.

INTRODUCTION.

I will here explain to you how to train yourself to dissect veins and 169
arteries in the best way. In my descriptions here also I shall propose as my intention and my aim to make my discourse clear and lucid to such a degree that it may be possible for one who studies them without ever having seen the dissection of an animal at all, after he has followed the account of the dissection of the veins and arteries as I have given it to him, to apply himself unaided to the study of them all.

CHAPTER I. DIRECTIONS FOR OPENING THE PERITONEAL CAVITY. THE GREATER AND LESSER OMENTA AND THE VESSELS THEY CONTAIN.

All anatomists uniformly call the veins and arteries specifically 'vessels'. And I do not think that anyone's lack of understanding of anatomy will extend so far that, when he hears me say: 'make an incision from the end of the sternum as far as the two pubic bones, an incision which passes straight over the body of the animal', he will not understand what I mean. Rather he will follow and keep to my instructions. There is no one who does not know that when he sets his hand to making an incision, in the first place the skin only will be incised, and that beneath the skin there extends a covering which intervenes between it and what is subjacent to it. Subsequently, after this fascial covering, the musculature appears. And when you cut through it completely, you then find the space that underlies it void, and in this space you find structures of which the first is an adipose tissue of the class of fascial coverings which spreads itself over the parts

found beneath [*greater omentum*]. And when you draw this off and remove it, you find beneath it the whole of the intestines, together with
170 the liver, the stomach, the spleen, and the remainder of the like abdominal organs. For the layer extended beneath the skin [*subcutaneous fascia*] is in a certain manner connected and joined to the coverings which invest the muscles lying beneath them, except that their combination and their connection is produced only by the very finest tissues, which resemble spiders' webbing [*arachnoid tissue*]. For that reason the covering can be detached and peeled off. But the attachment of the muscles to one another and their combination takes place in more ways than one. On their deep aspect they are invested by the covering which one calls 'peritonaion' [*peritoneum*], a name which means 'that which is spread circularly around'. It is so called for this reason only, that it invests and spreads itself circularly around the whole of the guts. This covering has also been called 'peritonaios'. The noun 'peritonaios' belongs to the class of masculine nouns, and 'peritonaion' to the class of those nouns which are neither masculine nor feminine. The Greeks call these 'oudeteron' which signifies 'neither masculine nor feminine'. The covering is also called 'dertron', that means the detachable, excoriable, although this name is not one of those which are generally and commonly employed. But as for you, should you call this covering by the Greek name 'peritonaios' or 'peritonaion', you are making use of names which the anatomists are already accustomed to apply. The covering, that is the peritoneum, adheres and is attached within to the structure that overlies the stomach and viscera, but not one of the parts underlying it adheres and is attached to it. But if you like to take the two borders of the incision, and to extend the incised line upwards, then the covering called 'peritonaion', that is, the peritoneum, can be lifted off without any of the subjacent structures following it. It is of course clearly to be understood that this operation should only be performed when the animal is lying on its back.[1]

And now, in order to examine more fully and clearly what comes next after the peritoneum, make two other incisions, either transversely
171 or obliquely. The incision should be made so that it crosses all the

[1] This last sentence seems to make it clear that with the animal lying on its back the viscera do not fall out through the wound, but remain in the abdominal cavity.

structures overlying the abdominal cavity which, as I recommended to you, you have just now divided by means of an incision passing in a straight line from above downwards. Make one of these two incisions on the right flank and the other on the left, and carry them so far backwards that they both reach the musculature of the vertebral column. When you have done that, then take everything superficial to the abdominal cavity that you have divided, and collect it together on one side. And should you wish to excise it completely and cast it away, that you can also do.[1]

Now at first you encounter the structure which I mentioned to you a short time ago, that is, the adipose membranous covering which is distributed over the whole of the intestines. Some anatomists call this structure by a masculine name, 'epiplous' and others call it by one of the class of nouns that is neither masculine nor feminine namely 'epiploon'. In our discussion we shall call it by either of these two names, whichever occurs to us at the time. We have already said that this covering, that is, the omentum, distributes itself over the intestines, and swims upon them. And I believe that those who gave it this name, I mean 'epiploon', so named it just for this reason, since its meaning is 'the thing that swims or floats on the surface'. It is a covering filled with many veins and arteries. It originates from the stomach in particular and from the hilum of the spleen. And it has yet another origin from the first part of the intestine, that is, the part which some anatomists call 'the offshoot measuring twelve fingers' [*duodenum*]. Further, it combines with yet other structures, all of which we have mentioned in connection with the anatomy of the internal organs. Here in this discussion it is not our concern or our intention to elucidate the nature of the covering called 'epiplous', that is, the omentum. But 172
because it is filled with veins and arteries, it is necessary that we should speak of it in connection with the anatomy of the veins and the arteries. Now since its interior forms a cavity to which there is no access from any direction, each of its two layers must be overlapped by the other after the fashion of two leaves of a book. Its lower layer you should leave spread out over the intestine. But raise up the upper layer and acquaint yourself with the many veins and arteries which are found there.

[1] This seems to imply removal of anterior and lateral abdominal walls.

All those veins and arteries commence on the convexity of the stomach. When you have sufficiently examined them, then draw upwards the free border of the omentum and place it on the thorax, lest it interpose itself between you and what you wish to examine after it. Similarly also, when you have seen the lower layer of the omentum, divide this too lengthwise into two halves, so that one of the two halves remains attached to the right side, the other to the left. Then draw these two halves obliquely upwards, and place them on the two flanks of the animal, one on the right flank, the other on the left. When you have done that, then acquaint yourself with the great vein which lies on the hollow aspect [*visceral surface*] of the liver. The easiest way by which you can find it and recognise it is for you to take the gall-bladder as your guide to it. For the gall-bladder lies upon the largest hepatic lobe, and its cavity extends as far as the outermost limit of the liver, while its neck extends to the hollowest part of the liver. From there originates that duct in which the bile flows in its natural course. But it [the duct], for its part, leads this [the bile] downwards, travelling past the liver, and pours it into the first part of the intestine [*duodenum*]. Close to it
173 you see, stretching out, a vein larger than all the [other] veins there [*hepatic portal vein*] and a very small artery [*A. hepatica*] which rides upon it. This vein there is, as it were, at the mid-point between the two in the long axis of the body of the animal. The artery extends over it in its upper parts, and the duct that receives the bile extends alongside it in its lower parts.

All these structures are clad and ensheathed in a delicate covering [*lesser omentum*], as are other structures which come after them in the region of the organ known as the pancreas. There is also similarly covered the first outgrowth of the intestine for which there is no name at all. For that reason the anatomists have simply called it 'outgrowth', but some speak of it also as 'the outgrowth measuring twelve fingers' [*duodenum*], because Herophilus has said that this is its length. But as regards the structure named 'pancreas', the case there is as I said before, to the effect that it is a body of fleshy substance within which only a small amount of the nature of blood is contained. Everything which belongs to this class [of substances] one calls 'adenes', that is to say 'spongy flesh'. You must now take care to detach the covering

from these structures, but you must aim at protecting as much as possible the venous branches attached to them. They should be preserved intact, without any harm or injury befalling them at your hands. For in the first place, there are attached to this covering many small twigs, which take their origin from the great vein which is called the 'portal vein', and their number is not the same in all the Classes of animals. Besides this you will not find in all individuals of the various animal species an equal number of these venules. It may be that those of them which are less full and smaller occasionally elude observation and discovery. Consequently these twigs, even when they are by nature always constant in their number, may not appear to be so. *174*
Many of them are fine, resembling capillary hairs in their appearance, I mean those twigs which go to the spongy flesh called 'pancreas' and the twigs which go to the place called the 'porta' [*porta hepatis*], together with those which go to the 'first outgrowth' of the intestine [*duodenum*]. For to this part of the intestine go veins whose condition is such as this, and often it is a single very clearly visible vein [*superior pancreaticoduodenal*], and at its side you see plainly a very small artery which extends along its length; and so also at its side there is yet another vein, which ascends to the place known as the 'porta'. It passes beyond this for a short distance, so as to divide at the end, that is, the terminal portion of the stomach. The extreme endings of this vein [*right gastro-epiploic*] unite themselves with the offshoots of other veins. This I shall mention to you later on.

As for the remaining veins, which branch off from that great vein whose origin is at the porta hepatis, each of these is of considerable size. And without exception they all reach as far as the stomach, the intestines, the spleen, and the great omentum. For to these structures alone go branches from the vein arising from the porta hepatis. But among the remaining organic structures there is not one to which a twig of this vein extends at all. The distribution of these veins does not always take place among all animals in one and the same manner. But in all animals there is one point in common, namely, that the veins which attach themselves and grow into the omentum, the spleen, the stomach, and the whole of the intestines, come off from the vein which originates at the porta hepatis. Accordingly we shall first begin with

a summary of what there is to see of that in the apes. For this animal
175 is more like Mankind than are the remaining animals.

CHAPTER 2. THE ANATOMY OF THE 'BRANCHES' OF THE HEPATIC PORTAL VEIN IN THE APE.

We say that from this portal vein there branches off first, a vein of no small size [*right gastric*], and this reaches as far as the flat aspect of the stomach [*lesser curvature*]. In general it divides and branches off throughout the entire right-hand half section near the lower end, the so-called porta [*pylorus*]. The remainder of it for the most part goes still further on, and reaches as far as the duodenum. Then it divides up and combines with the endings of another vein of which I shall speak later. After this comes another somewhat larger vein whose origin is contiguous to that of the first one. Frequently the origin of the two is single and common to both. This vein [*splenic vein*] stretches itself out, travelling in the direction of the spleen. It supports itself, however, at first upon the 'spongy flesh' called pancreas, and to this there attach themselves coming from it three or four veins of extreme tenuity. And these veins cannot be seen at all if the blood contained within them has emptied itself out. I believe that some of the old physicians call such veins as these by the Greek name 'apanthismoi' which has the same meaning as 'lines'. But as for me, I am accustomed to call them 'capillaries' because they resemble hair filaments in tenuity. Now when this vein, that is, the second [*splenic*] has travelled beyond the 'spongy flesh' called pancreas, you see it arriving at the spleen. On its way there it is swimming, or floating. I am in the habit of applying this expression, I mean 'swimming or floating', to all such veins as are without resting-place, support or firm emplacement and which are, as it were, suspended or clinging. And my precursors among the anatomists have applied this epithet exactly in this way. This condition only occurs amongst
176 vessels when their course lies in a hollow space, where no sort of body encounters them upon which they can lean, or by which they can support themselves. In the course of this vein as it travels to the spleen, other veins break off from it in the hollow aspect of the spleen. And these are sometimes few in number, and in diameter small at first, and finally capillary-like. Sometimes also, that great vein [*splenic*] is

present alone, without those small offshoots. Again this great vein is on occasion solitary and undivided, and at other times it is divided into two. Yet however it may be, it does nevertheless distribute itself on the flat aspect of the stomach [*left gastric vein*] until it reaches the cardiac orifice. And this vein also, that is to say, the one which goes to the spleen, and of which we said that those twigs shooting off take their origin from it, courses over the hollow aspect of the spleen. It then divides into two equal parts. And each of its two halves passes over the hollow aspect of the spleen, where it is 'floating', suspended, and mounted upon a membranous sheet which is folded on itself in two layers.[1] From one of the two branches many twigs spring off which sink into the hollow aspect of the spleen, and extend as far as its upper end. The other half extends downwards as far as the end of the spleen. In this fashion, their division breaks off with a large remnant of considerable proportions being left over from each of the two. Of the two, the upper branch [*short gastric*] goes up towards the convex side [*greater curvature*] of the stomach, the lower [*left gastroepiploic*] reaches the leftward side of the omentum. Now at the place where that vein mounts over which at first lies above the spleen, you see close at hand a single vein coming from the spleen to the stomach. But as for the
vein ascending directly upwards, of which we spoke (that is, the one 177
which comes up from the upper end of the spleen and ascends over the convex surface of the stomach which lies on this side), I have often found that, before it reaches the highest part of the spleen, it goes to the stomach and removes itself from the spleen a little above its middle region. But as for what remains over from it, that reaches as far as the upper end of the spleen, and what then still remains over, goes to the stomach, and distributes itself to those portions of it which are in the nearest proximity to the upper end of the spleen. And the branch which ascends to the convexity of the stomach proceeds onwards, riding on it 'floating' and suspended, with no contact with the body of the stomach. For between the two, obstructing their contact, lies a membranous sheet, which is folded over in two layers in the same way as that which I have described to you in regard to the omentum.

This sheet, when it meets and comes in contact with the vein, covers

[1] The two layers of the lienorenal ligament of peritoneum.

it all and cloaks it, encircling it with its two layers. Then these two layers unite and coincide with one another over the vein, and from them the initial stage of the upper reticular sheet comes into existence. But from the vein of which I said that it comes from the upper end of the spleen, and rides over the convexity of the stomach, there branch off very many twigs which combine together with one another. And they all reach the stomach, travelling within the folded membrane. And from it there branch off twigs which go to the omentum, in number corresponding to them. These branches travel within the folded-up membrane from which the upper part of the omentum is brought into being. But as for the ending of this vein, after it has distributed itself in this way, it joins on to the end of another vein, and combines with it, I mean the one which begins at the portal vein [*right gastroepiploic*]. That is a vein which extends over the right side of the convexity of the stomach in the same way as that vein which I mentioned previously, I mean the last one of which I spoke. For the disposition of the stomach is oblique, and the part called the 'mouth of the stomach' lies on the left side of the animal's body, but the place called
178 the 'gateway' [*pylorus*] lies on the right side. To the upper distended part of the stomach very many twigs betake themselves from the two veins described. By 'the two veins' I mean the one of which I said that it comes from the spleen [*left gastroepiploic*] and the vein [*right gastroepiploic*] which meets and combines with it. That [the latter] is the one of which I shall presently have to speak.

From that great vein springing out from the porta hepatis, which some call the portal vein, another, third, vein now branches off after those two that we have mentioned, and this distributes itself in the last mesentery [*middle colic and inferior mesenteric veins*]. Its origin is on the left side of the portal vein, just as is that of those two veins of which we have spoken already, that is to say those of which I said that they are often two subdivisions of a single offshoot. Nevertheless, for the present, with reference to all that you will hear further on about numeration, we shall simply take as a principle that these are two veins. But among those animals in which these two veins may be found as offshoots sprouting off from a single root common to both, the number of the sum total of the veins which we are about to mention further on is reduced by one, so that the fourth branch will become the third, the fifth branch will become the fourth, and so on for all in succession. But for the present, take it that there are two principal veins in accordance with our previous description. After them comes another, third, vein, and that is the one which goes to the last mesentery [*middle colic and inferior mesenteric veins*]. Now pass on with us to the account of the fourth vein.

This vein [*right gastroepiploic*] has its origin on the right side of the so-called portal vein, and it goes to the convexity of the stomach. It is the one of which we said not long ago that it divides itself up in this fashion, and its end combines itself with the end of another vein, I mean the one of which we said that it comes from the spleen to the stomach [*left gastroepiploic*]. Indeed the whole of the right side of the 179
upper portion of the great omentum originates from the right side of the stomach, just as its left side takes its origin from the left side of the stomach. And the veins which are found in this place branch off in the same manner as those veins which lie on that side and they pass on, as do those, in between the two membranes from which the great omentum takes its origin. As for the upper layer of the great omentum, there make their way to the right side of this veins resembling branches which diverge from that vein of which I said that it is the fourth of those that sprout off from the portal vein [*right gastroepiploic*]. In the same way to the other side of the great omentum, that is to say the left side, veins make their way which break off from the vein distributing itself in the spleen. But in the remaining portion of the great omentum, that is, what is spread out beneath its upper portion, of which I said that it has its origin on the convexity of the stomach, there are fine veins which commence on the 'flat side' [*lesser curvature*] just like those upper veins.

Let us now begin to repeat what we said about these veins and let us recall them one by one. Then afterwards we shall pass on to give an account of the remaining veins. We say, then, that the first vein springs out from the portal vein on its left side, and goes to the 'flat' side of the stomach [*right gastric vein*]. The second vein comes to the spleen having arisen from this same root. From this vein a branch [*left gastric vein*] distributes itself in the flat part of the stomach lying above and

to the left. But the other, larger branch goes on in the direction of the spleen. After it has distributed itself to the spleen, one of its two extremities mounts up to the convexity of the stomach and the other goes on to the portion of the great omentum found here on the left side. I said previously that from the place in which this part is to be
180 found near the spleen, a vein goes also to the stomach. Another vein, a third one, is found here which betakes itself to the last mesentery, that mesentery which reaches as far as the rectum. So these three veins have their origins on the left side of the portal vein. But the fourth vein, following after them, springs out on the right side [of the portal vein]. And that is the vein of which I said that it goes over across the porta [*pylorus*] to the convexity of the stomach [*right gastroepiploic*]. Before this vein courses onwards over the stomach, branches which reach the great omentum spring off from it, and in constitution and usefulness these are analogous to the branches of the vein which we mentioned previously [*left gastroepiploic*], that is to say the one which is on the lower end of the spleen, and which divides itself in the subdivisions of the great omentum found there. Now just as that one is distributed to the left side of the whole lower part [of the great omentum], so this divides itself up in the whole of the right side as far as its lower margin.

We have now given a sufficient and adequate account of the veins which go to the stomach, to the spleen and to the great omentum. Next we must follow that with an account of the veins which go to the intestines. Accordingly we say that the mesenteries which invest the intestines number three in all. One of these is the mesentery of the veins of the thin intestines—by 'thin intestines' I understand that portion of which the first part is called the 'fasting intestine' [*jejunum*]—and it lies intermedially between them. The other mesentery, the second, is that of the veins which go to the right-sided subdivisions of this intestine called 'colon'. The third mesentery is that of the veins going to the parts lying on the left side of this, as well as to all the parts that connect it to the anus. By the colon's connecting parts I mean the so called 'straight' intestine, that is, the rectum. You will see that in this mesentery there is distributed the third of those veins which we mentioned. But in the right-hand one of the two mesenteries of the colon, that is, the one which has its place on its first subdivision, there

is distributed on its right-hand side another vein [*right colic*] which
springs off after the four which we specified, and of which we said that 181
they take origin from the portal vein. The remainder of the great vein springing out at the porta hepatis is distributed in the mesentery of the small intestine [*superior mesenteric vein*], and its end divides into two halves. One of these two divisions divides itself up on the caecum [*ileocolic vein*], the other reaches the right flexure of the colon, then travels a little further and unites with the end of that vein [*right colic*] of which I said that it is the fifth following the four primary veins which I mentioned and which spring from the portal vein.

I have now given you an account of the division of the vein which springs off at the porta hepatis so far as it takes place on the underside [*visceral aspect of the liver*]. Its division within the liver itself is analogous to and the counterpart of this distribution. That is because from the porta hepatis there spring off and emerge veins, one of which goes to each of its lobes. Each of these veins then divides into many parts in the lobe to which it comes, and finally it travels to the extreme margin of its lobe. And along each vein and its subdivisions there extends and divides itself a branch of each of the two vessels of which I said at the outset that they are closely connected with and adjacent to the portal vein. Of these two vessels, one is the duct which receives the bile and the other is the artery [*hepatic*]. Further, you will see in the mesentery besides these veins which we have mentioned, others [*lacteals*] each of which ends at a portion of 'spongy flesh' [*mesenteric lymph gland*] specially associated with itself. And you will see how the final parts, the extreme endings, of these veins [*lacteals*] which lie in the coverings of the intestine, unite and combine themselves with those veins which come from the portal vein, inasmuch as they travel in the mesentery to the intestines. If you do not see them [the fine veins] clearly, then note the following advice which I give to you, and employ it generally in regard to all veins which may prove difficult for you to see. You must, I say, stretch out the whole of the material which surrounds that vein, away from the place in which it lies in the direction of the
mesentery. Next turn to the small veins, and fill them with blood by 182
compressing as strongly as possible the large veins which have their place above them. That is most likely to succeed when the air is warm,

and if the animal which is to be dissected has not been strangled long before that time. Now just as this is something from which you derive benefit in the study of the small veins, so also the contrary holds good, when it happens to the person engaged in the dissection that an uncertainty arises in the dissection of some vein or other. For he misses these veins because the blood flowing out obscures the view of them, especially in the bodies of apes, since the blood of apes is thin. It flows and streams out easily and quickly, even if the animal should have been dead for many hours previously. But the blood of the dog, that of the lion and other animals resembling these is very thick. Do you then remember what I have said throughout any attempt you may make to investigate and scrutinise the minute veins, and to study such of them as are only with difficulty accessible to one's view. For my part, I now return to that which I had in view, and on which I commenced.

CHAPTER 3. THE 'DISTRIBUTION' OF THE INFERIOR VENA CAVA, FROM ITS 'ORIGIN' IN THE LIVER TO VISCERA AND TO THE WALLS OF THE ABDOMEN.

I say that when you have examined the interconnection of the veins which go from the intestine to the 'spongy flesh', you should then realise that you have carried out to its ending the dissection of the veins which come from the portal vein. For besides these ones which we have mentioned you will find no other vein which combines with the one which has its origin at the porta hepatis, although there are very many veins there, in the great omentum, in the two flanks, in the lateral lumbar regions, on the urinary bladder, on the uterus, and, in general, in the whole of the region between the diaphragm and the two pelvic
183 bones. But the state of affairs in regard to all those veins is the same as that which applies to the rest of the veins throughout the whole of the body, namely that they all originate from the great vein which some call the 'hepatic' vein, others the 'hollow' vein [*inferior vena cava*]. Occasionally one finds that certain of the veins springing from the vena cava are combined and united with the veins in the leftward mesentery. An example of that is what we experienced recently, when we saw clearly a vein running transversely which united the vein going to the right testis with the vein which divides and splits up in the left

mesentery. As for the vena cava, its whole source is also on the liver, and yet it does not grow out like the portal vein from the excavated aspect of the liver, nor again does it originate from a single region on the convexity of the liver, but it takes its source from all of the veins which are found there. It is as though it has combined and coalesced from various roots and it mounts upwards like the trunk of a tree which divides into two. One of these two divisions goes upwards to the diaphragm, the other goes downwards to the kidneys.

Now in this method of dissection which we have described you will be able to see the whole of the veins which spring out from it. And you will see them most easily if you take out the whole of the intestines. Sometimes one removes the intestines together with the mesentery, at other times without the mesentery. Should I wish to remove them together with the mesentery, then with a fine flaxen thread I ligature the vein which comes from the hollow aspect of the liver [*portal vein*], and besides that I ligature the arteries which ramify together with it, especially when the animal that I am dissecting is only just dead, so that blood does not bespatter me either from the veins or from the arteries, and thus, without the blood pouring over me, I am enabled to study the branches of the descending part of the vena cava. But if *184*
I wish to remove the intestines without the mesentery, then I detach the membrane surrounding them externally and leave it with the mesentery. I have already said previously, where I dealt with the organs of nutrition, that this membrane is united with the peritoneum, and firmly attached to it. Consequently it can be separated and stripped off from the intestine with very little effort. You will not need the ligature if you take out the intestines in this way, especially when the ape has already long been dead. But if you take them without shelling them out in the manner we have just described to you, then indeed you require the ligature. However, if you remove them in this other manner, it is easy for you to discover and to acquaint yourself with the branches of the vena cava. You see these branches most clearly when you strip off the whole of the peritoneum which lies on the lumbar region. For the peritoneum is spread out there, over all the veins and arteries found in this place, and over the muscles of both the [right and left] lumbar regions. One portion of it extends over the kidneys, and similarly over

the stomach, the liver, the diaphragm, the uterus, the urinary bladder, and, in short, over all the structures lying between the diaphragm and the pelvic bone.

Now before you detach the peritoneum, you see delicate veins dispersed, which break off from the vena cava, and go to the renal membrane, that is, the covering which encircles the kidneys, and to the region thereabouts. Sometimes these veins appear only indistinctly on examination, at other times some of them will not be seen at all; it seldom happens that they are all visible. However, their appearance will always become more evident when the peritoneum has been detached, that is, at the time when it is being detached. But soon after the detachment of the peritoneum from them, when they have been exposed, they with-
185 draw themselves from view much more than before they were exposed.

As for the clearly visible veins which you see coming from the downgoing vena cava, these are what I am about to describe to you. The first is a vein [? *left phrenic*] which comes to the left side, somewhat above the kidney that is found on this side. A twig from this not inconsiderable vein joins and connects with the spongy flesh [*suprarenal gland*] lying there. The second vein [*renal*] goes to this kidney itself. Sometimes you find that if the first vein is not present, there springs from this one, that is, the vein going to the kidney, a vein which distributes itself to those parts in which the first broke up into branches. As for the right kidney, you find no other vein above that one which goes to it, except fine capillary venules, and these are the ones which I mentioned earlier. But on the right side a recognisable vein of noteworthy size resembling the vein on the left side is certainly not present. But the arrangement is often such that from the vein [? *phrenic*] of the left side alone without [the participation of] the vena cava, fine shoots branch off which go to the renal sheath, that is, the covering of the kidneys, especially when the branches split off only from the veins going to the kidney. The veins which nourish both the renal sheaths, I mean the two [right and left] coverings, extend themselves as far as that portion of the peritoneum which is connected to them both, so that the urinary ducts are either joined by very small veins which derive from these ones, or else this happens at the spot where those veins have their first halt on the kidney.

After these branches, you see the great veins which travel away from the vena cava to the kidneys. And you will see that from one of them, that is, the one which goes to the left kidney, a vein arises and goes to the left testis. And often a branch which comes from the vena cava itself
connects itself with this vein. On the right side, the arrangement is 186
reversed. That is to say, usually it is only from the vena cava itself that a vein goes to the right testis. In rare cases I have seen in addition a small twig springing out from that vein which goes to the right kidney, and then a single vein is formed from the two in combination. Of these veins [*testicular*] it is to be understood that they are very lengthy, since they travel down, and forwards near the heads of the femora, in order to arrive at the testes. It is also clear that on their course they are suspended, floating, since they are borne upwards, and gradually displace themselves from the lumbar region. And consequently a share of the peritoneum found in the lumbar region is apportioned to them, which surrounds them and supports and adheres to them until they reach the two long ducts. For on its own side each one reaches the testis. Now also, just as in the lumbar region the peritoneum is spread over these veins and over other veins and arteries, so also it descends with them in an unaltered condition until it arrives at the testes, being in the same state as it was when it started. And these veins, before they reach and attach themselves to the testes, twist themselves up in convolutions with manifold loops [*pampiniform plexus*], and their accompanying arteries circle around with them.

To those veins which branch from the vena cava as it is lying upon the lumbar region, there belongs yet another pair [*lumbar veins*] which goes out from it below the kidneys. And from this pair fine veins sink downwards until they reach the spinal cord, and a branch from them goes to the muscles of the vertebral column. Similarly also from hte upper veins following the diaphragm, a branch makes its way into the interior of the vertebral canal and reaches to the spinal cord. And again,
from them a branch goes to the muscles of the vertebral column. The 187
remainder of each single vein goes upwards, however, to the lower part of the abdomen, and divides into two halves. Of these two, one mounts over the first muscle, of which I said that it is in contact with the peritoneum and attached to it [*M. transversus abdominis*], and the other

half travels across the oblique muscle [*M. obliquus abdominis*]. Indeed the nourishment of these muscles in this region is derived solely from these veins. The position is the same with the veins springing off from the vena cava, and the whole of their offshoots to each one of the lumbar vertebrae, with the sole exception of the veins in the muscle ascending longitudinally directly upwards (*M. rectus abdominis*). For these are connected from the inner aspect. Their origin is twofold, as one of them comes from above, from the veins which emerge from the thorax, of which we shall speak later on [*internal mammary and superior epigastric veins*], and the other [*inferior epigastric*] from the vein [*iliac*] which, one on each side, goes to the legs, at the particular place where there originate the veins that go to the uterus. For the vena cava, in the lumbar region, divides itself into two heads near the broad bone, the sacrum, after a branch on each of the vertebrae has gone away from it to the places which we have mentioned. You can see the artery on this bone as though it were placed above and not below the vein as was the case above. And after this vein has divided itself, numerous offshoots spring
188 from it again before it proceeds outwards, making its way through the muscles to reach the inguinal groove. You find among them twigs which go to the lateral lumbar regions, travelling up and down and traversing the apertures and the large passages through the pubic bones [*obturator veins*]. Besides these offshoots yet other twigs branch off from it [*the common iliac vein*] which make their way to the whole of the structures lying on that wide bone, the sacrum. These structures comprise the muscles which lie there, the urinary bladder, the uterus in female animal bodies, the penis in males. To the testes, as we have already described, go veins from the region of the kidneys, while to the penis come the veins from the region about the broad bone, the sacrum. As for the female animal body, those veins which approach the male organs from places in the vicinity of the kidneys go to the ovaries, and to the cervix uteri come veins from the region of the broad bone, the sacrum. The cervix uteri of the female is the counterpart of the penis in the male. Furthermore these two [*veins, i.e. ovarian and uterine*] are the roots of the veins in the uterus. The vein which comes from the kidneys to the ovaries distributes itself also in the uterine cavity, and as for the vein coming from the region of the broad bone, the sacrum,

it distributes itself also to the cervix uteri, and to that which is attached to it. These veins lie within the peritoneum and go, one on each side, to the cervix uteri, close to the muscles.

Now there branch off from this region two other veins [*inferior epigastric*] which at first travel in an oblique direction upwards and forwards together, and apply themselves to the vertically directed muscles of the abdomen [*Mm. recti abdominis*]. Then from here on they pass vertically upwards, and go through beneath the muscle which *189*
I mentioned and both combine and join with those veins which descend from above [*superior epigastric* 'branch' of *internal mammary*]. These latter emerge at the thorax from both sides of the so-called xiphoid cartilage. Then fine offshoots branch off from them, which come out to the region of the mammary gland, descend in a deeper place from above downwards, and encounter those veins of which we said that they travel from below upwards together with the fleshy rectilinear muscle. Those are the two veins of which we last spoke. Some of the branches combine and unite themselves with the veins which are found in this place, others continue as independent veins [*superficial epigastric*] and descend on both sides near the exterior of the body on the surface side of the whole of the abdominal musculature. The view of these veins is most clear in the bodies of such animals as have little subcutaneous tissue, when much blood remains in them. With these veins also there meet two others, whose source comes from those great veins [*femoral*] that travel to the lower limbs at the place where they first pass through and emerge from the whole of the abdominal muscles and mount upon the groin. Consequently, just like the others which we mentioned previously they have a superficial position. On the bodies of such animals as have but little subcutaneous tissue you see them clearly beneath the skin. And when you detach the skin they are there in the first layer that you then see, lying beneath the skin, as I said, superficially to the muscles.

But with regard to the other veins of which we spoke, that is, those found within the muscles, the condition of both the external and internal elements of these is one and the same in this respect which I am about to explain to you. That is to say, there come off at one and the same point two veins, one on each side [*external pudendal veins*] and

190 they reach to the terminal parts of the skin of the penis and of the testes. And there goes to the testis, making its way over the spot which is called the 'posterior union and junction', a very small fine vein which is not visible in the bodies of all animals. But if the animal is of large size, and its body is full of blood, and if you compress this vein at the instant of the animal's death, before it has become at all cold, and if you drive the blood forcibly into its fine twigs, then this vein will become visible. In the same way this pair of veins which we have mentioned goes in the female body to the pudenda, and its course runs towards the meeting place of the two pubic bones.

Accordingly it amounts to a communication of a twofold kind between the veins of the thorax and mammary regions, those of the uterus, and those of the remaining genital organs. In the one instance, communication is established by means of the deep veins, of which we said that they have their places underneath the two upright fleshy muscles lying in the long axis of the body, and in the other through the connection with the external veins, that is, those last mentioned.

CHAPTER 4. FURTHER OBSERVATIONS ON VEINS WITHIN THE ABDOMEN, WITH NOTES ON TECHNIQUES TO BE EMPLOYED IN THEIR DEMONSTRATION.

After what has been said, the description of the dissection of the veins on the lower limbs should follow. But since we have already dealt with that in Book III of this work, I must begin an account of the dissection of the veins in the other organs that remain. But first I must add and join to the account that I gave what remains to be said about it. I have already mentioned that you can remove the intestines of the animal in either one of two ways. You can ligature the large veins and arteries that are at the head [*root*] of the three mesenteries, or else you can turn to the region of attachment of the mesenteries to the intestines
191 and cut these away and detach them, as the butchers are accustomed to do. If we do that, then the mesenteries alone remain behind, without the intestines, and all their veins and arteries remain, preserving their connections with one another unchanged. But as regards the performance of this operation, you must learn of the following defect. When we remove the intestines in this way it often happens that some

blood streams out from the veins and the arteries which we have cut through, especially when the ape is full-blooded, and when one has commenced its dissection immediately after its death. And if in addition it happens that its blood is by nature even thinner than that of other apes, and that the atmosphere of the place in which one dissects is warm, that makes it more likely that the blood will conceal what one requires to observe of the nutrient veins in the peritoneum over the lumbar region, since all of these are the finest of veins. For to this part of the peritoneum there go veins with very many branches, arachnoid veins. But most of them come off from those which go to the testis. Consequently you must now direct your careful attention to ensure that no blood flows out there, so that all the veins may show themselves clearly to you. That also happens if the ape has died a considerable time before being dissected. Before one takes in hand this task, then, the ape must be drowned, either in the afternoon or in the evening, as I have already explained, and then dissected the next day in the early morning. But if one makes the dissection on a dog, and dissects it immediately after its death in the method here indicated for the dissection of the mesenteries, then no blood is to be seen pouring out, much less a remarkable quantity of it, because of the thickness of its blood. It is just the same *192*
among [other] animals whose teeth interlock with one another, especially lions.

Now the dissection made in the way set out, I mean by the detachment and the extraction of the intestines, is fully suitable for the inspection, collectively and briefly, of the veins which we have mentioned, and also for the dissection of all the arteries discoverable within the peritoneum. That is to say, when you extend the mesentery, you will be in a position to get a good view of the arteries stretched out at the side of each individual vein. Should the task be carried out in a well-lighted place you will also see a small nerve stretched out at the side of the vein and the artery [*sympathetic plexus of nerves*]. But in this place we have not in view the discussion of the anatomy of nerves. I shall leave them, then, after making a single point. This is that you should bear in mind the mesentery which you have uncovered and exposed in this way so that when, later on, we come to an account of the nerves, we may not be compelled to repeat precisely what we have already said.

So I return once more now to the description of the veins, so that the continuity and the scheme of the discussion may not be interrupted by the insertion of a digression in the middle of an account of the arteries. Remember now that from the convexity of the liver, the vena cava lying in the lumbar region [*infrahepatic portion of inferior vena cava*] grows off as a tree-trunk grows from its roots, and so does the vein which mounts upwards to the heart [*suprahepatic portion of inferior vena cava*]. And you must be acquainted with this fact also which I am about to describe for you. It is that if anyone takes the view that these three veins may be regarded as a single one, I mean the vein which I have just mentioned in this discussion of mine and of which I said that it lies in the lumbar region, the vein on the convexity of the liver, and the third vein which ascends to the heart and the concavity of the
193 neck, he does not err, because many physicians have called this vein by this name, I mean 'the hollow one', [*vena cava*] on the assumption that it is a single one, whereas others call it the 'hepatic' vein. Nevertheless, the matter, as I have repeatedly said, is such that whoever has as his end aim the understanding and knowledge of the objects should not worry or concern himself about names. Consequently I have come to employ names and to put them into circulation as it suits me. But attend to me now, so that we may begin at another starting point. I say, just as all the lower veins, with the exception of the veins on the stomach, on the spleen, and on the intestine, are simply branches of the lower vena cava, so also all veins above the convexity of the liver have their origin from the vena cava ascending upwards. That is, as soon as it first emerges from the liver and makes contact with the diaphragm, which almost completely surrounds it, there sprouts out from it immediately a vein on each of the two sides [*inferior phrenic veins*]. Very rarely have I seen on both sides two unequal veins. One of the two was then a branch of the other, which is constantly visible. Among other animals one sees them not uncommonly thus, both together on both sides. I will describe what kinds of animal these are when I have completed the review of the apes and begun my account of those other animals, showing the details of their nature which you discover by dissection. However as regards the dissection which you are making here in order to study and to see clearly the veins which originate from the vena cava,

you must aim at gaining the clearest possible information about them. And 194
that can be done by pursuing the following course in your study of them.

CHAPTER 5. THE SYSTEMIC VEINS OF THE THORAX.

You must carry an incision, running in a straight line along the length of the thorax on its right side, where lies the cartilaginous part of those ribs which reach as far as the sternum, in such a way that the ends of the ribs connected with the sternum remain attached to it. As for the remaining part which the incision has separated and divided from the sternum, it forms a single fragment, so that the two parts may be removed one from another. Since that is so, when you break away this part towards the vertebral column you can clearly view the vena cava, and see that it ascends vertically through the whole of the thorax, so that it arrives at the 'cervical groove' [? *suprasternal notch*]. The first thing that you must investigate clearly and thoroughly, without negligence or carelessness, concerns the first branches of the vena cava, which go to the diaphragm. But since the body of the diaphragm is, in the strict sense, a muscle only, and since on this there are spread out the peritoneum below, and above it the basal portion of the membrane [*parietal pleura*] which applies itself to the ribs from within, it consequently amounts to three leaf-like layers, superimposed one upon another. You must therefore search and observe closely, between which of these layers or leaves is the position of the diaphragmatic veins. That can only be observed by the removal of the two membranes which invest it on its two surfaces, I mean the membrane which descends from above from the ribs [*pleura*], and the membrane continuous with the peritoneum. I will now describe to you what I constantly find with regard to this. You too are bound to see it similarly. For you will find that both the two veins are concealed between the diaphragm and the membrane which clothes it from above, [continuing] downwards from the membrane applying itself to the ribs from within. And at the same time you will see that the walls of these veins are as delicate as [those of]
the veins on the convexity of the liver and the rest of the veins there. 195
For the walls of all the veins on the convexity of the liver are slender. But when the vena cava passes through the diaphragm and enters the thorax, then its walls become stronger than previously, and a membrane

also is wrapped around it. This membrane is a portion of those [*mediastinal pleurae*] which divide the whole of the thorax lengthwise from above downwards. When you reflect it from the veins you get a better view of the venous wall, and you learn to what extent its thickness has increased over and above that of the veins of the liver. Before you detach the membrane, investigate those fine veins which distribute themselves [*mediastinal veins*] in it off from this vein [*V. cava*]. Further, there are among these veins twigs which attach themselves to the membrane which clothes the heart, its sheath [*pericardium*], upon its inferior parts. For it is joined and connected on both sides to the membranes which divide the whole of the thoracic cavity. And yet these veins are merely arachnoidal or capillary-like in size.

But the veins of notable size are these, which I will describe to you. I say that between the diaphragm and the heart no vein is found at all. Upon the heart there is a very large vein indeed which is peculiar to the part named 'the heart's ear' [*auricle and coronary sinus*]. And you will find that the blood which flows through this vein at this spot is in some animals, mankind among them, divided into three portions, but in others, including the ape, into two portions. Most of it goes to the right hand one of the two heart cavities, but the remainder goes to the veins which encircle and wreathe round the whole heart [*coronary veins*]. There are a few anatomists who have called these veins by this name,
196 that is, 'those which surround and encircle the heart'. Their situation is in the actual substance of the heart near its exterior.

In the human body the vein which supplies the lower part of the thorax [*V. azygos*], that is, the eight lower ribs, takes its origin from the right-hand one of the two auricles of the heart. But in the body of the ape there splits off from the vena cava, after it has passed beyond the cardiac auricle, a very large branch, and this travels downwards within the thorax on the right side, not on the other side as is its course in the human body, in the pig, and in other animals. And whether it lies on the right side or the left side, this vein goes onwards to the vertebral column, and it halts and supports itself on the centrum of the fifth vertebra. That is, first of all, it simply rests upon this vertebra, which is the one that primarily supports, holds, and fastens it, whereas before it approaches the fifth vertebra it swims or floats, suspended, although

the membranes wrapped round it which, as it were, mark it off from its fellows, protect it, fasten it and secure it. From here onwards it takes the direction of the lower thoracic region, alongside the oesophagus and the largest artery upon the vertebral column [*thoracic aorta*]. On its course, there branches off from it an offshoot of considerable size, at each one of the intercostal spaces. And from these veins branches are transmitted and pass through to the so-called vertebral-column muscles, and to the muscles encircling the whole of the thorax [*intercostal muscles*]. Other small branches go down and sink into the vertebrae. You see how, in manifold fashion, they invest and distribute themselves in the two sheaths [*meninges*], the dura mater and the pia mater which come from the cerebral membranes and envelop the spinal cord. Now in the body of the ape you see that this vein, as I have stated, when it travels towards the right side to the fifth vertebra, divides itself visibly *197*
before it mounts on this vertebra. And the vein branching off from it goes to the fourth intercostal space. Again, from this another vein ascends to the third intercostal space. You see now how this vein ascending upwards combines with another capillary vein resembling it in tenuity. This takes its origin from yet another vein which is called 'that which nourishes the upper thoracic parts' [*superior intercostal vein*], just as the other vein, that which reaches the fifth vertebra, is called 'the one nourishing the lower thoracic parts'. And you will see how this vein branches off right-handed from the vena cava, before it divides into two.

CHAPTER 6. REMOVAL OF THE CLAVICLE. THE VEINS AT THE ROOT OF THE NECK AND THEIR 'BRANCHES'.[1]

The first point of division of the vena cava is where it encounters the clavicle. Consequently we must of necessity cut away the clavicle in

[1] Precise identification of vessels referred to in the next two chapters is often very difficult or even impossible. In modern anatomy the wide range of variation in venous patterns is well recognised, and we tend not to give names to any but the larger and more constant vessels. For Galen, with his theory of the distribution of blood from the liver by the veins, the anatomy of venous patterns was all-important because it was by these pathways that all parts of the body received their nourishment.

A difficulty of another kind arises with regard to identification of the veins at the root of the neck: Galen had no name for the right and left *innominate* (as we still call them) veins, and has to use a periphrasis which might be equally applicable on occasion to other veins at the root of the neck. B.T.

order to see clearly all the veins lying here. The clavicle is very often cut away in this way. Should the ape have only just died, a great quantity of blood pours over you, more than the calibre of those veins properly accounts for, when you happen to cut or lacerate them in any spot. You must, then, take care to set it free from the membranes wrapped around it, from its end on as far as its root, and to detach it from those parts connected with it, leaving it as it is at its root. You must raise it and move it from place to place from time to time as may be needed. These veins feed the highest part of the muscles that rise from the anterior thoracic region to the shoulder joint, that is the part of the muscles near each of the two clavicles. They branch off from the
198 great veins which are found in this region, those which we wish to set free and bring into view without allowing any blood to flow out over us. It is best now if you cut the muscles away from the clavicles. In deepening your incision you must go only so far that the attachment of the fascial tissues still remains plainly visible to you. For after that you must take great care not to carry the incision deeper.

In this fashion also set loose from the upper parts of the right clavicle the muscle attached to it, that is, the muscle of which I said, in the place devoted to the description of the muscles, that it descends from the skull [*M. sternocleidomastoideus*]. And now, when you have detached and set free from the clavicle the muscles that lie on it and under it, then direct your attention to the vein which is wrapped round [? within] the convexity of the clavicle [? *internal jugular vein*]. Its place on the clavicle is near to that end which is connected with the sternum. Should blood gush out from this vein it cannot easily be stopped, and that spoils and impairs the work for you. Since this is so, the best thing for you to do is to start by ligaturing and securing the vein on both sides of the clavicle, I mean above it and below. Then cut through the articular ligament, so that you detach the clavicle from the sternum. Next go to the end of the clavicle, grasp it with your fingers, draw it upwards, twist it at the same time little by little, and cut away all connections between it and the structures passing by it. You should continue doing that until you reach the vein which you have ligatured. I have said already that this vein lies not far from the clavicle. The most correct and the easiest procedure is to divide the vein between the

ligatures, and then with the greatest care and precaution to pull the 199
clavicle upwards. At the same time you should bend and twist it towards the acromion process and cut away with a knife the membranes attached to the clavicle. The incision through these should be so contrived that it runs to and fro along the clavicle so that none of the parts round it are cut through until, when you gradually get as far as the acromion, a muscle confronts you which, as it were, lies opposite beneath the clavicle.

This muscle [*M. subclavius*] has its insertion on the clavicle. It goes in the direction of the anterior thoracic region downwards, and near it [*the clavicle*] is attached to the first thoracic rib. When you have cut away this muscle from the clavicle or from the rib, or from both, then cut away without hesitation all parts which are attached to the clavicle, after you have wrenched it towards the acromion. Eventually, in the course of time, it will not be difficult for you, if you are confident of your manual strength, to tear away the clavicle in its entirety without excising or ligaturing the [*jugular*] vein. You will be helped to do so by cutting through the attachment of the clavicle and at the same time lifting up towards the neck and bringing into a higher position the end adjoining the sternum. For the vein that encircles the clavicle does not at once enter into communication with the deeply-placed vein, but sometimes it joins and unites with this only after it has ascended one-third of the way up the neck. Frequently, also, it does not unite with it until it has travelled about half way up. For that reason you can pull up and raise the clavicle as far as the uppermost region of the neck, after which you can remove it. You can also cut out the end of the clavicle from the joint on the acromion, and then draw it away without further ado, and force it from whichever side you prefer to the opposite side. For the present, assume that you are tearing it completely away, or that you bend it or wrench it out in the direction of the acromion.
Thereupon you can examine everything that lies beneath it without 200
anything at all being there that might render invisible or indistinct the things you wish to see. For in this region your ape will resemble an animal which has no clavicle. Now I return to the systematic order of my exposition, and will speak of the small veins which you see in this place before the extraction of the clavicle, and of those veins which will become visible after its removal.

I say that before you take out the clavicle there are many very small veins to see, which travel obliquely forwards, in the direction of the throat, from out of the vein which wraps itself round the clavicle. And you will always see that they collect together with one another when they come to the throat. When I say here throat, that is the gullet, I mean the hollow depressed region where the clavicle is attached to the sternum. Here, then, one also finds small veins which take their origin from this very one where first it passes beyond the clavicle and mounts on the neck. And also before these veins and below that place one finds sometimes small veins, and sometimes a single vein of no great size, with many offshoots. They ramify in the organ called the thymus. By thymus one understands the great spongy flesh [*gland*] which lies at the division of the great vein [*superior vena cava* 'giving rise to' the *innominates*]. It is at its maximum size in newly born animals, and afterwards it diminishes steadily and gradually, in inverse proportion to the rate at which the animal grows and increases in size. One finds there also another vein which comes from the vena cava a little below its point of division upon the membrane which envelops the heart, that is, the cardiac sheath [*pericardium*]. And through this vein this sheath is nourished, and, beside it also, the parts found there of those membranes which divide the thorax [*mediastinal pleurae*]. And to these same membranes there also go very fine arachnoidal veins which spring
201 from the vena cava. All these veins are small. Somewhat larger than these is the vein which comes off from the one which encircles the clavicle. It is that vein which ascends up to the acromion. This vein proceeds towards the upper clavicular region from the commencement of the so-called 'shoulder vein', that is the 'cephalica', until it arrives at the shoulder. Frequently one finds beneath this yet another recognisable vein, which ramifies and splits up in the great muscle which lies on this part of the anterior thoracic region. As for the remaining parts of this muscle [*pectoralis major*] which are found in the anterior thoracic region, they are supplied by the veins which lie in the intercostal spaces, and these spring off from the vein which comes from the vena cava slightly below its division on the right side. This vein also, while it goes forwards and before it encounters the intercostal spaces, wends its way upwards, between the first rib and the clavicle, and from it there

splits off an easily recognisable branch to the first intercostal space. This offshoot I have already mentioned, and here I will once more say that this vein extends to the second intercostal space, and that a small twig from it also branches off to the third intercostal space. This branch [*superior epigastric*] combines and joins with the vein which ascends from below [*inferior epigastric*], so that when you look at them the two seem to be a single vein. What remains over of it runs superficially between the first and second ribs, and is lost in the muscles found there.

As for the largest branch of this vein which runs obliquely upwards [*innominate*], it proceeds in the region behind the sixth vertebra, and ascends towards the shoulder. On its way a branch splits off from it and goes on the right side to the vertebral foramen [i.e. in the *transverse process*]. After this branch [*vertebral vein*] has passed beyond the sixth vertebra it ascends vertically and then reaches the foramen in the fifth 202
vertebra, thereafter the foramen in the fourth, the foramen in the third, and so onwards as far as the first vertebra. In the interval between the vertebrae a small vein branches off from it, from which the structure enveloping the spinal cord, and likewise the spinal cord itself, are nourished. But with that part of the vertebral vein which passes beyond the first vertebra, there interweaves itself the small vein [*deep cervical*] which comes to this region from the deep jugular vein and descends together with it.

But now, in regard to all those veins which we have specified, and of which we have said that they come from the vena cava [i.e. after its 'division' into innominate veins] and penetrate into the interior of the vertebra, you must learn that there is to be found this one factor common to all of them, namely that the nourishment of the vertebrae also comes from them. And since the supply of nutriment which is being drawn from them is but scanty, it happens that on the small vertebrae no recognisable vein whatever is to be found, whereas on the great vertebrae of the lumbar region veins are visible which attach themselves to one aspect of the vertebra itself and grow into it. As for the veins in the thorax, you must learn that they have in common something which I am about to describe. This is that there go from all of them small branches to the so-called vertebral-column muscles, close to the joints of the vertebrae. Other branches, of larger size than these,

reach as far as the convex portions of the ribs, near the origin of their cartilaginous parts, and of each of these veins [*posterior intercostals*] the ending ascends to the place where the ribs are attached to the sternum, passes outwards, and there is combined and is united with the small external veins of which we said previously that they come outwards, passing by the convex sections of the thorax. At the so-called 'hinder-ribs' [*false ribs*], on the contrary, the end of the vein goes to the muscles of the abdomen, and you see that the first and greatest muscle [*M.*
203 *obliquus abdominis externus*] is especially nourished, over a wide stretch of surface, from these veins. Its deeper portion receives its nourishment from the veins which emerge from the vena cava lying on the lumbar vertebral column. But in this place I break off the discussion of these matters, and I return to the stage at which you have cut away the clavicle, whereupon I now leave the right side and begin upon the left side.

We find that the disposition of the vein which nourishes the upper portions of the thorax [*superior intercostal*] is not the same on this side as it is on the right side. For on the right side the vein springs off from the vena cava before its division. As for the vein on the left side, there do not branch off from the subdivision of the vena cava many veins going to the thorax.

But there do branch off from it, to the six first vertebrae and to the concave surface of the scapula, great veins of considerable dimensions which all arise from a single root, just as on the right side. From one of these veins the region of the spinal cord is nourished, in addition to parts of the muscles in that region which attach themselves around the vertebrae. But from the other vein the muscle [*M. subscapularis*] on the concave side of the scapula is nourished, as also the posterior muscle which connects the base [vertebral border] of the scapula with the vertebral column [*M. rhomboideus*]. Besides these, it nourishes the majority of those muscles which are found on the nape of the neck, from the back of the head downwards.

This, then, is what you see on both the veins, that on the right side and that on the left (i.e. the two just mentioned). But as for the place
204 at which the vena cava divides itself, with the result that two fully identical veins proceed onwards from it [*innominate veins*], between the roots of those two veins there branches off from it a single vein which

arises from its anterior aspect. This vein [*internal mammary*] goes towards the right side of the sternum at the mammary gland. But the vein at the left mammary gland, which likewise makes its way towards the sternum, takes its origin from that vein [*left innominate*] which comes from the vena cava after its division. This is the one lying on the left. The exit of these veins from the thorax is near the ensiform [*xiphoid*] cartilage. After they have come out, branches from them approach near to the mammary glands, and afterwards they divide into two portions. Of these, one wanders superficially downwards beneath the skin. The other descends by the two fleshy rectilinear muscles [*Mm. recti abdominis*]. We have already described previously how other veins meet them, which come upwards from the region below. And through the union of these veins with them there comes into existence the association between the mammary glands, the thorax [*thoracic organs*] and the organs of generation.

CHAPTER 7. THE VEINS OF THE NECK AND HEAD.

Now, after that pair of which we have described both the [constituent] veins, there branch off from each of the two parts into which we have said that the vena cava divides, three veins on each side. The origin of these veins is from roots which lie actually beneath the clavicle. One of these three, the one which springs from the highest root point, travels vertically upwards, so that its course goes superficially along the neck [*external jugular vein*]. But the other, that one whose origin lies on the lowest point takes the direction straight downwards, then divides at the outer region of the clavicle and combines itself with that vein which springs off from the upper parts of the root. And the last portion of it mounts up to the shoulder and travels along the length of
the clavicle. This is the one of which I said that it is called the shoulder 205
vein, the 'cephalica'. As to the way in which this shoulder vein, the cephalica, divides itself, that I have described to you already in the place in which I dealt with the anatomy of the arm.

Now from both the veins which encircle the clavicle, I mean the one placed outwardly and the one placed inwardly, there break off, before the one unites with the other, branches which split up in the neighbouring structures. These structures are: the lower portion of the

muscle which runs from the skull to the sternum and to the clavicle, the expanded muscle which lies next to the skin [*platysma myoides*], one on each of the two sides—the anatomists do not specify it and have overlooked it—the fasciae investing it, and the skin. To these organic structures you will find that veins always go from those in the lower regions of the neck, which overlap the clavicle. But as for the remaining regions, you find that the veins running to them are not always of one and the same pattern in all bodies of apes. That is because these two veins (I mean the vein behind the clavicle and the one on the outside of it) do not always meet and combine with one another in the very same manner. For sometimes they do not join and combine with one another until they have passed along the whole length of the neck, so that from the two of them a single vein comes into being, that is, the superficial jugular vein; but sometimes they combine after they have traversed only a third of the total length of the neck. In most cases they will be found to have joined in the former way. But as for their junction and union after they have passed only one third or little over a quarter of the neck, that is rarely met with. Yet in one ape we once saw that the two veins neither ran over into nor combined with one another at all. The arrangement in this ape was remarkable,
206 in that there were to be seen six veins lodged in pairs alongside each other. These were the two outer [superficial] jugular veins beneath the skin and the thinned-out expanded muscle [*M. platysma*] beneath it, then the two deep jugular veins in the depth of the neck, and in the middle, between these two pairs, yet another third pair. When the two veins unite more speedily with one another, then there branches off, from the superficial jugular, a vein which mounts obliquely to the muscle which goes from the bone of the first vertebra to the scapula [*M. levator scapulae*]. But when they have travelled far before joining and combining to form a single vein, then smaller veins spring out from each of them. The twigs sprouting out from the more deeply lying veins go specially to the musculature. But those veins which sprout out from the superficial vein, that is the one of which I said that it swings round encircling the clavicle, go to the fasciae, to the skin, and also to the upper portions of the muscle [*sternomastoid*] which descends from the skull to the sternum and the clavicle, and in fact they [*fasciae*,

skin, muscle] are nourished from these veins only. That is, from these two veins, after they have met and combined with one another, small veins occasionally branch off after their junction. That happens as soon as a single vein has arisen from the two superficial jugular veins. Sometimes no branch whatever comes off from that vein. That happens when the two do not unite and join immediately after crossing over the clavicle. They are then only affected by the division which they experience after they have run a long way, and not immediately. For 207
this superficial jugular vein, which takes its origin from the two veins mentioned, must necessarily and under all circumstances divide up. One of its branches mounts up to the delicate region of the lower jaw at the cheek, and then wanders along the side of it until it reaches the end of the lower jaw, the part which is called the chin. And twigs which go to the neighbouring parts split off from it along the whole of its course. From this vein [*external jugular*] branches also combine and unite themselves with the deep jugular vein. In particular, one very clearly visible vein joins and unites with a fairly large section of the deep jugular vein at the spongy flesh of the larynx [*thyroid gland*]. To this there goes in addition a vein which travels especially to the inner and upper parts of the gland. Consequently, if the ape which you are dissecting has not long been dead, and the blood has not yet coagulated to any great extent, you must take care and guard yourself against cutting into this glandular tissue and from tearing it and removing it from these veins. For this is a region where, when even a small quantity of blood flows out from a vein, it spoils your view of everything that you want to see. But as you cannot see the junction of the veins unless this glandular tissue [*thyroid gland*] is cleared away, you must try to arrange that the animal which you dissect has already been dead for one day in advance. But should it happen that it has only just died on the self-same day, then set free this glandular tissue from below and from the two sides, but protect and take care of its upper portion where it is in relation with the veins and arteries lying beneath it, and enters into union with them through the medium of a small vein that is attached to it. At the same time there ascends from this glandular tissue upwards to the tongue the vein [*lingual*] springing out from the deep [*internal*] jugular, together with a branch which breaks off

from the artery which is called 'carotid' (that signifies 'the artery of stupor').

208 Now both these two, I mean the [*lingual*] vein and the artery, at the organ to which they betake themselves are larger than its dimensions warrant. Close by, on both sides of them, and ascending with them, lies the nerve of the seventh pair springing out from the brain [*N. hypoglossus*]. This goes to the muscles of the tongue and distributes itself in them, and its course towards them leads to the side of the artery and the vein. It is clear to you that all these things which we enumerate are to be found on both sides of the whole neck, as well as of the tongue.

One of the branches of the superficial jugular is a vein of not inconsiderable size. And from it also, the slender muscle which goes from the hyoid bone to the scapula [*M. omohyoideus*] is nourished. Most frequently there goes to each complete half of it a slender vein branching off from the former one, since it is a peculiarity of its upper part, which is near the acromion, that one normally finds branches going to it from the veins which betake themselves to that region. Besides this yet other fine twigs enter into the skull, and these effect their entry through the bony sutures of the cranium, especially at the so-called coronal suture, and also through its outlets [*emissary foramina*]. When they enter they meet with those veins which go from within outwards through the foramina through which the nerves come out. For the deep jugular veins alone nourish all the parts of the two cranial membranes, and together with these membranes they feed, in particular, the brain. For from them there break off branches which make their way inwards from their ends. And they meet with the small veins coming from within. In the place in which I deal with the anatomy of the brain I will describe for you how and in what manner the veins which go to the brain divide themselves up, and similarly I will describe the disposition
209 of the veins which betake themselves to each one of the other bodily structures and organs, as for example the eye, the tongue, the larynx, the lung and the heart. But here it is enough to speak of one detail. It is that the two deep jugular veins, after branches have come off from them which break up in the deep regions of the neck, sink and flow down into those parts of the suture which resembles the letter Λ of the Greek script [*lambdoid suture*] where there is found the foramen [*jugular*

foramen], the channel out of which emerges the nerve which is called the nerve of the sixth pair of those that sprout outwards from the brain [*Nn. glossopharyngeus, vagus, accessorius*]. Before either of the two [deep jugular veins] has made its entry there, and besides the other capillary veins—these are overlooked for the most part—there branches off a single vein which enters into the space between the first vertebra and the skull. Of this vein the endings unite and combine themselves with the one [*basilar vein*] which lies on the spinal cord at the posterior subdivision of the brain.

Now just as we have dealt with the mode of division of the cerebral veins in the place in which we discussed the anatomy of the brain, so also we have mentioned the disposition of the veins in all the other bodily parts where we dealt with the anatomy of each singly. By the expression 'other bodily parts' I mean the tongue, eyes, lungs, liver, heart, kidneys, uterus, urinary bladder and other parts like them. Similarly we talked of the veins in the arms and the legs, in a discussion which was devoted especially to those parts in the requisite place. Nothing, then, has been left unsaid with regard to the veins, except for the point which I am about to make with reference to the jugular veins only. Since there are six of them, the superficially lying pair goes to the spongy flesh beneath the ears [*parotid gland*], and the middle pair goes to the two [right and left] soft places on the jaws. Consequently you find that where these two veins have united with one another and
have then separated (I mean the vein which travels [outwards] above 210
the clavicle, and the one lying below and inwards from it) there comes directly in continuation of the inner vein the one [*anterior facial*] which goes to the softest part of the jaw and cheek, and as the 'outer' vein [*posterior facial*] you find the one which travels to the 'spongy flesh' [*parotid gland*].

CHAPTER 8. THE ABDOMINAL AORTA AND ITS BRANCHES.

But as we have now finished with the veins, it is time to proceed to the discussion of the arteries. I have already said of all of them in general that together with every vein which is attached to a muscle there is also attached an artery. Arteries also accompany the veins which go to the stomach, to the spleen, and the whole of the intestines. But you will not find in every bodily structure to which a vein is attached that just there, at the side of that vein, an artery also lies. For though all the bodily structures are in need of veins for their nourishment, not every one of them requires an artery, because not every one of them stands in need of the service which the artery supplies. I have already summarised that in a chapter which I devoted to it and with which I combined nothing else. And since that is as I stated, then the discussion of the arteries must be made shorter than that of the veins. Though that is so, however, and though in many respects the position of the arteries is intimately connected with what we have previously described in relation to the veins, yet we must deal with it from the beginning. So now, my friend, if you wish to expose freely all the arteries of the abdomen, then you should immediately take in hand the dissection of the muscles also, in the way which I described for you previously.

Secure the arteries by ligatures a little below the mammary glands, where the arteries found in this place [*superior epigastric branches of internal mammary arteries*] sink into the deeper parts beneath the upright fleshy muscle [*M. rectus abdominis*] together with the veins of this region. For
211 the other pair [right and left] of veins which contribute in common to the mammary glands and the uterus, I mean the two [*superficial epigastric veins*] lying superficially beneath the skin are without arteries. Then as you come to the arteries within the peritoneum [abdominal cavity], inspect them all adequately. Commence your investigation with the three mesenteries.[1] For the arteries begin to divide from that region. But that part of them which lies above this region as far as their earliest points of origin extends along the line of suspension of the mesenteries. The root of the suspensory ligament [*root* of *the mesentery*] lies close to them [i.e. the points of origin of the arteries] and takes its origin from the bones of the vertebral column themselves. It is understood that when I say 'vertebral-column bones themselves' you must take me to mean the actual stem composed of the vertebrae. You should not wonder that the suspensory ligament must have its origin on a bone since the substance of this suspensory ligament lies between the diaphragm and the kidneys. Now, as for the greatest artery [*aorta*], since it is stretched out over the mid-line of the vertebrae, branches come off

[1] Namely, the mesentery proper, the transverse mesocolon, and the pelvic mesocolon.

from it which meet this ligament. They have to do that because the place of their meeting with it is on the anterior parts of the chief artery. You will mostly find that each of these two branches has at its source a special root peculiar to itself alone, and yet, occasionally also, you find that the two arteries have a single source and origin common to both. But each of the two divides itself immediately as soon as it has arisen. The upper portion [*coeliac axis*] distributes itself to the stomach, the spleen and the liver. But the other, that is, the lower [*superior mesenteric artery*], distributes itself in the mesentery. You find likewise that when the origin of the two comes off from two roots the upper one invariably distributes itself to the stomach, to the spleen, and to the liver, and you find that the lower artery distributes itself in two 212
mesenteries, namely in the whole mesentery of the small intestine, and in that one [*transverse mesocolon*] of the other two mesenteries in which is the intestine called the colon, which is the one to the right side of the two. To the third mesentery, which is on the left side, not one single twig goes from these arteries. In spite of this, though, the disposition of these arteries is not clear-cut, but merely that together with each of the veins there also travels an artery which divides with it as is the case with the other veins which distribute themselves in the liver, the spleen, upon the stomach, upon the small intestine and the caecum. The branch upon the left side of the intestine called the colon [*inferior mesenteric artery*] lies upon the first subdivision of the third mesentery, which is arranged on the left side. The origin of this artery, which is much smaller than the upper ones and becomes visible only with care and difficulty, comes from the artery [*aorta*] lying on the vertebrae, from its anterior surface. It is unpaired, without a fellow, and its origin comes after that of the pair consisting of two large branches which go to the kidney. But the two other great arteries, those in the mesentery, are spread out alongside everyone of the veins found in it. They take their origins from the great artery [*aorta*] which lies in the lumbar region in the interval between the diaphragm and the kidneys.

Let us now recapitulate what has been said, from its commencement onwards. We say that the veins which nourish the whole body all have their origin from the vena cava, except that, since the vena cava has two subdivisions of which one makes its way ascending upwards, and the

other descends downwards, we must construct our exposition as though we were dealing with the stem of a tree. We must act in the same way
213 when discussing the arteries. Thus, since the arteries have a single root on the left of the two cavities of the heart, and this root becomes immediately like a bifurcated tree-trunk, we must consequently summarise the branches which arise from each of the two trunks. Of these branches, some resemble the great limbs of a tree, the others resemble the small twigs and the leaves.

As a commencement, we shall point out the disposition of the artery which goes to the lower parts of the body. This mounts on the fifth thoracic vertebra in the place upon which there lies also the vein [*azygos*] which nourishes the lower thoracic region. And this artery travels with this vein and distributes itself together with it, and branches [*posterior intercostals*] sprout off from it which go to the intercostal spaces, just like the twigs of that vein. And from these arteries branches go outwards which travel with the veins to the outer thoracic region. For their origin is beside that of the veins, and they distribute themselves similarly to those muscles to which the veins are distributed. But as for the venous branches lying superficially beneath the skin, not one single artery is to be seen joining them. Now when this main artery [*aorta*] pierces the diaphragm, to this, on its course, it often gives off branches of considerable size, and sometimes small branches. In the same way a branch to the left side, which is sometimes visible, sometimes indistinctly seen, springs off from it, after it has passed beyond the diaphragm, at its first entry into the regions found below the thorax and within the abdomen in front of the kidneys. After this branch come two arteries, and these are those which I have already mentioned previously, and of which I said that they extend to and distribute themselves in the liver, spleen and stomach and in the whole of the mesentery with the exception of a small portion. These arteries are not coupled
214 in pairs, but the one comes off after the other. They have their origin upon the anterior part of the main artery. But all the other arteries coming after them have a paired origin. Of these, two very large ones go to the kidneys. And after them come two other small arteries, whose origin is paired, like the origin of the veins on every single vertebra. Also their course is to just the same places as those to which the veins go.

With regard to the unpaired artery which has no fellow and which arises below the kidneys [*inferior mesenteric*] we have already said that it breaks up in the lower mesentery. Accordingly there is no need for a long account, or for us to concern ourselves, because of the two following considerations. In the first place, although there go to the peritoneum numerous veins of arachnoid or capillary tenuity, springing from many veins, but mainly from those that go to the testes, with no single one of these veins do we find an accompanying artery, although we have already gone into that with extreme care, and although we have investigated and sought it out in all animals, especially in those of large size. For we hold it best to investigate and to study the details that are difficult to see in the bodies of large-sized animals, I mean in oxen, horses, asses, mules and others like those. But even in the elephant, let alone any other animal, we have never found arteries at the side of these veins. The other reason we have to record is this. A number of anatomists have erred, so I say, in their assumption that the arteries which encircle the urinary bladder [*superior vesical arteries*, the *umbilical arteries* of the foetus] connect with the great artery on the vertebral column [*aorta*] and combine themselves with it. For they do not reach
to that artery but only to the obliquely directed ones [*iliac arteries*] *215*
which branch off from the great artery and go to the lower limbs, passing across upon that broad bone, the sacrum. From these, branches break off which subsequently hang freely without entering any one of the structures lying in this place. And you will find that there are always two of these branches. On rare occasions I have found a third delicate twig, hardly visible [*middle sacral artery*]. These branches split, divide and break up upon all the structures which overlie the broad bone. But the two arteries which result from the division of the artery lying upon the vertebrae extend as far as the upper ends of the thighs, after passing beyond the lower ends of the muscles of the abdominal wall. There is one of them on each side of the animal body, I mean the right and the left. Before they mount the upper ends of the thighs, branches spring off from them which go to the muscles around the joint [*deep circumflex iliac arteries*]. But after they have mounted the upper ends of the thighs they distribute themselves completely in all the subdivisions of the lower limbs as I have indicated in Book III of this work.

CHAPTER 9. THE DISTRIBUTION OF THE THORACIC AORTA, AND A NOTE ON FOETAL BLOOD-VESSELS.

I have now described for you how there distributes itself the artery [*descending aorta*] which makes its way onwards over the fifth thoracic vertebra. And here is the place in which I have to speak of the artery above this one. I say, then, look immediately at that small twig which is single, unpaired, and lies beneath the lung [*left bronchial artery*] at the place where it [the *aorta*] joins the vertebral column. This is the twig of which some of the followers of Erasistratus believe that offshoots from it distribute themselves in the lung. But in the dissection of the lung we find no other fourth class of vessel except those which all anatomists have recorded, I mean the class of the 'rough arteries' (*bronchi*), that is to say the subdivisions of the trachea, the class of the
216 'smooth arteries', that is to say the subdivisions of the 'venous artery' [*pulmonary vein*] which goes from the heart to the lung, and the class of the 'veins' [branches of the *pulmonary artery*].

Over above this twig which we have mentioned you see the great artery [*aorta*] dividing itself. And before its division you see its origin from the heart. This is something that everyone sees in the dissection by reason of its great size, just as also every one sees the left one of the two ventricles of the heart, from which it takes its origin.

And now I will turn to an account of the points under discussion, and accordingly I will start from the heart which, for its part, is the starting point for all the arteries in the body. I say that from the heart springs out an artery in the same manner as does the trunk of a tree from the earth. And this artery is the largest of all the arteries in the body, and from it these latter have their origin. First of all it divides itself into two tremendous portions, which resemble large limbs of a tree. Then each of these two divides itself into others, and it keeps on dividing frequently in this way until all its subdivisions come to an end and a conclusion, just as the division of the branches of a tree finds its end in the small twigs, the spicules and the leaves. Now on the great artery, before it breaks up into two subdivisions, you can see two offshoots like that which emerges from the seed of a plant when it germinates. And of these two, you see that one is wider and longer than the other, and you find that it encircles the whole heart in a ring [*left coronary artery*], and surrounds it at those portions at which its two cavities [*ventricles*] unite with one another and adjoin each other [*descending branch*]. But the other offshoot [*right coronary artery*], which is narrower and shorter, distributes itself especially to those portions of which Aristotle holds the view that they are a third cavity of the heart. He did not, however, know that this is only a part of the right [one] of the two cavities of the heart.

After these two offshoots [the *coronary arteries*] you see the two mighty 217
arteries into which I said that the artery springing out from the heart divides itself just as the trunk of a tree divides into branches [*ascending* and *descending* aortic branches, i.e. *brachiocephalic trunk* plus *left subclavian*, and *descending part* of *aortic arch*]. Of those two, the broader is that artery which distributes itself to all the lower parts of the body, the narrower that which distributes itself to all the parts of the body upwards from the heart. I have already finished describing to you the distribution of the artery passing in the direction downwards. Now I will point out to you here the distribution of that artery which makes its way upwards. I say that this also, as soon as it branches off from the artery which turns downwards, divides itself. It is not yet supported by anything, but hangs suspended in the cavity of the thorax. One of its two subdivisions, that is, the greater of the two [*brachiocephalic trunk*], inclines towards the right-hand side and passes on until it reaches the meeting-place of the two clavicles with the sternum [*suprasternal notch*]. This place is called the throttle, that is, the hollow of the neck. The other subdivision [*left subclavian artery*] travels to the left axilla. Should you wish to dissect whichever of these two portions you like, you can see, with regard to the arteries branching off from it, that so long as they stay within the thorax they continue to divide up like those veins which we mentioned a short while ago. But when they come outside the thorax, then notice the manner in which, at their first emergence, the veins immediately separate themselves from the arteries and turn to the region of the skin. For in the parts above the thorax you will nowhere find an artery without a vein, but you will find many veins without arteries. Indeed, why should we mention small veins, when we find veins of the greatest size, I mean the super-

218 ficial jugular veins, without arteries? These latter arise at the place at which, as soon as the greater jugular veins reach it, there sprout from them those other veins of which you have already heard an account in the place where I have dealt with them for you. Afterwards those veins which lie externally to it encircle the clavicle at their first encounter with it. They are the ones of which I said that after they have mounted upwards to the neck and have united and combined themselves with other branches from the deep jugular veins, then there come from them the superficial jugular veins lying beneath the skin. Now the veins which spring off from them are without arteries. But with few exceptions those which branch off from the deep jugular veins are almost all accompanied by arteries. And in fact those are the capillaries which ramify and spread themselves in the fascial tissues. Of those veins which are connected to the muscles, there is no single one without an artery. Consequently, should you follow up the veins which I mentioned to you, together with them you will come upon the arteries and discover them. Now, as you will see, the artery of which I pointed out that it comes obliquely upwards to the 'hollow of the neck', when it meets with the vena cava, follows its example by dividing itself into two, so that there arise from it the [two] arteries which are called the 'carotids' (this means 'stupefying'). And they are also known under the name 'stupefying blood vessels'. These then pass upwards, alongside the two jugular veins, until they reach the skull bone. But as soon as they get near this, they part company [with the veins] and penetrate the cranial bones as far as the brain. For their entry [*vein* and *artery*] does not take place in a single foramen, but in two. The jugular veins make their way through a separate foramen peculiar to them, and the carotid arteries through another foramen peculiar to them, lying in front of it, I mean higher
219 up. The foramen of the veins is common both to them and to the components of the sixth pair of nerves arising from the brain [*Nn. glossopharyngeus, vagus, accessorius*]. And the foramen of the arteries belongs to these together with the nerves combined with them throughout the whole of the neck [*sympathetic trunk*]. The nerves then separate themselves from these [the arteries] in the thorax, and descend lengthwise on the ribs, downwards as far as the region below the diaphragm. But from the ends of the arteries, after they have pierced the skull, immedi-

ately upon their first entry and passage into its cavity, there proceeds the so-called 'reticular network' [*rete mirabile* of some quadrupeds]. As for the ends of the jugular veins, they ascend to the upper surface of the brain and then split and branch out from that region throughout the whole of the brain. Out from the rete mirabile, again, there ascend two arteries which encircle the brain together with the delicate meninx [*pia mater*] after the fashion of a girdle, just as do the veins as we have described in the exposition of the anatomy of the brain.

I have now finished my description for you of the whole of the ramification of the artery which mounts up to the jugular vein. But as for the artery which goes to the left shoulder, to the axilla, and to the arm, no branch at all comes from it, but it distributes itself with the veins which are found in these parts. Further, it does not distribute itself with all these veins, but only with those which nourish the muscles. For the superficial veins beneath the skin are all without accompanying arteries. Further, as for the veins which pass on and mount upwards through the foramina in the first six vertebrae, the arteries which here run upwards together with them are very slender. When I say 'foramina of the vertebrae', I mean the foramina in their lateral processes. I have on rare occasions found that foramen in the seventh vertebra as well. The veins and arteries which pass through the foramina originate from the veins and arteries which go to the shoulders deep down at the place where the sixth and seventh vertebrae meet. *220*
Consequently, the sixth joint is larger than the remaining joints of the neck. For it receives certain of these veins and arteries which branch off and shelters them in its cavity, and supports and holds fast the other arteries and veins which mount obliquely upwards, so that it [the sixth vertebra] becomes their resting-place and their support, through which they establish themselves. It secures them in the places through which they pass, they being these veins and arteries in the foramina which lie in the processes of the vertebrae. No branch whatever comes outwardly from them. But there spring off from them in the intervening spaces, the narrows between the processes of the vertebrae, arachnoid and capillary twigs which reach to the spinal cord. These twigs penetrate through the foramina out of which spring the nerves arising in pairs from the spinal cord. In the whole of this region (I mean where the

veins and arteries lie which proceed in the deeper parts to the shoulder) dissection is very difficult and tedious, and must necessarily be so. For in this place are not only numerous offshoots of the veins and arteries which penetrate the vertebral foramina, but also other veins and arteries besides them. I should like you very thoroughly to examine these, so that you may understand how they penetrate and how they join up with one another. You must now cut loose the whole of the bone from around the foramina on each individual vertebra. It is of course evident to you that that can only be done when you have previously removed the clavicle. What is also difficult to dissect is the vein and the artery at the skull-joint [*occipitoatlantic articulation*], if here
221 also you wish a thorough examination of those arteries and veins which plunge themselves into the deeper parts. For you must cut away those of the bones that hinder clear inspection.

Now these things are only visible and accessible to inspection in the bodies of mature animals. As for the animal which is on the point of being born you will see in it the two arteries which go from the placenta to the foetus, travelling in the umbilical cord, and those are the two of which we spoke earlier [*umbilical arteries*], likewise the artery [*umbilical vein*] which runs to the liver near to that part of it which is called the porta hepatis. This place is rightly named 'porta', since through it there enters the blood which comes from the pregnant mother to the foetus in the same way as provisions for nourishment reach the interior of the body through its portals. For from this spot the blood which the mother transfers to the offspring arrives at the convexity of the liver and the hollow surface of the liver of the offspring. From here the blood which reaches the hepatic convexity passes to the vena cava, and this vein delivers it and distributes it in the whole of the body of the foetus, just as it will be delivered subsequently in fully formed bodies. But that blood which comes to the hollow aspect of the liver travels further in the portal vein until it reaches to the intestines, the stomach, the omentum, and the spleen. In the bodies of animals already aged [post-natal individuals] you will see that vein dried up to a slender strand containing no blood at all [*ligamentum teres* and *ligamentum venosum*]. And the case is just the same with the arteries encircling the urinary bladder [*umbilical arteries*], and with the blood-vessel [*ductus arteriosus*] which connects the chief artery [*aorta*] with the arterial vein [*pulmonary artery*] in the lung.

CHAPTER 10. VEINS WITHOUT ACCOMPANYING ARTERIES, AND ARTERIES WITHOUT ACCOMPANYING VEINS.

As regards the other things that you see in the arteries and the veins,
there is no difference between mature and foetal bodies. But now, since
Erasistratus and Herophilus, and other anatomists who lived after them,
when they had completed their discussion of the dissection of the veins 222
and of the arteries which have no veins alongside them, wanted to
enumerate these in a single list, but never included them all, I think
that I should supplement here my description as already set out, and
add to it by an enumeration of these veins and arteries. That I will set
about by commencing with the vein in the foetus of which I said a
short time ago that it reaches the liver and has its origin at the umbilical
region of the foetus. This vein has no artery. Next comes the whole
vena cava, since there is no artery neighbouring on that part of it which
runs on the convexity of the liver. Similarly no artery accompanies
that portion which comes from here on to the vertebrae or the part 223
which travels to the neck-groove. And so also among the other veins
lying on the convex side of the liver there is none which has an
associated artery nearby, just as there is no artery associated with the
veins of the diaphragm, of which we said that they sprout off from the
vena cava, at the place of its passage through, and its penetration of, the
diaphragm. Similarly also, the vein which nourishes the thorax [*azygos* 224
vein] is without an artery before it lays itself upon the vertebral column,
that is, the one of which I said that in apes it springs out above the heart.
Likewise without an artery also is the vein, no less large in its proportions than this one, of which I said that it is called the 'shoulder vein' [*cephalic*]. Resembling it also are all the offshoots from it with the exception of a single one, that of which I said that it originates from the elbow-joint, and sprouts out from the depths just as is the origin of the medial vein, of which I explained that it traverses the axilla, that is the basilic. For these two veins alone travel in the depths of the forearm with two arteries accompanying them. But all other veins of the forearm, those in the superficial level, are without arteries. Of three

or four of them I have already said earlier that they branch off from the vein which traverses the axilla. Another vein much stouter than this is the one arising from both, that is the 'blue-black' [*median cubital*] vein. All these veins, then, on both the arms have no arteries associated with them, just as that vein also has no artery which crosses round the upper arm, encircles it, and subsequently travels onwards in the hinder districts until it reaches the region beneath the skin. It then goes towards the side of the upper arm furthest removed from the torso until it arrives at the forearm. For this vein also, including all its branches, is without an artery. The case is the same with the superficial jugular veins, inclusive of their branches on the neck, and those which stretch out to the shoulders, and those small ones of which we said that they break off from the roots of these and split up and bestrew themselves in the region adjoining the clavicle. For all these also are without arteries. You will also find that only an inconsiderable portion of the veins of the face and of the whole of the head, numerous though those may be, are accompanied by arteries, as we said earlier where we
225 spoke of the veins on the temples and of those behind the ears. In sum, you will find no arteries in the neighbourhood of any one of the veins lying superficially under the skin, neither on the back, nor over the ribs, nor yet on the whole of the thorax, or the whole of the abdomen, since among the veins which, as I said, emerge from the region of the costal cartilages and combine themselves with the veins which ascend in a superficial position from below upwards, there is not a single one in the neighbourhood of which an artery may be found to run, as those do which border the veins which travel in the depths and combine themselves with the inward parts of the 'upright' muscle [*M. rectus abdominis*]. For all of these have arteries close by them, and similarly an artery lies close by the veins in the deeper parts which descend from above downwards. Whereas those of them [the superficial veins] which ascend from below upwards and whose ends combine with these are without arteries. Likewise, no arteries are near those veins [*lacteals*] which pass up from the intestines to the spongy-flesh bodies [*mesenteric lymph glands*], or the veins on the broad bone, the sacrum, with the exception of those among them which go to the musculature. Thus, as for those branches, there is no single one among them which has an artery. And similarly

you find that all those veins of which we said that they go to the pubes [*pudenda*] and have their origin outside the muscles [*superficial external pudendal veins*] are without arteries. This is also the case with those veins which are in the thigh beneath the skin, and those which lie superficially in the lower part of the leg. For you find here also that, after the threefold division of the great vein [*popliteal*] shortly above the bend of the knee, one of its branches, that which with its offshoots travels in the depth, has arteries which are its neighbours, but that among the veins which move away towards the surface and come onwards to the skin there is no single one in the neighbourhood of which there is an artery.

I have now enumerated for you the veins which are free from arteries. *226*
But the arteries which lack veins are as follows. While the animal remains in the uterus as a foetus, the arteries [*umbilical*] which encompass the urinary bladder and encircle it persist. Those are the ones of which I said that they come from the umbilicus and combine themselves with the branches which spring off from the great artery [*aorta*] after that has divided. Likewise also, you will find alone and lying without a vein the offshoot [*ductus arteriosus*] which breaks off from the great artery [*aorta*] and goes to the arterial vein [*pulmonary artery*] and blends with it while the animal remains in the uterus, it being an offshoot of which the structure and use are those of an artery. Among the arteries there are still some others which lack veins, not only in animals while they are in the uterus, but also in those that are already fully formed. Among these are the great arteries which come from the heart. One of these is the artery lying on the fifth thoracic vertebra [*descending part of aortic arch*], the other one is the artery [*brachiocephalic trunk*] which mounts upwards to the hollow of the neck, and the third, besides these two, is the artery of which I said that it goes to the shoulder and to the axilla of the left side [*left subclavian artery*]. For each of these travels far onwards without a vein being found alongside it. That one which goes to the fifth thoracic vertebra has no accompanying vein until it rests upon that vertebra, nor has that which goes to the hollow of the neck until it reaches the spongy flesh which is called the thymus. The one which travels to the left axilla is without a vein until it arrives at the first rib. Amongst these arteries can also be counted the one which mounts upwards from the artery of stupor, one branch of it lying on

227 each side, and arrives at the retiform meshwork, since to it there belongs a special foramen [*carotid canal*] far removed from that of which I said that the ending of the jugular veins mounts upward through it in order to reach the brain [*jugular foramen*]. To them belongs also the retiform meshwork. For all these arteries have no veins beside them. Further, there also belong to them the arteries which branch off from this meshwork and travel towards the pool [*infundibulum*], taking an upwards course. For on their way no single vein is in their neighbourhood before they begin to divide. Others of them are the arteries in the diaphragm. For these also have no connection with any vein until they combine themselves with the ends of those veins of which we said that they distribute themselves in the diaphragm itself, coming from the vena cava. And amongst them can be counted the initial stages of the branches going to the liver, to the stomach, to the spleen, and to the intestines. For these also have no connection at all with any vein before they commence to divide.

The Thirteenth Book of Galen's work on Anatomy has been finished with God's help and aid.

BOOK XIV

THE CRANIAL NERVES

In the name of God, the compassionate, the merciful. The Fourteenth Book of the work of Galen on Anatomical Dissection. In it the anatomy of the nerves arising from the brain will be discussed.

CHAPTER I. MACERATION OF SKELETONS FOR STUDY OF NERVE-FORAMINA. NOTES ON OTHER ANATOMISTS AND THEIR VIEWS.

Galen says: The dissection of the nerves is a toilsome and difficult matter *228*
for many reasons. Among these is the fact that a thorough examination of the nerves springing from the brain and the spinal cord cannot be made unless you cut away, as completely as may be necessary, the bones which surround their sites of origin. But if we do cut away those bones, though the parts of the nerves that encircle their inner portion remain intact without having been cut or torn through, I mean the parts which emerge from the thicker of the two meninges of the brain and of the spinal marrow, what lies in the middle of these parts, which are like bark round the wood of a tree, does not remain uninjured, even though it is not cut or torn through. For its root, its site of implantation, is found in a soft tender body, I mean in the brain and the spinal marrow. Further, there is the fact that the fleshy tissue of the muscles veils and covers those nerves which distribute themselves in the musculature. Also, on account of the enveloping fat, many of the nerves elude the view. Another reason is that the isolation of many of them can only be achieved with the greatest difficulty on account of their combination with other nerves. Also, on account of their small size, many are hard to see, especially in the bodies of apes.

Consequently I believe that, in regard to the very small nerves, a number of anatomists simply follow what they find to be the likeliest
and most reasonable course, that of adopting what others have said *229*
without having seen those nerves with their own eyes. Many of them

have also made unsatisfactory statements about them. But their errors are quite evident, inasmuch as they have dissected hurriedly. In the enumeration of the nerves they have completely overlooked many organs and not included them in their account, just as if there were no nerves in them at all. They also pass over the grooved surfaces of the bones of the vertebral column, or again many of the foramina which lie in those grooves, as for example the foramen in the first vertebra which the anatomists have overlooked, together with the nerve which, after its origin in the spinal medulla, runs through it [*first cervical nerve*], and the foramen in the very massive bone, that is, the cross-bone [*os sacrum*]. Thirdly, they ignore the foramina in the skull, and fourthly, that in the upper jaw. All these foramina you will see with your own eyes in a cadaver in which all that overlies the bones is decayed and the bones alone remain, in their connections with one another, without separating from each other. These can be seen in such human cadavers as you happen to look at, as we pointed out at the commencement of Book I, and also in the bodies of apes when we have buried them for four months and more in earth that is not dry. For when they have remained in the earth for this length of time they decompose well, and from those foramina there fall away all ensheathing tissues [membranous parts] which are found on them. It is better for them to have become macerated and clean than that they should be so desiccated and hardened as to become like tanned hides. For what we wish to see in the remnant of the cadaver is not that the objects emerging from the foramina have come to be like leather thongs and stay fixed in their places; what we really want is that all of them should have fallen completely away,
230 since these structures, should they remain as they were, hold together and bind to one another the bones which they meet. In this state the orifice of each of the foramina and its intrinsic curvature are made indistinct. An example of this is that just this type of inspection has led some [anatomists] to the firm conviction that some skulls have no sutures at all, and that others have not got the full complement of sutures. I advise all of them to try what you have often seen me do. For I have always at hand a large number of specially prepared bones of apes, and you also will reach an understanding of the matter by preparing these bones and procuring them for yourselves, especially

when you get skull bones and vertebrae. For here particularly you require actually to see and to examine carefully the foramina of the skull and of the vertebrae. Also, you have seen that I have ready at hand the skull and the vertebrae of an animal with interlocking teeth. But so far as the hyoid bone is concerned, I have examples of it not only from the bodies of these animals that I have mentioned, but also from the bodies of those others which we dealt with previously in Book I, those being the animals whose nature is not far removed from that of Man, and of which there are six kinds. Here I have provided ready to hand the hyoid bones of all these animals, including the bones which support them and secure them to the skull, bones which in arrangement and structure are unlike each other. I have also the first of the vertebrae of the osseous spinal column.

For in this bone equally there are found foramina which have escaped the notice of the surgeons who have written books on anatomy. As for those who have published no works, I cannot divine their views, about which there is the greatest mystery. I myself think, either that they did not possess this knowledge at all, or else that, possessing it, they concealed it from us and grudged it to us, con- *231*
sequently teaching us nothing of it. That was what Quintus did, a man who was distinguished and pre-eminent in the time of Hadrian, in the city of Rome. He had become widely known, and had gained a not inconsiderable reputation through anatomical perspicacity. But he composed no writings on anatomy such as Marinus did, and Numisianus also, who in Marinus' life-time had already become pre-eminent in Alexandria. He was a man of profound learning, who had valuable ideas on the subject of anatomy. He wrote many books, although during his lifetime these did not reach a wide public. Because of that, after his death, since his son Heraclianus wished to secure himself in the sole possession of all that his father left, none of these books were shown to anyone. Then, when Heraclianus also was on the point of death, they say that he destroyed them by fire, although otherwise he was one of those who, in the days of my residence in Alexandria, had given me the most hospitable reception. The sponsor of my acquaintance with him was a man who was one of the circle of his most intimate friends. I constantly rendered him the most zealous service, so much so

that, contrary to my first impression, I almost admired him to adulation. But none of that availed to procure for me any of the writings of Numisianus, which had not yet been shown to many. For Heraclianus used to put off giving me those books, and he was continually hinting at reasons for this delay. He was not one of those who have no knowledge or any understanding of anatomy. Rather, he had views on anatomical science which he explained to me, just as did Satyrus, who
232 had a clearer recollection than anyone else of the theories of Quintus. Pelops also, who was the principal pupil of Numisianus, for his part did not expound them, nor did he show any of them to anyone. For he preferred that certain theories, as yet unknown, should be attributed to himself. Pelops also wrote some very valuable books, but after his death all were destroyed by fire before anyone had copied them, since he used to keep them in his house, and he repeatedly postponed their publication. The numerous books on anatomy by Pelops which are found in the hands of the public are only such writings as he used to hand over to his pupils, and to which he appended the work on the Introduction to Hippocrates; these he would present when his pupils wished to return to their homes, so that he might equip them with something of which, when they pleased, they might avail themselves in order to elucidate what they had gathered from him. But the 'Anatomy' of Pelops had a far wider scope and greater usefulness than has this book, which comprises these sections of his, though even his 'Anatomy' is neither exhaustive nor final. Similarly, the book by Satyrus is neither final nor exhaustive. As this is how the matter stands in regard to these works, then I need refer to none of the other pupils of Quintus, all of whom I took great pains to meet, and whom I found to be inferior to Satyrus and to Pelops. Far inferior to either of these is Lycus the Macedonian, author of a book on anatomy which at the present time enjoys a wide circulation, although he is a man who, in his lifetime, had no great reputation amongst the Greeks. Had that not been the case, then most certainly I would not have omitted to go and see him also. In regard to these works of his which in this our own
233 day I have seen in the possession of many, it is clear that they are constructed out of the writings of Marinus, but they are all full of errors, and are moreover less comprehensive even than the books of

Marinus himself. For Marinus had accumulated no small experience in dissections, and it was he himself who had set his hand to and had observed everything that he explained in his writings. In his great Work, he had established the record of the bones with the greatest thoroughness, and he had laboured to trace all the foramina which perforate the skull and the vertebrae, and to exhaust their study, although now and then we may discover him in error, as I have proved on repeated occasions in the city of Rome, in distinguished company in the presence of all the notable surgeons.

Now here I commence with an account of matters which you have often seen me explaining to special friends, and also, on not a few occasions, to large audiences, after I have first summarised the meaning of the names which I employ in this discussion.

CHAPTER 2. NOMENCLATURE OF NERVE, LIGAMENT AND TENDON. OLFACTORY BULBS. THE OPTIC (FIRST PAIR) AND OCULOMOTOR (SECOND PAIR) NERVES.

Of that which the various names 'nerve', 'ligament' and 'tendon' signify.[1] In this Chapter my aim is to describe the dissection of the nerves which come off from the brain. Hippocrates named the nerves collectively from the Greek 'tenōn'. This is a word derived from the Greek 'teinein' which means 'to stretch'. And this name for the nerves is derived from the fact that some individuals believe that the nerve stretches. In Greek, too, the nerves were also called 'neura' which comes from 'neuein' and means 'to bend'. The term is used because the limbs of the animal extend and flex themselves in this or that direction primarily by means of the nerves, since it is the nerves alone, when they have joined the muscles and grown into them, which bestow upon them voluntary movement; but all voluntary movements, as we have set forth in the work 'On the Muscular Movements', are actually *234*
produced by the muscles only. And already in this Work also I have described at length the anatomy of the muscles. Whoever retains in his memory what I said about their anatomy will know very well that in the animal body the muscles are the instruments of voluntary movements. There exists also in the body a structure [tissue] which resembles

[1] This is probably a heading introduced by a scribe. B.T.

that of a nerve, and proceeds outwards from the bones. You find this structure sometimes rounded, resembling the nerve, and sometimes you find it has a certain breadth, which is either greater or less. That is to say, it often thins out, and spreads itself out so far that it reaches the degree of width and tenuity of fascial sheaths. This class of simple and self-contained structures and organs in the body lacks sensitiveness. It is whiter and harder than the nerve. I call it 'ligament' lest a similarity of nomenclature become a cause of obscurity in the subsequent discussion. But the great majority of surgeons call this body also 'nerve', although they add to this name a distinction by which means it becomes recognisable. They talk of a 'binding nerve', just as it is their custom to call the other nerves 'voluntary nerves' or 'sensory nerves', thus appending one of these two adjectives to the noun.

There exists yet another genus of bodies resembling nerves, which we call 'tendons'. The tendons are just like the ligaments in regard to the differences in form, and in the multiplicity of their peculiarities. In respect of hardness and pallor, they come between the nerves and the ligaments, but this variety of structure [*tendon*] is not devoid of sensitiveness, as the ligament is. It invariably proceeds from a muscle, and for this reason it can be called a 'nerve'. So now you must retain
235 the significance of these names quite distinctly in your memory, and remind yourself constantly that when we say 'nerve' we only mean that which springs from the brain or the spinal marrow, and when we say 'ligament' we mean by it only that which grows out from the bones. And when we say 'tendon', then we only mean what takes origin and issue from a muscle. In this way we turn our application of the nouns which indicate the meanings which we have mentioned. But now it is time that we should turn to our original object.

On the processes which reach from the brain to the two nasal fossae.[1] From the brain two long horn-like processes spring out, which reach to the two nasal fossae. Besides being lengthy, these two processes are hollowed out internally by an excavation which resembles that of a tubular flute, and their substance is exactly like that of the brain. But nerve-tissue is not like that. On the contrary its substance is dense and tough, and consequently a nerve is of firmer consistence than the brain.

[1] Probably a later scribal addition to the text: the olfactory bulbs. B.T.

Besides this cavity which you see in the two processes that go to the nasal fossae, you will see no other cavity in the nerve since, although admittedly a hollowing out is found in the two processes [*optic nerves*] making their way to the eyeballs from the brain, yet this [hollowing] is not so large as that other one, and also it does not reach so far forwards as that. On the contrary, it is only a small hollow passage, difficult to expose to view. It can only be detected by the insertion of a fine probe, a hog's bristle, or something else of similar tenuity.

The material substance of these two [*optic*] processes is also dense and compact. Nevertheless its density and compactness are less than those of the substance of all the other nerves. The measure of the contrast between it and them is the same as between milk which has just begun to curdle, and milk which has already curdled, and whose curdling is *236*
so complete that it cannot be stirred up. In addition, the material substance of this nerve is farther removed from that of the brain than is the substance of the rest of the nerves from that of this one. This pair of processes is the nerve known as the optic nerve. Its place is behind that of the two processes which come to the nose on a similar course. You can obtain a good view of this nerve pair after you have detached the surrounding bones from the skull as we have indicated in the ninth book of this work. In regard to what I have further to say and to describe for you, you must understand that you are to base yourself on the fact that the brain is constructed as I there described it. And you will find that the origin of each one of these two nerves extends upwards as far as the thalamic region, belonging to the two anterior ventricles of the brain, which comes into existence near the oblique lateral deviation of the cerebral ventricle. Then the two processes [*optic tracts*] make their way from this region and come to the middle region, where the one process meets and blends with the other. Next, after that place, each one of the two separates off from and leaves the other and they go obliquely to the chambers of the eyes, and so their disposition comes to resemble that of the Greek letter chi, which is written like this: 'X'. Neither of the two processes passes to the opposite side of what lies over against its origin, but that nerve which originates from the right side of the brain gets to the right eye, and the nerve which originates

from the left side of the brain gets to the left eye. Now when either of the two gets to the chamber of the eye [*orbit*], then it passes out of the cranial cavity through a circular foramen situated there. And after it has emerged from and passed beyond this foramen, it grows into the eye.

After you have examined these two nerves you see two others, hard
237 nerves, whose origin springs from the anterior parts of the brain [*Nn. oculomotorii*]. Both of these extend as far outwards from the mid-line as we previously mentioned that those other two nerves do. And these two proceed in their turn out from the skull to the situation of the eyes [*orbital cavities*] through two openings [*superior orbital fissures*], each one of which is in close relation with one of those two openings which we mentioned previously, that is to say those which encompass the two optic nerves. Those last two nerves are softer than these other two and much larger than them. After the two optic nerves have reached the eye, they break up, and each of them becomes the retinal covering [*retina*], as we have described earlier in the tenth book of this work. But as for that pair of nerves [*Nn. oculomotorii*] which is much harder and much smaller than those, each of its components splits up in the muscles which move the eye to which that nerve comes. Of that also we spoke in Book X of this work.

Whoever desires to enumerate simply the processes arising from the brain will say that the first pair of nerves springing from the brain goes to the two nasal cavities, and its course travels along the middle region of the skull. The second pair is that of the optic nerves, and in their course its two components travel one on each side of the nerves of the first pair. The third pair is that of the nerves which move the eyes. Nevertheless anyone who does not wish to reckon simply the processes, but the nervous processes and their points of origin, will count the optic nerves as the first pair, and, as the second pair, that of the nerves moving the eye. For as we explained previously in our description of the eye, the eye is moved by means of the pair of the 'hard' nerves [*Nn. oculomotorii*], but the things which it perceives with its gaze
238 it apprehends by means of the pair of 'soft' nerves [*optic nerves*], whose two components the anatomists call 'canals', for the reason that these two nerves alone are tunnelled by perceptible and recognisable channels.

I have already dealt exhaustively with these nerves in Book X of this work. But in regard to what concerns the other pairs of nerves, I have decided to discuss them in this Book.

CHAPTER 3. COURSE AND DISTRIBUTION OF THE TRIGEMINAL NERVE (THIRD PAIR) AND ITS MOTOR ROOT (FOURTH PAIR).

Of the third and fourth pairs of the nerves arising from the brain.[1] Here now, after these two pairs of nerves with which we have dealt previously, there is found a soft nerve-process. This is the process that some anatomists designate by the name given here, I mean that of 'soft nerve-process', although this pair [*N. trigeminus*] is not softer than the pair of optic nerves. Those who study each one of its parts separately, and who do not concern themselves with what they see of the whole of its place of origin, imagine that this pair is softer than the pair of optic nerves. That is because, if you grasp it by putting your fingers round it, its parts cleave together and are set in motion. The reason is that this pair has a plurality of roots and not, as has the optic nerve-pair, one single root. Since these roots are loosely attached and connected to one another, when anyone fingers them with a twisting movement, they become supple between his fingers, and on this ground one regards them as softer than those nerves which have an undivided root. The optic nerve has another quality which distinguishes it from the other nerves, namely that the outside of it is harder than what is found beneath it, in the depth. And indeed, the contrast herein is not insignificant. But all the remaining nerves are of an entirely uniform *239*
texture in the whole of their substance, or else the difference between their outer and inner portions is slight.

Now as for the third pair of nerves [*trigeminal*], that of which I said that it possesses numerous roots, there occurs in respect of it something exceptional, which is found in no other pair. For you see that after its origin each one of those other nerves approaches the skull bare and uncovered, without having upon it any portion of the thicker of the two cerebral meninges. Then, when it enters the foramen piercing the skull, it is encircled by the dura mater, and in this condition it passes

[1] Probably a scribal addition. B.T.

through and out from the foramen. The portion of the dura mater applied to it now travels continuously with it further onwards, just as though it were a protective covering, a sheath which envelops it.

But the third pair [*N. trigeminus*] sinks into the depths of the dura mater underlying the brain so far that anyone who sees it thinks that the path which it is about to follow leads to the lowest section of the skull, and that it will pierce through the part of the skull underlying this meninx. But it does not, in fact, pierce through this or traverse it, nor does it pass out to the lowest part of the skull. On the contrary, it goes only to the region at the front of the head, just like the first and second pair. Amongst the details which show that is the fact that, at its exit from the skull, it places itself close to the second pair [*Nn. oculomotorii*]. This third pair you must follow up, and first you should cut away the part of the dura mater into the depths of which it sinks at its commencement. When you do that, you will see that it does not continue on the course which it had followed, sinking into the depths in its downward path. On the contrary, it pauses, and then bends away forwards, and in the whole of its course it invests itself with the dura mater which frequently makes contact either with the whole of this
240 pair as a body, or with individual parts of it. Besides what I have described with reference to it, you see also that it does not lie upon the naked cranial bones, but it applies itself to a part of the dura mater. For in Nature something invariably clothes a naked nerve should that meet and connect with a hard substance. And consequently in this place a part of the dura mater is found beneath this nerve. And since what I have described is the case with this nerve, then that which first happens to other nerves at their passage through the skull must apply to the nerves of the third pair from the beginning. That is to say, it is encircled by a part of the dura mater which comes to be like a tube around it, and this nerve enters into the hollow of it, and continues with it in this state till it reaches the opening that leads through the skull. From here onwards a subdivision of the dura mater accompanies it in order to protect it and to shelter it all around.

You will also see the path which this nerve follows till it reaches the skull after you have cut away the meninx and set it free round the nerve. And when you come to this place at which the nerve meets the skull, then cut away all the bone found encircling the nerve, that is to say the frontal bone and its two supra-orbital arches and the eye-sockets. Also take away, just as they are, the two eyes, in the way which I have described for you in the tenth book of this work. For otherwise it will not be possible for you to examine the course of this nerve.

Now when the eye has been removed, and also the bone between the eye and the brain, that is, the bone in which the cavity which surrounds the eye is situated, first study carefully the whole of the path which the two nerves of the third pair follow until they reach the eyes. After that, *241*
see how this nerve splits up in the skull, and how the fourth pair [*motor root of the trigeminal*] soon after its origin combines with the third pair. This latter is far more massive, and it is compounded of many roots. But the fourth pair is very small, and therefore as soon as it blends and unites with the third pair, it will be difficult for you to see how it cuts itself off from the other, and separates. Now, in order that nothing may escape your scrutiny of these nerves which are interwoven, as soon as the third pair has united with the fourth, first expose with care and attention, in the manner which I have described for you, the whole course and path of the nerves. That you should do by removing the dura mater from round the nerve, cutting it and freeing it with a sharp knife. Follow this by incising next the part of the layer spread out beneath the nerve. After this, raise it with a hook, and lay freely open the whole of this region, until you can see the bone that underlies it, and all that is to be found hereabouts. For this is the only way in which you will be able to see that one portion of the nerve between the two layers breaks off on the course which both nerves pursue, and that the dura mater is perforated, and beyond it also you will see the portion of the bone adjoining the dura mater there. If you carry out this operation which I have described for you, then soon afterwards you will be confronted by that interlacement of the arteries which ascends to the brain and becomes like a net [*rete mirabile*]. This network encloses, in those regions which lie in front of it, the spongy flesh [*glandular tissue*] which resembles the runner bean [*hypophysis cerebri*] and which projects from the brain-cleft into free space and stretches to the place which is known as the 'pool' or 'cistern'. For it is convex, and it is provided with an empty cavity. You must now cut away this *242*

part also and simultaneously with it the glandular tissue, but in your incision of these parts which you sever you must take care and guard against dividing, along with them, some part of the nerves at their origins.

But if you make no mistake there in the application of the knife, you will sometimes see in that position a nerve which the anatomists have neglected. It is one which passes out from the skull through an orifice beneath the auditory meatus, in which the carotid artery mounts upwards. It is clear and well known that on each side of the head one of these two nerves [*sympathetic plexus*] arises. As for these arteries, they divide themselves profusely, and are many times interwoven so that the net-like [*retiniform*] anastomosis arises from them. Further, this isolated nerve arises in the place [interval] between the origins of those two pairs and the place of their subsequent course forwards. Now take care of this nerve, and preserve it uninjured from all damage. If you do that with it, you will learn that it comes from the fourth pair. As for the region to which it goes, you must attend to what I shall say about it in a subsequent discussion. Here I will only mention this one point, namely that this nerve leaves the skull, as it travels through the bone surrounding the auditory foramen (that is, the bone which one calls petrosal), through a certain part of it in which the so-called foramen caecum is found. Later on I will deal with this for you, but for the present go with us to the chamber of the eye [*orbit*].

Arrange the cut in such a position that from the third pair of nerves, which travels under the floor of the two eyes, you clear the delicate bone separating the two from one another. For only thus will every-
243 thing that you wish to make visible show itself to you, if you cut away the whole chamber of the eye, not only from above, as I told you to do shortly before this, but from underneath as well. For as I have already said to you, it is here that the nerve of the third pair lies. If you now expose the parts underlying these bones you will immediately see the temporalis muscle also, which many anatomists have seen only indistinctly. In order that this muscle should so appear that you can get a complete view of it, cut away the whole of the zygomatic bone and everything that adjoins it and lies in close relation with it. Then, when the whole of this muscle has become visible, it will not prove difficult

for you to examine the muscle [*M. pterygoideus medialis*] concealed in the mouth, I mean the one whose origin proceeds from the groove between the two wing-like processes [*pterygoid plates*] and which joins and connects with the broad part of the mandible. In order that you may be able to study exhaustively this muscle and the other parts lying in its vicinity, divide the mandible at the place of its symphysis at the chin, separate its two halves from one another, and then cut loose from it the other muscles attached to it and what is conjoined to it of the membrane that invests the tongue. Cut these from both its sections, and draw them to one side. When you do that, you see clearly the two muscles [*Mm. pterygoidei*] by means of which the mandible is drawn upwards, and you also get a good view of the branch which comes off from the third pair of nerves [*mandibular division of the trigeminal*] and proceeds onwards to the two muscles. When you follow this branch and trace its track along its whole course, then you can cut away all the muscular tissue which interposes itself between your view of the connection of the nerve. For after this same nerve has emerged from the skull, a branch from it makes its way to the joint fixed between the mandible and the skull, passing outwards in front of the auricle *244*
[*N. auriculotemporalis*]. This branch will show itself clearly to you as soon as you dissect away the so-called muscular carpet [*M. platysma myoides*].

From the third pair [of nerves] a massive branch separates off which takes a downward direction [*mandibular division of the trigeminal*]. From this branch twigs go to the two muscles [*Mm. pterygoidei*] of which we spoke, then its remnant divides up, and a twig from it [*N. lingualis*] applies itself to the membrane which invests the tongue, as we have previously described in Book X, where we dealt with the anatomy of the tongue. The other part of it penetrates into the mandibular bone through the foramen which is found near the molar teeth. In all animals this is a recognisable and conspicuous aperture, and its situation is on the mandible at its expanded part, one on each side internally. Through this aperture enters a nerve [*inferior dental*], by no means small in size, which establishes itself firmly in the region where the roots of the teeth are placed. That is to say that the canal extends along these roots throughout the whole length of the mandible as far as the situation of the incisor teeth, which are the lateral and the medial incisors. The portion of the bone through which this nerve makes its way has an exceptional texture, that is to say that it is more spongy and less dense than all the remaining portions of the bone. Now from this nerve branches break off which distribute themselves to the roots of the teeth. On each side of the mandible one of these nerves is present. But the main nerve which emerges from this canal divides up and distributes itself to the lower lip. And this is the termination of one offshoot of the third pair of nerves, the one which after the emergence of this pair from the skull breaks off from it and then starts to make its way in a downward direction.

As for the remaining portion [*maxillary division of the trigeminal nerve*] it proceeds, as I have described, to the infra-orbital region, and from it branches spring out, of which the first goes to the uppermost region of the mouth [*greater and lesser palatine nerves*] to which there comes no
245 portion of the nerve previously discussed, that is to say of that nerve which distributes itself to the covering of the tongue [*N. lingualis*]. Following upon this there branches off from it an offshoot travelling deeply to the nose, and to the region adjoining the nose. And of the remainder of this nerve a part passes on in the upper jaw and reaches the roots of the teeth found there. Its course is like that of the nerve which travels in the mandible, and the branches which split off from it at the roots of the teeth are just like those which split off from that one. Then it passes right through the foramen near the incisor teeth, and distributes itself to the upper lip, just as that other nerve is distributed to the lower lip. After these nerves have divided and split themselves up as we have described, the nerve-shoot next to these, which is still outstanding from the third pair, passes outwards through the bone which is called the 'cheek-apple', that is, the prominence of the cheek. In this bone there are sometimes three, sometimes four foramina. And from these nerves sensation and movement reach the upper jaw in all its parts, I mean those of its parts which lie superficially beneath the skin, the muscle known as the 'chewing' muscle [*masseter*], and the muscle which moves the region on the nose which is called the nasal ala.

You have now seen clearly how the matter stands with regard to all the nerves of the third and fourth pairs, and you have acquainted your-

self with them. And before you proceed to the dissection of the fifth pair you have one matter to attend to, and this is something which you must remember to carry out in the dissection of the sixth pair also. This one thing that I have to say to you is, that you must set free the nerve [*sympathetic*] which comes out from the hole of which I said that it is found in the petrosal bone, I mean the foramen [*carotid canal*] towards which the terminal part of the stupefying [*carotid*] artery makes its way. Begin at exactly that spot in the animal which you are dissecting, on the one side, after you have cut away the bone which surrounds the artery and this nerve. And if you do not cut or damage 246
either one of these two structures but follow up their path within the skull, you then see this nerve quite plainly from its first place of origin, and you can also see from which pair of nerves it proceeds [from the *vago-sympathetic trunk*, i.e. from the sixth pair].

CHAPTER 4. THE FACIAL AND AUDITORY NERVES (FIFTH PAIR).

Of the fifth pair of nerves growing out of the brain.[1] I have already said above that when we speak of 'processes' of the brain, and of nerves, this has not in both cases the same significance, since from the brain to the nasal fossae two processes which are not nerves make their way. Indeed every nerve which takes its origin from the brain is one of its processes, but not every process branching from the brain is necessarily a nerve. And since that is so, then by rights the first of all the pairs of nerves must be the optic nerves, the second pair must be those moving the eyes [*oculomotor nerve*], the third pair following these must be the so-called 'soft' pair [*trigeminal nerve*], and, next to that, the fourth pair must be the one which is close to the third pair and which unites itself with it [*motor root of the trigeminal*]. The fifth pair, which follows these ones which we have mentioned, is that which takes origin from two nerves whose two individual origins come off close to one another, although their passage out from the skull is not through a single aperture [*facial and auditory nerves*]. Therefore one might well assume that this is not a single pair, but rather two pairs. Nevertheless, since Marinus has treated the two as a single pair in his enumeration, and as

[1] Probably a scribal addition. B.T.

our teachers have followed him in that and have imitated him, then let us also call this the fifth pair. Thus when we say in our future discussion of them that on each side there are two nerves, and that the path of each of these double nerves goes through two apertures, and when nevertheless we reckon the two as a single pair of which the constituent parts lie close to one another, there is nothing in that at all injurious to our
247 knowledge of the significance of the facts. Harm can only be done here by ignorance of the fact that, as regards the so-called blind or one-eyed canal [*canal for the facial nerve*] the earlier anatomists were firmly of the opinion that it is blind or one-eyed, because it is bored crookedly through the bone. Its place is close by the auditory meatus and the nerve through which auditory sensations are conveyed, and from it there comes out an undivided nerve, in the part of the skull behind the ear, in the place to which goes the canal also. And since that is so, then it is self-evident that this canal and this nerve both lie posteriorly but that the auditory meatus and the auditory nerve lie anteriorly, except that this nerve [*facial*] when it has traversed the tortuous canal which pierces the skull sinuously, next moves forwards in the direction of the root of the ear below its lobules. It then arrives at the face, and is united with the nerve of which we have previously spoken, when we said that it comes off from the third pair of nerves, in the direction of the temporo-mandibular joint [*N. auriculotemporalis*]. From it [*N. facialis*] there spring off branches, some of which are all found invariably one and the same in all animals, while others are found neither invariably nor amongst all animals. Certainly the first branch has frequently been clearly visible to me in the bodies of those animals of which the temporalis muscle is massive, and I have seen that it joined and connected itself to the external part of this [muscle] at the back of the head. But as for those branches which come off from it to divide in the structures lying in front of the auricle, they distribute themselves superficially over this muscle and the adjacent regions. But the main body of the nerve extends onwards to the cheeks, and from the 'chewing' muscles it splits up and distributes itself at the margin of the broad masseter muscle.

Investigate all this, and study it on the head. You must have a skull lying before you which you have prepared thoroughly, so that all its

foramina have become evident to you, and you can discover them and identify them clearly. That becomes possible when all the structures 248
in the skull, I mean the fasciae, veins, arteries and nerves, have been removed by putrefaction. It is understood that this must be the skull of an ape, if you are engaged upon the anatomy of the ape, and of a goat when a goat is studied, and similarly in respect of all the other animals, whichever you happen to be investigating. You must have the skull of your animal in a mature state in order to examine and investigate it. Then, in accordance with that, you can set your hand to the dissection of whatever part of the head you select. Your examination and investigation of this skull will prove to be extremely helpful in enabling you to work correctly, and it will guide you on the right way to a thorough understanding of the matter. This is something which I have already mentioned to you previously, and perhaps I will return to it in the future. For the things that you have to do are numerous, so that you must continually remind yourself of them. But I will bring my exposition to an end with the assumption that the skull, which I have described, lies in front of you.

CHAPTER 5. THE VAGO-GLOSSOPHARYNGEAL COMPLEX (SIXTH PAIR), THE HYPOGLOSSAL NERVE (SEVENTH PAIR), AND THEIR CONNECTIONS WITH THE UPPER CERVICAL NERVES.

Of the sixth and seventh pairs of the nerves arising from the brain.[1] Our forerunners among the anatomists reckon as the sixth pair of the nerves arising from the brain that which emerges from the extreme end of the lambdoid suture [at the *jugular foramen*]. This pair has three nerve-roots [*glossopharyngeus*, *vagus* and *accessorius*]. And because these three all emerge from a single foramen, and a single sheath envelops them, those who look at them imagine that they become a single nerve. Consequently you must try to observe them by cutting away the musculature of both sides of the neck. Nor is it unknown to you that that must be done after you have first removed the muscle known as the 'muscular carpet', together with the skin. This is something you must constantly bear in mind, even if on occasion we do not mention it.

[1] Probably a scribal addition. B.T.

249 In the neighbourhood of this pair [the sixth] there lies another pair of nerves, and this [*N. hypoglossus*] is the last of the nerve-pairs which take their origin from the brain. Its position is so close to that of the sixth pair that it may be thought that the two together constitute a single pair, that is to say in animals of small bodily dimensions, a class which includes the apes. One of the reasons why one imagines this to be so is that the sheath investing them envelops both in common. After the two have travelled onwards over a small distance, there enters with them in the investing sheath that pair of nerves which penetrates through the petrosal bone, and which the [other] anatomists have overlooked [*N. sympathicus*]. And now, when these three pairs [IX, X, XI reckoned as a single pair, XII, and *N. sympathicus*] have become associated and combined together, there attaches itself to them a fourth pair [*first cervical*] as an accretion. This combines and associates with those nerves which we mentioned earlier and it is in fact the pair which takes its origin from the first cervical vertebra. Next there is intertwined with those pairs mentioned the one which takes its origin from the second vertebra. In this place is the terminal position of the so-called 'artery of stupor' [*carotid*] and the end of the jugular vein travelling in the depth of the neck. That there is one of these veins on each side of the neck is evident and well known, one being on the right side and the other on the left. Whenever you hear anything spoken of as situated on one of the two sides, you must simultaneously assume that occurrence for the other side also.

The terminal branch of the artery ascends to the rete mirabile and it runs through the canal in the petrosal bone. But the terminal precursor of the jugular vein passes through from the terminal part of the lambdoid suture. This nerve and the artery and the vein proceed on both sides through precisely the same foramen. So far as the hinder part of the
250 foramen is concerned, here descends the sixth pair, and it has, as already described, three roots [*glossopharyngeus, vagus, accessorius*], and the end of the deep jugular vein goes upwards and ascends as far as the head of the lambdoid suture. As for the anterior aspect of this foramen, there ascends from it that artery [*carotid*] known as the artery of stupor, and there makes its way downwards from it a nerve which traverses the canal in the petrosal bone [*canalis caroticus, N. sympathicus*].

Accordingly, all these structures that we specified, artery, vein and nerve, lie in one and the same small place close to one another. Some of them meet and touch others, simply making contact with them. Others are joined and blended, and then unravel themselves in one way or another. Some are joined to others by fascial sheaths which surround and encompass them all together. Since this is so, the anatomists have good reasons when they teach many diverse views on these points, inasmuch as the separation and liberation of each single structure from the others is in the highest degree difficult.

But do you first reflect the sheaths investing and surrounding them, then cut through those sheaths which bind them up with certain other parts lying there. At the conclusion of that, study what comes after the first and second vertebrae. For if these parts are visible and uncovered for you, I will give you some notification and information about the recognition of all the things that I have mentioned to you. Together with these you must also dissect the special muscle of the mandible [*digastric*]. The best thing to do with regard to this muscle is, at the very commencement of your task, to cut it out and remove it, because that helps you to a clearer view of the above-mentioned nerves, vein and artery. Besides this, dissect away the muscle [*M. stylohyoideus*] which has its origin at the base of the awl-like [*styloid*] process, and the muscle [*M. mylohyoideus*] which connects the lambda-like bone [*hyoid* *251*
bone] with the mandible. In addition to these, dissect away the muscle which runs from this bone to the scapula, being elongated and slender [*M. omohyoideus*]. And when you have done that, then your view of the nerves, and of the vein and the artery which we have mentioned to you will no longer remain obscured.

Now just as the first pair of those nerves which have their origin on the spinal medulla does for its part also interlace and interwine itself to a small extent with the nerves which come out in the sixth pair [*glossopharyngeus, vagus, accessorius*], in the same way there interlaces and entangles itself with both the pair which emerges from the petrosal bone [*N. sympathicus*]. As for the third [? *spinal nerve*] it is intimately blended only with the nerve at the broad scapular muscle [*M. trapezius*]. The whole of the nerves, veins and arteries which lie here, can be separated from one another in the following manner. You must first

incise and reflect from them all the fascial sheaths enveloping them, so that you can see each single vein, artery and nerve remaining alone by itself. It will be clear to you that the first of those structures which separates itself from them and diverges is the nerve which forms part of the seventh pair [*hypoglossus*]. It is 'harder' than the remaining nerves which are contiguous to it. For the nerves of the sixth pair admittedly differ in 'hardness' from one another by a small amount, yet all of them are less 'hard' than the nerve of the seventh pair. As for that nerve which traverses the canal in the petrosal bone, it by no means falls short of these others in this respect, but rather it is still 'softer' than they are. And as for that nerve which is the hardest of all those, I mean the nerve of the seventh pair, it first breaks off from them and begins to progress obliquely upwards in the direction towards the tongue-muscles. This
252 is the nerve of which we spoke in Book X of this work, and we pointed out how one can expose it in the shortest possible time while the animal is still alive, if one wishes, and then secure it by means of a ligature, or destroy it or cut it, and thereby paralyse and deprive of movement the whole of the tongue musculature to which it is distributed and in which it ramifies. I have often seen that from this nerve a very fine twig [*descendens hypoglossi*] branches off to the muscle which goes from the lower corner of the hyoid bone to the thyroid cartilage of the larynx. And in an ape it once appeared to me as though the nerve to this muscle came from the sixth pair [*vagus*], as also to that muscle [*M. sternohyoideus*] which runs from the hyoid bone to the sternum. To the muscle which extends toward the scapula [*M. omohyoideus*] whose origin is connected with and adjoins the origin of that other muscle [*M. sternohyoideus*], I have also seen the nerve to its upper belly coming from the seventh pair. And also, occasionally, I have seen that the nerve to its lowest part [*inferior belly*] came to it from the sixth pair.[1]

Now in this dissection which we have in hand, you must clearly and exhaustively inform yourself about the ligament [*stylohyoid*] which connects the lesser cornu of the hyoid bone to the free end of the

[1] In the human body the XIIth nerve may appear to arise from the Xth nerve. Once a student submitted to me a dissection in which he had found 'the XIIth nerve coming off from the Xth nerve'. The combination is not rare, but of course only temporary, and it occurs outside the skull. It might illustrate the anomaly which Galen records here.

styloid process. For it is perfectly round to such a degree that one who sees it thinks it is a nerve. In the bodies of apes, in which alone it can be seen, it is more slender than that nerve of which we have said that it mounts upwards to the tongue [*N. hypoglossus*]. I have already said previously that Herophilus calls the process of the skull which others call awl-pointed or needle-pointed, and which is a slender cartilaginous process, styloid. That is because many people in Alexandria, and many others besides them among the peoples inhabiting the regions of the
Orient, who speak bad Greek, call 'styloi' the pens with which one 253
writes upon waxed tablets. Now the free end of this process which looks like the end of the pen which one uses for writing on these tablets, that is, the process which is called awl-like or needle-like, consists of pure cartilage. Similarly also, the end of the lesser cornu of the hyoid bone is cartilaginous. And the ligament which binds together these two cartilages is extremely rounded and slender, just like one or other of the individual nerves of the neck. It also resembles one of the nerves of the seventh pair, except that it is less thick than that nerve, since that is thicker than this ligament.

Now, if either this ligament or certain fascial sheaths or spongy flesh should hinder the thorough-going inspection of the more deeply lying structures by interposing themselves in this place, you must completely uproot and clear away those obstructions. When you complete this kind of clearance, then in addition to the rest of what comes to light there will clearly show itself to you that special pharyngeal nerve [*N. glossopharyngeus*] which lies more deeply in the neck than the nerve of the seventh pair. Moreover, this nerve is distinctly more slender than the other. And, for both these reasons it comes to escape notice to such an extent that you think that it does not exist at all. However, do what I told you in the way of removing and excising the structures immediately related to the veins and the arteries. When you do that you will see this nerve also along with other structures, and you will
see that from it fine twigs branch off which run to the muscle of the 254
pharynx, itself merely a small muscle [*M. stylopharyngeus*], and then further onwards so as to reach the whole of the rest of this region as far as the root of the tongue. In no animal have I ever yet seen a third structural part to which offshoots of this nerve extended. Now this

nerve is one of the three which contribute to the sixth pair, and in fact it is the most slender of all the three. And to this pair belong further two other massive nerves, of which the one associates itself with the third pair of nerves coming from the dorsal medulla [*spinal cord*] and stretches towards the shoulder [*N. accessorius*], while the other [*vagus*] lies next to the artery of stupor [*carotid*] along the whole of the neck.

Now that nerve [*accessorius*] which passes upwards and proceeds in the direction of the shoulder has its place of origin beneath the wide-spread muscle [*trapezius*] attaching itself to the partition wall [*spine*] in the middle region of the scapular bone, and actually this is the first muscle underlying the muscular carpet [*M. platysma myoides*]. You sometimes see the termination of this nerve entering this muscle, and sometimes you also see that a twig finally branches off from it which passes from it to the muscle [*M. deltoides*] which ascends from the upper arm. There are here related to the shoulder two nerves, which I am going to mention to you now, so note them well. I say that you will see a branch which splits off from this nerve [*N. accessorius*] at its junction with the second and the third nerves springing from the spinal medulla, and this branch runs to the muscle [*M. sternocleidomastoideus*] which goes from the skull to the breast-bone and to the clavicle. And you will see another branch which goes to that muscle which takes its origin from both sides of the first vertebra and joins itself to the upper region of the shoulder. In the pig I have also seen that to this muscle that has been mentioned there proceeds one of the nerves that arise particularly from the second vertebra. Consequently I advise you to investigate thoroughly, and to make yourself absolutely sure about these networks into which the nerves enter with one another, in accordance
255 with what I have also told you earlier. And if at any time you observe one nerve approaching another and uniting with it, then concentrate your attention and note whether both nerves remain after this association just as they were previously, or whether one of the two is more slender than it was and the other one larger. For if the two nerves are two exactly similar stems as they were before, then the reason for their combination in nature with one another is a seeking on the part of both of them for security and protection. But if their sizes differ, then the one whose size is lessened and reduced is the one from which nerve

fibres have been taken away, and the nerve which has become larger than before is the nerve to which those nerve fibres have come as an increased growth. In addition, the combination and interlacement of the nerve fibres, and the manner of their ramification reveal to you from which of the two large contributory nerves it is that the smaller nerve springs, approaching, joining and combining with them.

CHAPTER 6. THE VAGUS NERVE AND ITS BRANCHES, WITH SPECIAL DESCRIPTION OF THE RECURRENT LARYNGEAL NERVE OF GALEN.

In another treatise I investigate the characteristics of the muscles to which there run branches of these nerves of which we are speaking, and there I discuss every single muscle separately, and I summarise how many points of origin, and how many roots the nerves making their way to them possess. But here it is time for us to begin on the description of the remaining nerve, that is to say, one [*vagus*] of the three nerves [*glossopharyngeus, vagus, accessorius*] which together leave the cranial cavity at the lower end of the lambdoid suture. And the discussion here also will be duplicated, by which I mean that it will have two sections. The first one of these will be concerned with dead animals, and in it we shall summarise the nature of every one of the branches of this pair of nerves [*vagus*], for example, what its dimensions are, from which of the subdivisions of the parent nerve it arises, and in what part or in which organ it is distributed. The second subdivision will be concerned with 256
living animals, dealing with what happens when nerves are secured by ligatures or bruised or cut (whichever one of these terms I use, you must understand me to include the other with it; it is a habit of mine to call them all by a name which may embrace them all in common, this being either 'damage' or 'injury').

When you dissect a dead animal, the first nerve branch that appears is one which you see going to the artery [*common carotid*] called the 'stupefying one' or the 'artery of stupor', and it comes also to the deeply placed jugular vein of the neck. The next nerve-shoots which appear after these are two which go to the larynx [*internal and external branches of the superior laryngeal nerve*]. One of these two goes towards the line that is opposite the thyroid cartilage of the larynx in its upper

part, and the other goes to the muscle which connects the thyroid cartilage with the oesophagus. Occasionally you will see that from the former branch, that is, the upper or higher one of the two, a nerve twig runs to a muscle [*M. thyrohyoideus*] which unites the greater cornu of the hyoid bone to the thyroid cartilage and connects the one with the other, and then proceeds to the muscle [*M. sternohyoideus*] which leaves the hyoid bone and reaches the sternum. The whole of the remainder of this nerve then penetrates into the deeper parts below the thyroid cartilage. Then again, in so far as the second of these branches is concerned, that is to say the lower one of the two, clearly visible twigs branch off from it and constantly run to the muscle which connects the oesophagus with the thyroid cartilage of the larynx, and to the muscle which connects this cartilage with the cricoid cartilage. The remainder of this nerve divides up in the muscle which passes from the thyroid cartilage to the sternum. I have often found that this nerve also supplies the other muscle which together with this one comes from the hyoid bone, but runs to the sternum, I mean the muscle whose
257 attachment to the other I have already described. In the upper parts of this muscle are unmistakable nerve-twigs, which you find taking origin sometimes from the seventh pair of cranial nerves [*hypoglossal*], and sometimes from the sixth pair [*vagus*]. And after these nerve-twigs you will not find in the whole of the neck any visible branches coming off from the sixth pair. But there are branches which proceed there to the oesophagus and the trachea and which are clearer and more obviously recognisable than this branch. They also, though, are slender, to the extent that all the anatomists have overlooked them. They unite and blend with that upwardly ascending nerve of which I will soon give you an account.

Below the neck, at the upper aperture of the thorax, nerve branches which are small but not inconspicuous go to the trachea. And these nerves are distributed to the sheaths of the lungs [*pleura*] without visible offshoots arising from them to go to the lungs themselves. This is a fact which, with your own eyes, you will find just as described in the bodies of the larger animals also, and not only in those of apes. Similarly one finds that, after the nervous twigs that have been mentioned, a nerve branch reaches the heart and joins it at the place where the encircling blood-vessel [*coronary*] comes off from it and also where the root of the sheath enclosing the heart, and called pericardium, is situated. On the heart you cannot see any obvious nerve which breaks up in its substance. Only in the bodies of very large animals will you detect there a nerve penetrating slightly towards its cavity. But among the remaining animals you will see no nerves which make their way into the cardiac cavity.

With regard to those nerves which we have reviewed in respect of the parts of the body to which they are distributed, the matter is clear. But as to what concerns that nerve stem which I myself discovered and 258
have named the 'upwardly recurrent' one [*N. laryngeus recurrens*], the origin of this nerve from the two sides, the right and the left, does not take place in the same manner, but they can both be detected in the same way. That can be done by two methods. One of these is for you to follow closely the vagus nerve, where it lies alongside the carotid artery, until it enters the thorax. Inspect it and observe it from every angle after its first entrance into the thorax, so that not one of the branches springing off from it escapes your notice. When you have done that, you will discover the head of the upwardly recurrent nerve and find that it does not behave in the same way on the two sides of the thorax. On the contrary, the nerve on the right side enters into its ascending stage much more hastily, after it has passed only a short distance from the upper end of the thorax, and there it approaches the artery found on this side, I mean that artery which ascends towards the axilla, its position being oblique [*right subclavian*, arising from the *brachiocephalic trunk*]. For the ascending recurrent nerve winds itself round this artery. But on the left side of the thorax its course and inclination are to the artery that springs from the heart. Thus among the branches of the right and left vagus nerves, which travel alongside the carotid arteries, you will see no sections which do not occupy precisely similar positions with the sole exceptions of these two branches. The remaining branches you will see occupying identical positions on both sides, I mean on the right and on the left.

Now with regard to the situations in which these two recurrent nerves first take their origin, you will certainly not wonder that the anatomists do not know them, because those are places in which lie

many veins, arteries, and fascial sheaths, and also because that portion
of each nerve which constitutes its origin and its root from which it
259 springs, is covered up and ensheathed. So too, you will not wonder
that the anatomists know nothing about the upward course which this
nerve takes in the neck when it returns upwards, because its ascending
course is concealed and covered by the fascial sheets alongside the
trachea. But as for its conjunction and union with the larynx, I do not
understand how those persons who interest themselves in the construction
of this part of the body and apply themselves to its dissection have
failed to recognise it. For its conjunction and union, even if not clear
and evident in the bodies of small feeble apes, nevertheless are certainly
so in the bodies of dogs, goats, and oxen. For it was these larger
animals that our teachers were always accustomed to dissect, because
all the vocal organs of these animals are of great size—and when I say
vocal organs I mean the larynx together with its muscles and its nerves
—and so there you can see this upwardly recurrent nerve large and
plain in its conjunction and union which takes place in that part.

You will succeed in the discovery and the study of this nerve most
easily if you go to the butchers who slaughter cattle and sell separately
every portion of them, and get them to produce for you the tongue complete
with the larynx. You must now uncover and remove the muscle
which comes from the oesophagus [*pharynx*] and encircles the larynx on
both its sides, that is, the muscle of which we said that it joins and connects
with the thyroid cartilage [*M. thyropharyngeus*]. You will at once
see clearly this upwardly recurrent nerve, as it is distributed to the muscle
behind the cricoid cartilage [*M. cricoarytenoideus posticus*]. And you will
see that it sinks inwards and, together with the muscles, it goes into the
deeper parts and is distributed in the muscular tissue on both sides of
the larynx and in the depths of the larynx. In the anatomy of these
parts you have already learned that what covers and closes the larynx
260 is the internal [deep] musculature, whereas what opens it is the muscular
tissue on both sides behind it. Here also the terminal branches of this
nerve combine with those of the nerve which we mentioned shortly
before, that is, the nerve [*internal laryngeal*] which comes from the
direction of the upper parts of the thyroid cartilage and sinks downwards
here into the deeper parts of the larynx. When you have seen

this nerve in the body of an ox, then pass on to those of swine, and investigate similarly in these animals its course and its distribution. For that also will be an easy and far from troublesome task for you. In fact, there are sometimes cut out [from the animal] the larynx and with it the whole of the lungs and the heart, and it is evident to you that, together with these, the trachea will be removed as well. All these organs collected together are named 'the pluck'.

Now afterwards, when with your own eyes you have observed the end of the upwardly recurrent nerve and have understood about it as a result of the dissection of the laryngeal region, then set aside the larynx and pass on from it to the undissected body of a dead animal, and in it cut away, as I have explained to you, the muscle common to the oesophagus and to the thyroid cartilage [*M. thyropharyngeus*]. But when you have found the early stage of the recurrent nerve, then proceed downwards along the trachea, travelling with the nerve. You should not leave this until you have reached the thorax, in which its first origin takes place, coming off from the same part precisely in the bodies of all animals which possess a larynx. And its distribution likewise is just the same in the various parts of the larynx. Uniform too is the combination of the nerve which joins and connects with the larynx, coming from the sixth nerve-pair, with the endings of this nerve. This is also true of the path followed by this nerve in its recurrent course upwards in the neck. Thus in all animals it is combined and joined, by means of a forked twig, with the great nerve [*vagus*] lying alongside the arteries [*carotid*]. Thus again, this combination and this fusion are among the details which anatomists have left out of account. *261*
We, however, have frequently separated and differentiated this nerve, known as the 'vocal' nerve, from all the structures adjacent to it, together with the great nerve [*vagus*] alongside the arteries, and we have demonstrated the manner in which the offshoots from this nerve [*N. recurrens*] combine and unite with the offshoots of that other nerve [*N. laryngeus superior*]. It is easiest to demonstrate that in the body of an ox, because of the great size of the nerve in that animal, and next to the ox, in the bodies of dogs and lions. For this nerve is very large in the bodies of these also. After these come the bodies of those other animals which have interlocking teeth, next the bodies of swine, and,

after them, the bodies of goats. I advise you to apply yourself to the study of this nerve with the greatest zeal, so as to find and acquaint yourself with it in the bodies of dead animals in two ways. One of these is that you commence its dissection from its endings at the larynx. The other is that you follow the great nerve [*vagus*]. It is best that in the detection and examination of this nerve you pursue both methods, that is to say that you follow the nerve which travels alongside the artery until you reach the thorax, and thence you trace the upwardly recurrent nerve. As you approach the thorax, then put traction upon each of the nerves separately, first on one, then on the other, and in making traction notice how you are led and brought by the tension from one to the other. If you do that, there will be clearly revealed to you the place in which this nerve commences and breaks off from the vagus. It is quite obvious that in order that you may thus seek out and make sure of the origin of this upwardly recurrent nerve, the thorax must have been opened previously in the manner which I described in the passage where I dealt with the dissection of the respiratory organs.

CHAPTER 7. EXPERIMENTS ON THE VAGUS NERVE AND CAROTID ARTERY.

Thus after you have acquired operative practice in the way which I have mentioned, on the bodies of dead animals, then proceed to those of living animals, and apply to these the method which I will here
262 explain to you. Divide and clear away all those structures which lie superficially to the nerve, in the region just below the larynx, in such a manner that you carry an incision of moderate length from above downwards, one on each side, so that you expose the nerves. As regards the upwardly recurrent nerves, each lies nearer to the trachea than the great nerve [*vagus*], of which one is found on each of the two sides of the trachea. But as for the two vagus nerves, their distance from the trachea exceeds that of the recurrent nerves, though they are not, in fact, very far from it.

Close beside each of the two vagi there is an artery, and they are held together by a fascial sheath, common to each artery and its nerve. But no structure lies near the upwardly recurrent nerve. Therefore when you have exposed these two nerves by means of the incision running from above downwards, then draw both of them slightly upwards by means of two blunt hooks such as are called one-eyed or blind hooks, which are perforated and through which a thread has been drawn. Next grasp with one of your hands the end of the thread and with the other hand withdraw the hook in the path which it travelled first, when you were inserting it beneath the nerve. When you have done that, it follows that when you raise the hook and remove it, the thread will still remain beneath the nerve.

As for what concerns the two vagi, the hook normally grips the carotid artery with each nerve unless you anticipate this by dissecting and splitting the fascial sheath common to both the nerve and the artery and enveloping them. Here also is lymphatic gland tissue which usually presents itself to you after you have made the incision, and it envelops and conceals from you both the artery together with the *263*
nerve. That most often happens in the bodies of pigs. Should you encounter this lymphoid tissue, then follow it up and cut it out, taking great care and proceeding cautiously. Then, if you go to work thus, the nerve sustains no injury. Also, after you have done this, you can reflect the sheath from the nerve if you have trained yourself in this task two or three times previously. And now, when with two hooks you have drawn upwards the two arteries together with the two nerves as well, grasp one end of the thread and withdraw the other end together with the hook. For nothing is lost if you draw upwards both structures with the thread, I mean the trunk of the artery and that of the nerve. If that is done with them then the separation of the one from the other is easier and less toilsome than when they both lie in the deeper parts. Amongst the things which add considerable assistance to the liberation of the two is if the hook, as we have chosen it purposely, is not in the highest degree blunt and absolutely deprived of point, after the fashion of those which some call one-eyed or blind, nor yet very sharply pointed. It should be, as it were, intermediate between the absolutely blunt one without a point, and the very sharp hook, in order that when in probing you press very hard and stick it into the sheath you are able to pierce the sheath with it, and when you only press lightly you do not pierce the sheath. Thus, when you adapt the hook in such a fashion

for yourself, then you can pierce the sheath without being liable to cut through the nerve or the artery. Also the thread passing through the
264 eye of the hook should be neither very slender nor yet very coarse. For in the latter case, if this portion of the nerve should be ligatured with it, you would then see on it something like the track of a saw upon wood. But it is best and most suitable that the nerve should continue throughout to be protected from injury so that after the slackening of the thread the animal may cry out and its voice may return to it. For if it happens that, after the slackening of the thread, the animal does not cry out and its voice does not return, then it may be that you have divided the nerve or destroyed or bruised it, or inflicted injury upon it in some other way, whatever that may be.

It is now abundantly clear from the description which we have given that the earlier writers did not hit on the right conclusion when they believed of these two arteries [*carotid arteries*] that they are the source of the disability which befalls the animal in this operation. It was for this reason that they named them—erroneously—the stupefiers or the 'stupefying arteries'. But again, for your part, be sure to expose the erroneous character of this belief and overcome its supporters, refuting and confounding their arguments by the following demonstration: first of all ligature those two arteries; if you then observe that the animal cries out just as it had cried out previously, though both arteries have been ligatured but not the nerves, then either on another animal or, if you prefer it, on the same animal, release both the arteries and ligature the two nerves. And if you do that, then you will see that when the injury has affected only one of the nerves, that is, one of the two great nerves or the recurrent nerves, the animal now retains one half of its voice. But if the injury has affected both nerves then the animal becomes completely voiceless, except that there remains a certain rattling sound which is produced when it gasps. Should you desire that this rattling should be completely suppressed so that the gasping may persist alone without it, then turn to the nerve branch
265 which leads to the root of the tongue [*N. glossopharyngeus*] before any part of it joins and connects with the muscle of the pharynx. It is best if you sever that nerve branch alone without interfering with the stem which goes from it to the tongue. Previously I have already said in

those chapters in which I was dealing with the causes of respiration, how you are to set free this nerve, and I have also distinguished and differentiated very clearly between gasping and the expulsion of the air in [normal] expiration. And in the chapters in which I was dealing with the nature of the voice, I distinguished and I drew the contrast between simple gasping and such gasping as is accompanied by hoarse rattling, and also the distinction between vocal sounds and spoken words. That is, I established the fact that the expulsion of air in expiration occurs in its spontaneous effusion, and that when involuntary expiration supplements and accompanies it, then gasping is produced. When this is combined with constriction of the pharynx, that causes gasping together with a hoarse rattling. When this gasping is put under pressure by the larynx, then vocal sound results. Then, when these sounds are differentiated and tone is distinguished by the tongue, speech is produced. And since that is so, then, if we paralyse and deprive of movement the whole of the thoracic musculature, as we have described, and inflict injury on the nerves which bring that musculature into action, leaving only the diaphragm sound and uninjured, the animal will still be able to exhale spontaneously, but will not be capable of gasping or of making sounds. But if the faculty of active exhalation remains intact and uninjured, and we paralyse the larynx and deprive it of movement, then the animal loses its voice, and only exhales laboriously. And when we injure the pharyngeal muscles as well, then the hoarse rattling comes to be lost by the animal, and it now exhales, but only inaudibly. But if the tongue-muscles only should be paralysed, and their movement be suppressed, then that inflicts no sort of damage either on the voice or upon deglutition. We have already described how we have to proceed in order to paralyse and to deprive of movement these muscles also, by *266*
dividing the nerve that comes to them from the seventh pair [*N. hypoglossus*].

Now all these things that we have explained in the chapters in which we dealt with 'The Uses of the Parts of the Body' were naturally unknown to our predecessors, because their explanation and proof belong to those details which can only be seen in the dissection of living animals. So we also find that the earlier writers had no sort of correct acquaintance with the nerves lying at the sides of the arteries which they named the 'arteries of stupor', 'stupefying arteries'. These names they applied because, according to their view, it is these arteries that bring about stupor, if an injury befalls them in the way which we have described, although this is a matter which requires intensive research and investigation. For it was certainly possible that they might not know of the nerve at the side of the artery. But they should not have been ignorant of the fact that, when an injury befalls the arteries and not the nerves, that causes the animal no harm which might lead to loss of sensation or mobility. For we are accustomed to see clearly that in such a condition the animal nevertheless moves and breathes without difficulty or hindrance, and nothing in it is affected except the voice alone. They may perhaps, then, have called the loss and the cutting off of the voice stupor, I mean those who endowed the artery with this name, that is, 'stupefying artery' or 'artery of stupor' on account of that symptom, that is, stupor. It has been reported to me that in our own time there was an individual who opposed and disputed with one of our colleagues on the point of whether the animal becomes paralysed and mute as soon as this nerve has been subjected to injury. It was however the man who opposed and disputed this view who was exposed and put to shame, in the presence of an assembly in which there were many who saw that and who formed a correct judgement on it.

But as for the people who have thus named these arteries, it does not
267 matter what really impelled and induced them to name them thus. And now we will leave them, and speak of another circumstance, which we have observed by ocular evidence in this nerve. I vivisected an emaciated sow in which I saw that the two nerves lying at the side of the arteries were very large. Accordingly I laid them free as far as the thorax. Besides these I also laid free the two upwardly recurrent nerves. Next I took hold of the right-sided one of the latter nerves, and drew it strongly upwards, taking care not to injure it as I did so. And as I drew this nerve slightly upwards, I took hold of it with the fingers of my left hand, and directed all my attention upon the great nerve, in order to see if any part of it were drawn downwards. And there I saw that that was obviously the case. And further, I saw that when the nerve was stretched, then something like a fold or bend appeared on the great nerve. I now cleared away from the nerve [*vagus*] all of the ensheathing

tissue which is found outside it, and then clearly saw the fascicles stretched. To those fascicles I paid attention, and I tried to pick out which was actually that part of the great nerve that was drawn downwards. Then, when I was holding each of the two nerves in one hand, I saw that when I drew upwards the portion of the great nerve, the recurrent nerve stretched downwards to the thorax. And now, as I saw clearly that I had discovered and reached the right conclusion regarding the portion of the great nerve that is about to go recurrently upwards, and that I had solved the problem, I separated off that portion of it and secured it with a thread, by means of which I ligatured it by itself alone. And then I saw that the animal immediately had [retained] only one half of its [normal] voice. Next I loosened the thread and com- *268*
menced going upwards with the intention of separating off that portion of the great nerve that lies opposite the recurrent nerve. However, I did not go up beyond the position of the branch which breaks off and goes to the larynx [*N. laryngeus superior*]. The reason was that I found here that the whole nerve was formed into a compact and firm structure whose unity and interlacement it was hard to separate and unravel. After that, I left this (the right) side and I set about carrying out the same work on the left side. I did not, however, hope for the same [success] as on the right, because of the remoteness of the positions of the bends and looping of the [left] recurrent nerve, which on this side is inclined over the principal artery [*aortic arch*] near the heart. And as now the circumstances did not favour my persistent endeavours I saw that I should certainly not succeed unless I employed the following device, which I will here describe. After I had fully reflected from the great nerve all the ensheathing fascial tissue lying upon it, until nothing remained over with the sole exception of the special unmixed nervous substance, that is, the substance of which I explained to you that it takes its origin from the brain, I then went on to find out which portion of this [the left side] nerve was the analogue and the opposite number of the nerve which I had previously dissected on the right side and of which I had completed my study. And after I had identified this portion, the opposite number to that [other] nerve, I separated it off from the great nerve by itself alone, and secured it by means of a ligature. When I knew for certain that I had attained and

had found the object of my search I was at once extremely glad. Then,
269 when I had made this manipulation, I repeated it many times. On a few occasions I make mistakes, because the proceeding is in itself difficult, and gives trouble in connection with the discovery and the searching out [of the parts desired]. And since that is so, then if once, twice or thrice you too miss your objective in that, you must not despair, but hope that you will succeed the next time. So do not shun making these experiments, and do not interrupt or abandon them. It is indeed shameful and disgraceful that everyone is accustomed to bring themselves to voyage across the great expanses of the sea for the sake of wealth, and thereby to endure very great hardships, but as regards the knowledge and the understanding of the nature of things, it is their custom not to undertake the repetition of the same task time after time, unless there is some money to be got by that.

CHAPTER 8. EXPERIMENTS ON THE MUSCLES OF THE LARYNX.

But now I base myself on the assumption that this has been done, and I will begin on another type of operation. First, though, I must remind you of something which I have frequently stated in various works: namely, that it makes no difference in destroying any activity belonging to the voluntary movements, whether you cut across, with an incision running transversely, the whole muscle which causes that movement, or if you divide the nerve of that muscle. And it is just the same as regards severing the tendon which grows out from the muscle. For the disability which results from that cross-cutting of any one of these three is the same. After we have pointed this out, and called your attention to it, now ascertain wherever it is possible for you to cut across the muscle, and then set your hand to its division. Admittedly this will not always be possible for you. Thus, for example, take what you will encounter among the laryngeal muscles. For you are not in
270 a position to cut across the musculature found in the cavity of the larynx without perforating the whole of it. But you can cut across the musculature lying upon it externally and enveloping it. When you learn this you can first divide the nerve [*external laryngeal*] of the muscle which is common to the oesophagus and to the larynx [*M. thyro-*

pharyngeus] and thereupon you can satisfy yourself as to the sort of modification of the voice that ensues. Subsequently you can also investigate this by cutting through the muscle itself. For as the consequence of the cutting across of one of the other muscles, the voice is not destroyed, nor does it disappear entirely. On the contrary, it will only be totally destroyed and cut off when that musculature is cut across of which we spoke previously and said that it opens and closes the larynx, that is, the musculature in which alone the recurrent nerve distributes itself. The damage which affects the voice, and the change which it suffers, is in proportion to the importance of the function of the muscles to which the damage occurs. We have already spoken of these functions in the work 'On the Voice' and in the work 'On the Uses of the Parts of the Body'.

Should that muscle whose head comes from the oesophagus and whose attachment and insertion is on the thyroid cartilage be paralysed and its movement lost, or should it be cut, this changes the voice in a certain manner, but nevertheless does not entirely destroy it. For the action of this muscle is only to draw the thyroid cartilage towards the oesophagus, and when the muscle draws it, this cartilage will be brought up to the second cartilage [*cricoid*], which it then overlaps and to which it adheres. It constricts the larynx, grasping this firmly by means of its sides. And now, when the nerve is cut which supplies this muscle, or when either of these two muscles be cut in two transversely, whether it be on the right side or the left side of the body, then the one which has not been cut across draws the larynx across towards the side opposite
to that on which the muscle has incurred the injury. One side of the *271*
cartilage, where the muscle is involved in the injury, remains, then, slack and bereft of movement. And when the nerve[s] on both sides are cut across, then the thyroid cartilage remains in an intermediate state of inclination, and each of its two sides will become slacker than is the case in their natural condition, and slacker also than is the case when the injury affected one nerve only. If you cut across the muscles on both sides, with an incision which goes right through them, then the thyroid cartilage assumes the highest degree of slackness and immobility. When that happens, as soon as the animal tries to make a sound those parts of the larynx which lie in front expand. And this

affects the depth of the voice, without, however, destroying and suppressing it. If you turn over the whole larynx a little after an injury of that kind has already befallen that muscle, you can then inflict an injury on its hinder musculature [*Mm. cricoarytenoidei*] by which the glottis is opened, and you can do so in one of two ways. For you can either divide the branch of the upwardly recurrent nerve that goes to it, or you can cut through the muscles themselves. These lie on the second cartilage, and when that muscle which connects the oesophagus with the thyroid cartilage [*M. thyropharyngeus*] has been detached and taken away, then those muscles [*Mm. cricoarytenoidei*] will be brought into view. But if you do not first turn over the larynx as described, then they will not be brought into view. As for the third cartilages [*right and left arytenoid cartilages*], on these you cannot inflict an injury in the same way as it could be inflicted on the thyroid cartilage or on the cricoid cartilage, unless you divide the nerve and not the musculature itself. That is because the principal mass of the musculature projects into the thoroughfare of the channel through the larynx
272 [*thyroarytenoid and lateral cricoarytenoid muscles*]. Were it possible to inflict an injury on these muscles as well as on those which lie behind, then as soon as that was done the larynx would come to a standstill, and no muscles would act upon it, with the sole exception of those which close and cover it over from within. One of two things would then be bound to happen. Either the voice of the animal would be damaged by this in the highest degree, or else the animal would be completely asphyxiated. That this account is entirely correct you will well understand if you remind yourself of what we said in the work 'On the Muscular Movements', in which we demonstrated that when the [contractile] movement is cut off and lost in one of two groups of muscles, of which one is opposed to and set over against the other, should this affect the muscle group that opens up some feature of the body and is responsible for this task, then that feature will be distorted by [the action of] the muscle which closes it and dragged towards this muscle. It will then remain fixed in that shape without relaxing from it.

If now, moreover, you injure the nerve of that muscle which attaches the lower part of the thyroid cartilage to the cricoid cartilage [*M. cricothyroideus*], the injury and the damage which the voice meets with is of

a very small degree. That is to say, the larynx will become more flabby in this section. And we have already said that when it becomes flabbier it broadens out and expands. When this happens, there comes about, as the necessary sequel, a lowering of the voice. And if you deprive of movement the upper laryngeal musculature and cut it transversely, that also causes the larynx to broaden out and expand. When I say 'the upper musculature', I mean that of which we have taught that its origin arises from the rib [*greater cornu*] of the hyoid bone, and that its attachment and ingrowth is on the thyroid cartilage [*M. thyrohyoideus*]. This is the muscle which we have also mentioned previously where we described the anatomy of the larynx and of the hyoid bone. Now just
as this muscle draws upwards the thyroid cartilage and, by means of *273*
traction upon this, draws up the larynx also, so the one which goes from the thyroid cartilage to the breastbone [*M. sternothyroideus*] draws downwards the thyroid cartilage and the larynx. And damage and injury take place only in correlation with the service performed by each individual muscle. This is a point which you must remember as being of universal application.

CHAPTER 9. THE CERVICAL AND THORACIC PARTS OF THE SYMPATHETIC TRUNK.

When you have studied the details of the larynx, it still remains for you to examine that nerve which is left over in the neck from those which descend from the brain downwards. This is the nerve [*sympathicus*] which emerges in the canal [*carotid*] which traverses the petrosal bone. It so happens in regard to this nerve that already at its origin it is blended with other nerves, as we have described, and it is secured by fascial sheaths, which are common to all of them. Consequently one immediately believes of this nerve that it is a branch of the sixth pair. There is a peculiarity which distinguishes it alone, namely a small structure which is formed on it [*sympathetic ganglion*] which resembles the firm consolidated structure [*ganglion*] that forms on nerves [? *tendons*]. For this nerve is small, and when you examine it you believe that it has now increased in thickness and become larger through the addition of this structure which resembles that firm consolidated body. For you do not see that this grows on to another as a separate structure.

That is to say that when you scrape off this structure you are not in a position to leave the nerve by itself in its proper condition, but you believe that what resembles a firm consolidated structure on it grew from it, out of the thickness and density of the whole substance of the nerve. Now this condensation is something which occurs to this nerve at the commencement of the neck, and again further down at its end in the region at which the nerve runs into the thorax. It may be imagined that in each one of those sections when it has been affected
274 by this thickening the nerve becomes thicker than it was in the preceding section.

This nerve [*sympathetic trunk*] travels downwards into the thorax, extends on to the roots of the ribs, and blends itself with the nerves of the intercostal spaces. Should you wish to see how it interweaves itself, you can do so by the following type of operation. From each individual rib, whichever it may be, detach the surrounding structures, and let the detachment take place at those of their parts at which this nerve, of which we speak, appears stretched out in the longitudinal direction of the animal's body, over the ribs. You can denude and clear the ribs either from the ventral aspects, in which case you are removing the sheath which applies itself closely to them internally, or else from the lateral structures, where you remove the intercostal muscles. Finally, you can clear them from the external outwardly lying parts, by removing the muscles of the vertebral column. In the whole of this task you must go to work with the greatest care and precaution, so that you avoid cutting through any portions of the two nerves of which you wish to examine the interlacement and anastomosis. For you will find that all the nerves of the intercostal spaces [*Nn. intercostales*] blend themselves, in one and the same manner, with that nerve which travels from above downwards. Thus when you remove, from around the ribs, all that is found in the neighbourhood of the nerves, and you clear this away until the rib becomes visible and you see it together with the nerve alone exposed to view, at this stage you also will find what we have previously found: that is, that the nerve running downwards from the neck [*sympathetic trunk*] joins with each of the nerves between the ribs and blends with them.

So now, just as when you clear away from the inner parts on each

one of the ribs the membrane which applies itself to their inner surfaces
you see that nerve which comes from the brain passing on and travelling
from above downwards, in the same way you will find on the outer
parts of each individual rib a small nerve stretched out which joins and 275
connects the two nerves in every two intercostal spaces. And if you
wish to obtain a more complete and clearer view of the reciprocal
association of the two nerves, then take hold of the root of the rib
which you have denuded, and move it slightly, so that you can see
clearly the joint between it and the vertebra, in order that here you can
cut through the ligament which surrounds and enfolds it. If you do
this properly, you can detach the rib without damaging or cutting
through any part of the nerves. And when you have detached the rib,
you see the anastomosis of the nerves with one another in the form of
an annular figure, since each of the two nerves in the adjacent intercostal spaces attaches itself to two other nerves, and combines and unites
with both of them. One of these two nerves lies on the ventral, the other
on the dorsal parts, though the nerve which lies ventrally descends from
the brain, but the external [dorsal] nerve takes its origin and has its commencement exactly in that place. It does not, however, branch off from
either one of the two anastomosing nerves, but it is as it were a third
entity, which has a substance peculiar to itself. Such a reciprocal association as this you may see also in the nerves of the axilla, among many
of their branches, and there you will see a third nerve stationing itself
transversely between the two others which combine with one another
frequently, without the mass of either of them increasing or decreasing.
That is something which takes place in all nerves which divide up, 276
since the nerve-stem from which another nerve branches off diminishes,
and the bulk which it originally possessed becomes smaller. The degree
of its reduction, its diminution, corresponds to the size of that nerve
which breaks away from it. But as for the nerve which passes over to
another and combines, blends and connects with it, you will see that
it increases the size of the nerve with which it combines and connects.
And it does that in proportion to its own mass. On this analogy, when
two nerves are bound together through the medium of a third nerve,
and it does not appear that they have become lesser or greater than
before, then you must regard the nerve that intervenes between the

other two, and is shared by them, as no more than a ligament for them. And since that is so, you will see that in the parts where you observe a slender nerve travelling and covering a wide track without becoming supported or fastened, this other common associated nerve is more properly a ligament for the neighbouring structures. When those parts on which this nerve travels find themselves in incessant movement, in that case it will require even more in the way of support and security, and consequently such a ligament will serve to secure it firmly. And since we see that the substance of the nerve descending from the brain and traversing the roots of the ribs neither gains nor loses in size, then the most appropriate thing to say about it is that it interlaces itself with the intercostal nerves, without either giving anything to, or receiving anything from them. Thus the path which this nerve follows in the thorax is of the kind into which you now have had an insight. But as
277 to how it associates itself with the nerves of the sixth pair, and with the nerves sprouting out from the lumbar vertebrae when it has passed beyond the thorax, that you can see and observe in the discussion on which we will embark after first having moved on to the great nerve, which is the nerve of the sixth pair.

CHAPTER 10. THE VAGUS NERVE AND THE SYMPATHETIC TRUNK IN THE ABDOMEN.

After it has passed beyond the heart, this nerve [*vagus*] encircles the oesophagus, places itself continuously alongside it, and is, as it were, bound up together with it. And when it has travelled further with it, it joins the mouth [*oesophageal orifice*] of the stomach and infiltrates it, so that this part attains such a high degree of nervous sensibility and of relationship with the components of the nervous system that it is pre-eminent above all the other bodily parts in this respect, and for this reason it possesses a surplus of sensitiveness. From this nerve, which reaches to the mouth of the stomach, small branches go also to the whole of the stomach, and thus the chief part of this nerve-pair, as I have described, remains on the stomach, but the rest, that part of it which is left over, blends itself with the nerve of which we have spoken already, that is, the one which traverses the thorax to the roots of the ribs [*sympathetic trunk*], and with one after another of those nerves which take their outflow from the lumbar vertebrae. Then it distributes itself to all the abdominal viscera, that is, the bodily organs in the abdomen below the diaphragm, and to the intestine.

I will here summarise for you how to obtain an adequate survey of the distribution of this nerve also. From the ensiform or xiphoid cartilage carry a single incision in a straight line onwards, so that it reaches the meeting-place [*symphysis*] of the two pubic bones. Then when you uncover the intestines and bring out the stomach together with them, so that you can see the course of the greatest artery [*aorta*] on the mid-line of the vertebrae, you will find here the suspensory band of the intestine [*root of the mesentery*], as it comes forwards to the vascular tissue surrounding the intestine. The tissue of this suspensory band is the same as that of a ligament, and its place of origin is on the vertebrae following the diaphragm. Here also you will find a single branch of the greatest artery [*aorta*] without an opposite vessel, and its place of origin is on the front aspect. This branch descends with *278*
the suspensory band of the intestine and divides into two portions. Often you will find at its commencement two roots, of which the first borders on the second, at the front aspect of the aorta. Whatever may be the origin of this branch, and whatever the way in which it first emerges (that is, whether it arises in two halves, or is single) it does divide into two branches after it has travelled a little further onwards. One part of it takes the direction of the stomach, of the liver and the spleen [*coeliac artery*] and distributes itself together with the veins that are in these places. The other part [*superior mesenteric artery*] distributes itself to both the viscera, I mean the right and the left. With this we have already dealt. Here it is enough for you if I make this one point. It is that when the arteries have come with the suspensory band of the mesentery, and commence their distribution in the mesentery, at that precise place you will find the nerve which comes off from the one already mentioned [*sympathetic trunk*] distributing itself with the arteries to all the coils of the intestine and to their inward parts. When you have seen that, now is the time for you to remove the whole of the intestine, leaving behind the mesenteries. You can only carry out this removal by detaching and removing from the intestines the covering which surrounds them outwardly, a sheath which, as we have previously described, is connected

with the peritoneum. In this manner also the butchers separate off the intestines, which are attached to the vertebral column. But in order that you may more surely and clearly become acquainted with the combining and unification of the nerves with one another, you must also remove the stomach. And when you have uncovered these parts and they have thus been clearly displayed, then you will see those nerve branches which go to the liver and the spleen. Those branches are very small. After them you see the branches which come to the mesentery. But as for the branches which go to the two kidneys, the greatest part of these proceed from the nerve [*sympathetic trunk*] which goes to the thorax, and combines and unites with other nerves, that is, with those which we mentioned shortly before [*Nn. intercostales*]. This, then, as
279 I have described it, is the distribution of the nerve coming from the brain. But to all other bodily parts go nerves that arise from the spinal cord. And in the book next following I will describe the anatomy of these nerves.

The end of the Fourteenth Book of Galen's work on Anatomy. To God be his due of praise. Blessing be to Muhammed the Prophet, his family and his companions.

BOOK XV

THE SPINAL NERVES

In the name of God, the compassionate, the merciful. The Fifteenth Book of the writing of Galen on Anatomical Dissection.

CHAPTER I. INTRODUCTION. EXPOSURE OF SUPERFICIAL NERVES AND MUSCLES OF THE NECK.

Galen says: when surgeons speak of pairs of nerve roots, they apply the *280*
name not only to those pairs of nerves arising from the brain, but also to the paired nerves growing out from the spinal cord, since the nerve roots are found on both sides, I mean on the right side and on the left. For branches break off either from the brain itself or from the spinal cord itself and become firmer and more dense, being braced together, and consequently they become different from the root from which they took origin. The texture of the spinal cord is just the same as that of the brain from which it starts out, but it is more indurated than the brain tissue. The degree of increase in this induration corresponds to the degree in which the nerve arising from the spinal cord is more indurated than the cord itself. It makes no difference to the exposition of Anatomy which we have in mind whether, considering the nerves arising from the spinal cord which we propose to mention here, we name the spinal cord according to the customary usage of the Greek language 'vertebral marrow', or simply 'marrow'. For Plato applies the term 'marrow' to the spinal cord, which he calls 'vertebral marrow', and to the brain also, which he calls 'cranial marrow'. It is clear that he uses this term (marrow, I mean) of every soft delicate substance which bones envelop. But the nature of this substance is not uniform. For the cranial marrow, that is, the brain, and the vertebral marrow, that is, the spinal cord, are the origin and root of all the nerves in the body. But as for the marrow *281*
contained in the bones, no nerve takes its origin from that. Between the two, furthermore, there exists this contrast, that you when you boil the bones you find, after the cooking, the bone-marrow very swollen

and sweet, whereas in the cranial marrow, that is, the brain, and in the vertebral marrow, that is, the spinal cord, that [alteration] is not found. However we allow free choice in the matter of names, so let everyone use whichever he pleases. But you know that these bodily organs of animals to which we apply the term 'nerves' absolutely, and which other surgeons call 'sensory nerves' or 'voluntary nerves', all take their origins from the brain and the spinal cord. In the preceding Book we have already dealt with all the nerves arising from the brain, and now we shall speak of those which take their origin from the spinal cord.

In Book IV we have already pointed out how one must reflect and detach the skin surrounding the cervical region. And I said that deep to the skin there are attached two attenuated muscles, united in one, which are spread out beneath it [*M. platysma myoides*], and further that our predecessors used to reflect both the skin and these muscles together. Consequently they did not recognise their existence. Whoever prefers not to call them two muscles can call them the muscular carpet. And, further, I said that you can dissect these muscles in either of two ways. One method is for you to remove them together with the skin, till you reach the spinous processes of the vertebrae, where the broad fascial ligament begins which the two muscles cover. The other method allows you to leave this thinned out muscle *in situ*, connected with the body of the animal, one muscle on each side, on the right and on the left. You then detach the skin from it, reflecting it and setting it free. I have spoken already, in the fourth book, of the nerves of this muscle,
282 and I have described how you must grasp and ligature them, seeking to preserve them as you reflect and invert them in the direction of the spinal cord, when you cut through the muscle. Similarly in Book IV, with reference to the nerves on either side of the neck, that is, the nerves of this muscular carpet, I remarked that you must secure them with a ligature and protect and preserve them in order that after you have dissected away the muscular tissue you may study the origin of every single one of these nerves, which anatomists are also accustomed to call 'roots', while others call these roots and origins, the branches.

It was our intention in that dissection which we expounded there to preserve the muscular carpet in its [natural] condition as a single sheet

without any gap in it, in order to instruct ourselves thoroughly on its whole nature, and to understand its functional activity. Now, however, our object and intention is to protect these nerves in their continuity from any damage or injury. We proceed thus to dissect away and to divide the muscular carpet, in which we see all these several nerves travelling, or on which we see them mounted. Of these nerves many are slender, and particularly in the ape, since in this animal all the cervical nerves are slender, and because that muscle where these nerves are distributed is small and feeble. So now with a sharp scalpel you must fully reflect the skin from the fascia adherent to it, so that this latter remains attached to the body of the animal, expanded and encircling the neck, the skin alone having been detached and reflected, *283*
without any portion of the other substances [tissues] remaining attached to it, neither fascial tissue, nor vascular tissue, nor nervous tissue. On your first attempt, content yourself with exposing only one of the two sides of the neck, the right or the left, whichever you please, in order that that thin subcutaneous muscle may be made visible, and that you may inspect the whole of it thoroughly, as I described it in the fourth book. If you accomplish that successfully and correctly, you will see there many minute veins, some forming arachnoid structures, and others capillaries, and all of them lying superficially. On that fascia you will further see the special nerves of the muscular 'carpet', and those which travel in it and emerge from it to reach the head. One part travels from the side of the neck as far as the head, as though it was making for the auricle, towards its front and back aspects [*great auricular nerve*], and another runs from behind towards the vertebral spinous processes as far as the head [*great occipital nerve*]. Thus the auricle has two nerves on each side, the right as well as the left. You may wish to restrict yourself to seeing clearly how this [last] nerve runs upwards, but you should also follow it up in its distribution. So reflect the whole of the skin of the head encircling the auricle as far as the hinder portions which extend upwards to the highest part of the skull and downwards to what is known as the 'nuchal' region and the occiput. To do this will prove very easy for you, for there is no problem here of the kind which you meet in the operation which you have to perform when you reflect the muscular carpet. That is because the muscular carpet is attached to the

skin covering it, but the whole of the upper part of the skin lying upon the head can be freed from what underlies it by peeling it off with very little effort. When you have reflected this you will see that, of the two
284 dorsal branches [nervous], one slender one runs straight upwards in a longitudinal course so as to reach the uppermost region of the head, and that the other branch courses obliquely and reaches the auricle between the two nerves of which we have just spoken. Stretch both of these two branches upwards, and clear away the fascia bound up with them, over which the nerve travels upwards in its ascending course. At this stage ascertain where the nerve first emerges from the deeper structures to the skin. You will see that it comes out near the spines of the vertebrae, because it travels in the upper part of the muscular carpet and in the muscles lying deep to this, that is to say, the muscles with which we dealt in Book IV of this work.[1]

The first of these muscles, of which there is one on each side, originates from the transverse line of the occipital bone. I have learnt that its end is attached to the whole of the spine of the scapula and is also connected to an upper part of the clavicle. As for the second muscle, which lies below this, it extends from the very narrow point of its origin on the occiput to the base of the scapula. There follow two other muscles which originate from the whole of the occipital bone. One of these two, which underlies the muscles we mentioned previously, has a single division. The other, which lies below it, has in general two divisions, and sometimes three. With regard to these muscles I have learnt that they incline the head backwards, together with the whole of the neck. These two nerves, then, penetrate the whole of this musculature and pass on to the spinous process of the vertebrae. When
285 you remove the muscles, you can get a good view of the nerves and see each of them at their very first origin, of which we shall speak later.

[1] This is a truly difficult section. There is evidence that Galen had actually described the nerves Great Auricular, Lesser Occipital, and Great Occipital, but the text as handed down and translated (perhaps more than once) may have suffered if any translator was not personally and fully acquainted with anatomy. The present version suggests that Galen was well acquainted with the general disposition of the cervical muscles and nerves, but a literal translation cannot be said to be free from ambiguity, especially, perhaps, in regard to the lesser and greater occipital nerves. It conveys an impression of personal investigation of dissected animals—and contrasts with the 'text-book' reproductions so characteristic of a certain type of examinee!

But before you extract and remove these muscles which we mentioned...[1] the rearwards course of this nerve lies between these small muscles that move the head-joint alone. There are four of these muscles on each of the two sides, I mean the right and the left. Since this is as I have described it, if you want to study thoroughly the whole of the distribution of the nerves springing from the spinal column, you must first dissect the muscles mentioned here, together with all the other muscles placed both at the side and at the anterior portion of the neck. If you do that, you will see on both sides a single muscle joining and connecting the head and the first vertebra. In the same way you will see two other muscles on each side in the anterior positions, one going a trifle obliquely from the skull bone to the first vertebra, and the other extended beneath the muscle which is at the front of the neck. You will also see the muscle which connects the second and first vertebrae from both sides, one on each side, and the two muscles which go from the head to the second vertebra. One of these is oblique and the other runs straight in a lengthwise direction, and is also connected to the anterior neck muscles.

CHAPTER 2. THE FIRST AND SECOND CERVICAL NERVES.

Now act on the assumption that these things which I have described for you have been prepared and got ready in the way which I showed you. For in the account on which I am beginning, of the dissection of
the nerves springing from the spinal cord, I am basing myself on the *286*
assumption that this has been prepared and arranged. I say, then, that you will observe that the structure of the bodies of the animals with whose organic parts you have a sound acquaintance as a result of your dissections resembles the structure of the human body in some degree. Of some of these animals, though, it was previously thought that their nature is separated widely from that of Man, as for example the classes of Birds, Fishes, Snakes, Worms, Wasps, Midges, Flies, Fleas and all other similar creatures whose structure is not known because of their small size. By conjecture, however, we can assume that these also are, as it were, related to those other animals, as we see that all of them have sensory organs placed in their heads, and we observe that their position

[1] Lacuna in the Arabic. M.C.L.

is precisely the same as that in which they lie in all the other animals. Similarly we see that they possess a thorax, feet [limbs] and bodily organs through which their excreta and evacuations pass out. But a profound knowledge of what lies within their body cavity is impossible to attain since one cannot dissect them because of their small size. But there is evident and clear proof that it is through the operation of a single source of wisdom, which concerned itself with them, that all the bodily parts of animals have been built up and created. We must then try to learn the conformation of that which is hard to observe in any one type of animal, whichever this may be, in other animals where that can be found and thoroughly investigated, I mean those animals in which such details are in their nature larger and more massive than those which in this [smaller] type are hard to see. Thus for example in the body of Man, in that of the ape and in those of all other similar animals the first vertebra is very small. And so also is their second vertebra in
287 correspondence with the first. But in bears, dogs, lions and wolves, and in general in those animals which have interlocking teeth, the first vertebra is very massive, and the others also large. In the bodies of horned animals the first vertebra is likewise large, although their nerves do not possess the same strength and massiveness as those of the animals with interlocking teeth. And therefore I have set myself to study these two first vertebrae in the bodies of those large-sized animals, and in the bodies of dogs, lions, and the other animals which belong to this class, because the great size of these two vertebrae, and the measure of the strength and size of the nerves, make it easy for the truth about them to be ascertained by those who concern themselves with their investigation. For as regards the majority of those who have written works on anatomy for us, I think that they simply wanted to become known by their writings to a great number of people, and desired that their reputation might be enhanced, not that they might extract and discover the truth. If you yourself investigate these animals which, because of the bulky dimensions of the first vertebra, have muscles there of great size joined by nerves of corresponding size, and if you first acquire a thorough knowledge and understanding of them and remember the sites in which the nerves arise and their course, then you will be able to recognise these in the bodies of apes as well.

After the muscle which covers the dorsal aspect of the cervical vertebrae has been dissected away, those muscles present themselves which move the joint of the head by itself, and which are arranged between it [the skull] and the first and second vertebrae as a triangular figure on either side, I mean on the right and left sides. And in the centre *288*
of the three sides of the triangle a small nerve can be seen which distributes itself to the muscles which we have mentioned [*sub-occipital nerve*, a branch of the *first cervical*]. If you detach and remove these muscles, you then see also a fourth very small muscle [*rectus capitis posterior minor*] coming from the skull and attaching itself to the first vertebra. To this muscle there also proceeds a branch from that nerve, one of whose branches is distributed to [each of] the four muscles we have mentioned. The other branch [*anterior primary ramus*] inclines obliquely backwards, passes through the foramen[1] at the side of the first vertebra, and distributes itself in the small muscles which lie on both sides of the joint [*right and left atlanto-occipital joints*] and to those of the anteriorly placed muscles which are, so to speak, placed opposite to the eight small posteriorly placed muscles we have already mentioned. On the first vertebra there are those other foramina in the processes which are on its two sides, and these are the foramina which are found only on the six upper vertebrae, present here just as in the other vertebrae [*foramina transversaria*]. There are on it [*the first vertebra*] four other foramina also, [only] two of which are found in apes, and two [others] in other animal orders. But one pair of them [the latter pair], namely those which are found in all [most] animals, is directed upwards, conceals itself and is covered over in the grooves which are placed in the first vertebra and which are entered by the processes of the skull situated there. Many [anatomists] among the Greeks call these processes by a noun 'korōna' which is neither masculine nor feminine. Others designate them by a feminine noun pronounced in the same way but spelt differently. And others call them the mastoid processes. But so far as the other pair of foramina is concerned, each is narrower, and each component occupies its place at the side of the vertebra

[1] Not the vertebrarterial foramen but one formed over the posterior arch of the Atlas by the ossification of the falciform margin of the posterior atlanto-occipital ligament—a foramen rare in Homo, but constant in lower mammalia. See text, p. 230.

289 [*vertebrarterial foramen*]. Both these foramina lie below the two upper ones composing the other pair.[1]

Now the nerves spring from the vertebral column on either side, I mean on the right and the left. Then each nerve divides immediately into two unequal portions, and is distributed to the muscles situated around the joint. And since the muscles lying behind the joint are more numerous and of greater dimensions, it is there that the larger branch breaks up and disappears. The other [smaller branch] wends its way obliquely to the side, and enters the pair of foramina there which we have mentioned, that is, the pair which it traverses and outpasses. And each of the two branches of the nerve reaches the small muscles on either side of this joint, and similarly extends to that muscle which alone holds the joint on the anterior parts. At this same spot this nerve blends and unites itself also with the second pair of nerves arising from the spinal cord, and with other nerve-pairs descending from the brain. The blending and union of this nerve do not always take place in one and the same manner in the six classes of animals, nor is its state in its blending and union one and the same in all the varieties of every class, just as it is not one and the same in every individual member of all the varieties of these classes. That is because things are so created that these nerves are bound to one another only because of the security and protection which that affords. That is done in some instances because the nerves are small, sometimes because they are soft and delicate, sometimes because they extend themselves over a great distance, and sometimes because they are entrusted with powerful and strenuous activities. Again, the blending and union of a nerve with part of another, or of part of it with the whole of another, does not constantly take
290 place in precisely the same way. It happens, in my view, in the way which nature finds to be the least burdensome and the easiest, being arranged and established in the most appropriate manner. So you find that those parts in which it makes no difference whether this one takes precedence over that, or that over the former, have not the same struc-

[1] The text suggests that Galen was used to tracing the foramen in the transverse process as from below the transverse process, then tracing it up to the upper border of the process and upper surface of the posterior arch where the first pair of foramina, formed by the roofing over of the groove, is found. The relative positions—upper and lower—as described above in Galen's text are made intelligible by this suggestion.

ture in all animals. Since this is so, do you bear it in mind and remember it in regard to all nervous unions and blendings which you will see. For it is a consideration which applies to them all in common. But now let us commence again with what we originally intended to discuss. We say that we most frequently find that pair of foramina of the first vertebra which we cited in those animals in which certain of the teeth interlock with certain others. After these we may expect to find it in other animals whose first vertebra is of large size. But as for those whose first vertebra is small, you may in rare cases find the vertebra imperforate, although even when the first vertebra is not perforated at both sides [over the posterior arch], the distribution of the nerves in such animals also is one and the same. And in fact the one branch of the nerve, that is, the larger of the two [*posterior primary ramus*], divides and ramifies in the muscles lying posteriorly to the joint, and the other smaller branch [*anterior primary ramus*] goes to the two sides and to the anterior regions adjacent to the end of the groove in which the processes [*occipital condyles*] of the cranial bones project. For as the muscles which lie posteriorly to the joint number eight in all, four on the left side, and four on the right side, and all are small, it happens that each of the two nerves ramifies and breaks up into three branches which
are similar to each other. But as regards that muscle which connects *291*
the transverse process of the first vertebra with the posterior [spinous] process of the second vertebra [*M. obliquus capitis inferior*], this nerve prolongs itself so as to reach one half of it. But for the remaining part of this muscle, which springs from the first vertebra and extends to the second, a nerve runs to it from the second pair. And usually you find that the terminal twigs of the two nerves which we have mentioned are combined and united together.

Of the nerves of the second pair of those arising from the spinal cord.[1] In their writings the skilled anatomists discuss the second pair of nerves arising from the spinal cord as though it was the first pair. That is because they do not correctly know either its origin or its point of emergence, or that it is posteriorly situated, and that it traverses a foramen in the vertebra. Thus in the conformation of both these pairs of nerves alike there occurs something which distinguishes them, and

[1] Probably a later addition, by translator or scribe. B.T.

which is found in no others of the remaining pairs of nerves of which the spinal cord is the origin and root. As for the first of these two pairs, it happens that its ascent and exit leads it through two foramina in the first vertebra, which [foramina] are not present in any of the remaining vertebrae. As for the second pair, it emerges below the first vertebra, without traversing a constant foramen. The second pair is of larger dimensions than the first, and one of its two branches is distributed to the muscles which lie on both sides and on the posterior [*dorsal*] aspect of the neck. For the first vertebra next to the second has a characteristic peculiar to itself alone, that is, the presence of muscles on each side [*R. and L. M. rectus capitis lateralis, and M. obliquus superior*]. This is something which none of the other vertebrae possesses. But as for the muscle [*M. rectus capitis anterior*] which comes from the skull and is attached to the anterior parts of it, you see in other animals in which the first vertebra is large that there is a linear marking which bounds
292 it and which singles it out by passing exactly round it. Whoever has accustomed himself to recognise that marking on it will find it. In the bodies of apes, this muscle on the anterior aspect blends with others and is hard to distinguish. In apes that muscle also is small which connects both sides of the first vertebra with the second [*M. obliquus capitis inferior*].

Throughout the whole of this muscle, branches of the second nerve-pair divide up and ramify, after it has come to the front. And this [the anterior division of the nerve] unites again with the nerves on the anterior aspect of the neck, but not however in one and the same fashion in all the animals of one class. Again, a small branch from the posterior division of this pair of nerves passes to the muscle [*M. rectus capitis posterior major*] connecting the hinder [spinous] process of the second vertebra with the skull. One can very often find that the muscle [*M. rectus capitis posterior minor*] connecting the first vertebra with the skull receives a twig from this nerve. That can most often be seen clearly in the lion especially. In the apes, however, all the nerves which contribute to this musculature are slight and attenuated, and it is difficult to see them. Moreover all these nerves, which are of very small size, take their origin from that branch which runs posteriorly from this nerve.

And in all animals this branch is recognisable and visible, and in the bodies of apes it can be seen just as well as in the bodies of other animals. In the other animals also, the path of this nerve leads at first backwards to the neighbourhood of the spinous processes of the vertebrae, and from this place onwards, after it has moved somewhat obliquely, it then climbs upwards and travels in the hinder part of the head, and in its course, till it reaches the uppermost part of the head, it ramifies in the skin and the subjacent scalp-tissues. Its passage, its tunnelling in its devious windings, and its reversed course from the spinous processes of the vertebrae to the head, take place just as in all those other nerves which *293*
are distributed in the muscular carpet [*M. platysma myoides*] of which we have spoken in Book IV of this work. But in those animals in which the temporalis muscle is so large that its origin reaches back as far as the occipital bone, as for instance in the animals with horns and in those with interlocking teeth, there springs a branch from this obliquely directed nerve which ramifies in the superficial parts of this muscle.

We have now submitted a sufficient and ample account of the details relating to the second pair of nerves, and we must take in hand the description of the third pair. But first we must remind you that the muscle [*M. obliquus capitis inferior*] which connects the transverse process of the first vertebra with the hinder process of the second vertebra has, as we said, two muscular 'heads', which are bound together at their ends. One of the two arises at the sides of the first vertebra, and the other particularly at the hinder portion [*spinous process*] of the second vertebra. It has been thought that this muscle employs both these two attachments, which exist between it and these two vertebrae, so that sometimes one acts as though it were its origin, and at other times as though it were its insertion. Thus when this muscle employs its attachment to the first vertebra as its insertion, it turns the first vertebra backwards towards the second, and when it employs its attachment as though it were its origin and place of commencement, it draws the second vertebra obliquely forwards towards the first.

CHAPTER 3. THE THIRD AND FOURTH CERVICAL NERVES.

Of the third pair of nerves arising from the spinal cord.[1] The third pair of nerves arising from the spinal cord passes through and emerges from the foramen which lies on both sides and which is the foramen common
294 to the second and third vertebrae, just as the other pairs of nerves emerge. This common foramen, which is completely circular in shape, originates between the two vertebrae, each one of which contributes one half of its circumference, as we have already described in the book in which we dealt with the bones. Of the two branches of this pair, which grow out first, immediately after it has divided, one subdivision makes its way backwards, and the other passes forwards. The branch which passes backwards [*posterior primary ramus*], extends in the direction of the spinous processes of the vertebrae, sends off branches in its course and, becoming arachnoid in form, it reaches the muscle [*M. sternomastoideus*] which is related to the head and the neck alike. These ramifications you will see clearly when you first dissect that muscle itself. Now as soon as the nerve has reached the spinous processes of the vertebrae, it passes beyond the fascial sheath, just as the nerves pass beyond the muscular carpet which accompanies them. It then passes from there beneath the skin obliquely just as though it were making for the auricle. Its path lies in those parts on which the boundary clearly shows itself which runs along the upper margin of the muscular carpet. Thereupon it divides and ramifies here as it distributes itself in the auricular muscles. Moreover a slender twig like an arachnoid filament branches off from it and this reaches as far as the temporalis muscle, that is, in those animals in which because of its great size this muscle extends far backwards.

That branch [*the anterior primary ramus*], however, of the third pair which passes to the anterior parts, blends and unites with the pairs in front of it. And indeed this conjunction and union takes place in any one animal in the same fashion as in another. From this branch there now springs an easily recognisable nerve, which goes in the muscular carpet. And from the whole of this nerve which has combined, as
295 I described previously, there proceeds to the auricle a nerve [*greater*

[1] Probably a scribal addition. B.T.

auricular] of considerable size, and this nerve distributes itself in that muscle [of the auricle] which draws it downwards at the side of the neck and turns it forwards.

By means of its end-branches this nerve often blends and unites with two nerves of another kind [*cranial*]. Of these, one [*the facial nerve*] passes forwards from out of the so called monocular or blind foramen, and this takes its origin from the fifth pair of the nerves arising from the brain. The other [*auriculotemporal nerve*] comes out to the side of the temporomandibular joint, and its origin, unlike the first, is from the third pair of the nerves arising from the brain [*N. trigeminus*]. Of these details we have already spoken in the place in which we dealt with the nerves arising from the brain. So now let us turn back to the discussion of the nerves arising from the spinal cord.

We say that the third pair of these, that is, those with which this discussion is concerned, communicates in these anterior regions which we have been discussing up to this point, with a branch from the sixth pair of nerves which arise from the brain. There belong to this pair on either side three nerves [*glossopharyngeus, vagus, accessorius*] as we have already shown in the place in which we dealt with them. As for this branch of the sixth pair, it is certainly not a nerve such as you could miss or overlook, when you make your dissection after having reflected the muscles around the neck, as I have already recommended to you. It [*N. accessorius*] proceeds to the broad massive muscle, the first of those which run from the head to the shoulder, to become visible beneath the muscular carpet [*M. trapezius* deep to *M. platysma*]. Now from these nerves which mingle with each other there comes out a nerve, and this also joins that muscle which runs from the first vertebra to the anterior part of the scapula. You will often see that the nerve which comes to this muscle does not branch off from this pair but from the *296*
pair following the third vertebra, that is to say the fourth pair of nerves arising from the spinal cord. Similarly too there comes to the muscle which passes downwards to the clavicle, and of which I said that it arises on the hinder parts, a nerve whose origin comes about through the union of the *N. accessorius* sometimes with the nerve following the second vertebra, sometimes with that which follows the third vertebra. In not a few cases it originates from both of these. And likewise you

will also see that nerves join and attach themselves to the arteries and veins that pass upwards from the lower part of the neck to the head. These nerves are some of those that combine below the first and second vertebrae. Here there are strong fascial sheaths clearly visible, which surround the veins and arteries, and in these sheaths you see that the nerves distribute themselves. As for the veins and arteries themselves, you cannot clearly see the conjunction and union of the nerves with them, unless the animal itself is of very large size as for instance the ox, horse, mule, camel or elephant.

Of the fourth pair of nerves arising from the spinal cord.[1] The fourth pair of the nerves arising from the spinal cord emerges between the third and fourth vertebrae through a foramen which is shared in common by both. It is evident and well known that the nerves of this pair are two in number, as are the nerves of the remaining pairs, one on the right, the other on the left side of the animal body. And these two nerves are both equally thick, and the foramina through which each of them passes are of equal size. Likewise each distributes itself to muscles which in size and number are on a par with those to which the
297 other is distributed. It is remarkable to see the agreement and concordance in this identical distribution of these two nerves. And that is something that you will see plainly on all pairs of nerves. Since that is so, you should know also that whatever you observe in a single nerve, no matter to what pair it may belong, you are bound to find the same thing in the other [opposite] nerve. And since that is the case, you can train yourself in dissection on the body of a single animal by giving yourself double practice on each one on the nerve pairs. The more you study each of them, the more will you remember and grasp the position of the nerve, its dimensions, and the muscles to which it is distributed. You need to remember these things because of operations you may attempt to perform in opening up abscesses in the neck and in dealing with neck wounds.

If you now wish to study the actual origin of the nerve, you must divide the vertebra as I have described previously at the end of the ninth book of this work. And if you desire to make sure of the distribution of the nerve from its root onwards, so you must little by little

[1] Probably a scribal addition. B.T.

split and free from it the muscle fibres surrounding it at its origin. These muscles comprise, in front, the muscle [*M. sternomastoideus*] which is common to the neck and the head, and, from behind, not only this, but also in addition the muscles known as the 'vertebral muscles', and, laterally to the origins of the nerves, the muscles which run downwards to the thorax [*Mm. scaleni*]. These are the ones of which I informed you previously that they enlarge the upper parts of the thorax. Also there are given off from this pair, and similarly from all the pairs lying on the neck, branches [arising] close to their sites of origin which pass to the muscle [*M. sternomastoideus*] belonging to the head and the neck in common. Their path to it leads from the anterior and posterior aspects of the neck. From it also, branches go to the vertebral muscles *298*
lying in the neck and to the muscle known as the muscular carpet. For although it is thinned out, a great number of nerves—more, in fact, than corresponds to its mass go to it. Of stouter dimensions than these nerves are those which mount upwards from deeper parts laterally to the vertebrae. There is a nerve for every vertebra, and these are the nerves of which I said that they pierce through and pass into an expanded thin sheet. Of this, when it is invested with fleshy fibrils, the muscular carpet [*M. platysma*] consists.

When all these nerves have travelled laterally until they have reached the [transverse] processes of the vertebrae, there go out from them very slender twigs running obliquely to the muscle common to the neck and the head. For all these twigs are inclined upwards. And after they have overrun the root of that sheet, they also extend over the sheet itself, and connect with the muscular carpet, with which they come to the jaws and cheeks. Furthermore, smaller nerves than these proceed to the muscular carpet from the anterior region from each single vertebra. The path and approach also of these nerves to this muscle conforms to the direction of its fibres, along which the nerves are extended. The stoutest of the nerves which go to the muscle known as the muscular carpet are those which proceed towards it from the intermediately situated nerve-pairs of those emerging from the cervical vertebrae. And it is one of these pairs of which our present demonstration treats. The same happens with the fifth pair and the sixth pair. But as for the small nerves going to it, and which are amongst those that are not identifiable

in all animals, such of them as lie in the lower regions are branches from the seventh and eighth pairs, and those which are in the upper regions are branches from the second and third pairs. But from the first pair, in no kind of animal will you find even the smallest of nerves pro-
299 ceeding outwards. For the muscles which act upon the joint of the first vertebra next the skull lie in the deep region, and similarly the first nerve-pair, since it alone is assigned to these muscles, is completely covered in and concealed in the depths [of the neck] and no branch of it reaches either to the muscle which is common to the neck and the head, or to the skin which envelops both. But from every other one of the cervical nerves a branch comes off to the skin, and its tenuity resembles that of arachnoid filaments.

These, then, are amongst the points which are common to the pairs of nerves found here. With them also are included the branches which go to the anterior and posterior musculature common to the neck and the head, and the branches that go to the musculature of the vertebral column. But together with the characteristics which the fourth pair shares in common with the others, it numbers amongst its peculiarities the fact that a branch runs from it to the muscle which goes to the clavicle [*M. trapezius, clavicular attachment*] and to the muscle [*M. levator scapulae*] which reaches the elevated part of the scapula, the path of which leads from the first vertebra on either side. From the same nerve comes a branch which, after it has passed over this muscle, is distributed to the upper parts of the wide-spread muscle [*M. trapezius*] which passes onwards to the whole of the 'septum' [*spine*] in the middle portion of the scapula. Yet another branch belongs to this, the fourth pair, with which we are dealing. And this is a slender branch which at once diverges from it at its beginning and whose course goes downwards, to the side of the process which borders on the fourth vertebra. This nerve blends and unites with the one whose origin comes after the fourth vertebra, as we shall describe in the discussion which we are about to undertake. Here and there I have seen it blend and unite with the nerve following the fifth vertebra.

CHAPTER 4. THE FIFTH CERVICAL NERVE, AND GENERAL EXPOSURE OF THE BRACHIAL PLEXUS.

On the fifth pair of nerves arising from the spinal cord.[1] The fifth pair *300*
of nerves arising from the spinal cord climbs upwards from the place between the fourth and fifth vertebrae. It has details which it shares with these other pairs of nerves associated with it, and these are the points which we have mentioned. Besides these common characteristics which it shares with others, it possesses some which are peculiar to itself, and it is of these that I wish to speak to you here. I have already said that from the fourth pair a nerve branches off which comes down beside the lateral process of the fourth vertebra. And this nerve unites with the fifth pair, of which it is our intention here to give an account, and blends and unites with it between the two sites of origin of two pairs, namely the origin of this pair of which we are here speaking, that is, the one which comes after the fourth vertebra, and the origin of that pair which comes next after it, that is, the one which, when you number off the pairs from the first of them, is the sixth, of which the site of origin lies between the fifth and the sixth vertebrae. But the nerve which comes to this branch, and of which we wish to give an account, blends and unites with that coming from the preceding pair, so that all these nerves then blend and unite with the branch following the fifth cervical vertebra. That branch is twice as massive as this nerve. And when the two have become merged in one, there branches from them an offshoot which forms the first portion of what, together with others, will afterwards comprise the phrenic nerve. After this branch, the nerve which follows the fifth vertebra breaks up in a way which will be described in what follows. It scarcely ever happens that that nerve which follows the fourth vertebra arrives opposite the diaphragm without joining and uniting with the branch which follows the fifth
vertebra, though this does occur now and then in rare cases. The nerve *301*
is sometimes joined immediately by a small offshoot from the nerve-pair following the sixth vertebra. It may then have an attachment from the pair following the seventh vertebra, or from both together, each contributing a very small piece. For never in any animal have I ever

[1] Probably a scribal addition. B.T.

seen in the phrenic nerve that its root was single and standing alone. On the contrary, I have seen that it has either three roots, or, in any case, two.

Of the sixth, seventh, eighth, and ninth pairs of the nerves arising from the spinal cord.[1] The pairs of nerves arising from the spinal cord which, four in number, follow the pair just mentioned, go to the upper parts of the scapula, and to its hollow excavated portion [the *fossa subscapularis*], to the upper region of the shoulder, and the upper arm. As for the sixth cervical nerve, this follows the fifth cervical vertebra, the seventh follows the sixth vertebra, and the eighth follows the seventh vertebra. And the place of the ninth nerve is within the thorax itself, after the eighth vertebra [i.e. the *first thoracic vertebra*], although some [anatomists] believe that no nerve whatsoever passes from the thorax to the upper limb. Even more than they deny this do they deny that any nerve from after the ninth vertebra goes to the upper limb. Once a man, one of those who are conceited and who boast of their anatomical skill, set about deriding one of our supporters for maintaining that a nerve [*intercostobrachial*] arising in the second intercostal space runs to the upper arm, despite the fact that the uncovering and exposure of this nerve is not difficult, and the same is true of the nerve following it, which emerges from the third intercostal space, and takes the direction towards the axilla. For although each of these two nerves is much
302 more slender than the nerve of the first intercostal space, yet nevertheless it is easier and more simple to make them visible, and to expose them for inspection, when the whole of the structures in and around the axillary cavity are properly cleared away and removed. From your dissection you must now exclude the muscle which the anatomists have overlooked, that is, the one which ascends from the flank to the shoulder joint [*M. latissimus dorsi*]. It is of the class of the fasciae and is delicate. Consequently, since the anatomists were accustomed to reflect it together with the skin, they did not recognise it. But as for you, let your dissection of it proceed here in the opposite manner to that which I described for you in the fifth book of this work. That is to say, there the best course was for you to commence from below, and then work upwards towards the head of the upper arm, passing in the axillary

[1] Probably a scribal addition. B.T.

cavity, where a wide tendon begins to take its origin from the muscle. But in the operation which we have in hand here, it is best for you to start from above and then to move downwards. Thus you first divide the tendon of the muscle, then with one hand you draw forwards and downwards the entire muscle with its tendon, and with the other hand, using a sharp scalpel but restricting the cutting, you incise the fascial tissues through which this muscle is attached to the underlying parts. Now proceed there very deliberately in consideration of the arteries and the veins which join and are connected with this muscle. For it often happens, when that animal which you are dissecting is a full-blooded one and you dissect it immediately after it has died, that from these arteries and veins blood escapes, which will disturb you and prevent you from thoroughly examining the structures which are situated in the axilla. For in this place, beyond the muscle which we have mentioned, and underneath it, lie the nerves which go to the whole of the upper limb, and accompanying these are those also which go to the scapula and to the upper region of the shoulder. There are 303
also found in this place the great artery and the two veins which ramify in the whole of the arm, accompanied by the branches which arise from each of them, and also the fascial sheaths which surround all these structures and fasten them one to the other, and the 'spongy flesh' [*lymph glands*] which supports the arteries and the veins at their divisions, and fills up the spaces between these [divisions] like milk in vessels which we prepare. There also one constantly finds fat which encircles the fascial sheaths, and the nerves as well, if the animal has a well-nourished body and is fat. When you have now dissected these parts, then cut out all those other structures, and leave behind all the veins, arteries and nerves. And if you see at any time that the arteries and veins impede the thorough study of the nerves, and interpose themselves between them, then cut these vessels out also, after you have ligatured with two threads each one of the two kinds of vessel, so that the part of the artery or of the vein which you cut out lies between the two ligatures. Otherwise, if you cut the artery or the vein without tying them or securing them with a ligature, then blood streams out.

First, then, you must prepare the structures in the axilla in the way I have described to you. But as for the method of uncovering the

muscles which surround these structures, and those which travel to the scapula, I have already described that in Book III of this work, and I will describe it for you here also. I say, then, in regard to the muscle [*M. pectoralis major*] which comes upwards from the thorax to the shoulder joint, that you should begin its dissection from the lower part. Do not pay attention to the nerves which go from the intercostal spaces to the outer regions of the thorax. For they do not concern you,
304 if you desire to dissect these four pairs upon which our discussion is centred. Rather, do you direct your attention solely to these nerves, I mean the ones which travel towards the cavity of the axilla. In the course of this dissection which is performed in this way, remove and take out the whole of the muscle which resembles the Greek letter delta—that is this, Δ—and of which the chief bulk of the fleshy mass of the shoulder is composed,[1] so that you reach the meeting-place of the nerves and the scapula. And when you set free this muscle which I have mentioned to you from the [other] muscles abutting upon it and in contact with it, be on the watch as soon as you see a nerve branch which arises from the nerve-pairs here in question, and which joins any muscle. Together with this branch cut out the flesh that receives it, so that afterwards it does not spring back to its root and place of origin. It will then be easy for you to study while the flesh still envelops it. And if you do not want to carry out the dissection in this fashion, then use a ligature and by means of it secure the nerve which is distributed to a portion of that muscle which we mentioned. Cut away the muscle from it, and continue the cutting as far as the tendon of the muscle. If you do this, you can then cut away the whole of the muscle, after you have first studied and memorised to which muscle it is that the
305 nerve branch which you have ligatured makes its way. For the first origin of this nerve is something which you discover at the end of the operation. But you will not be able to see the muscle to which it goes, and with which it joins and connects after you have reflected it and cut it away. When you have done all this properly, then make the scapula stand away from the thorax, and free the muscle on the concave

[1] Ḥunain says: In the Greek MSS. which we have seen this portion has been defective. It was not as we have translated it, but we understood the meaning to be on the lines of our translation.

hollow part of the scapula from the structures which lie beneath it. Immediately after this you must dissect the very massive muscle which lies outside the axilla. I have already dealt with this muscle in the place where I described the anatomy of the muscles which move the shoulder joint.

If you do this properly and you cut away from the muscle which goes to the thorax from the neck whatever blocks your view of these nerve-shoots and interposes itself between them and you, you can then see clearly all the points of exit from which the nerves of these four pairs, of which we are here speaking, emerge from the spinal cord, and you see their intermingling, when they become entangled with one another, and also the long nerves which, beyond the plexus, extend to all these regions. Of these nerves the one which runs more upwards comes to that particular part of the scapula where its neck commences and where the uprising part of the septum [*spine*] which is found at its middle point begins to ascend and to extend towards the top of the scapula, though this can be seen even before the region of the axillary cavity
has been freely exposed. The second thing you see after this consists of *306*
small nerves, mostly three in number, rarely two, which go to the hollow concave surface of the scapula [*Nn. subscapulares*]. In the third place, after those minglings and amalgamations, you see another nerve, in the depth of the shoulder joint [*circumflex nerve*], and this is the one which passes beneath the shoulder joint and reaches its external aspect.

Of this nerve also the path is to be found in the hollow concave surface of the scapula, and from it a small branch makes its way to the muscle whose origin comes from the lowest part of the scapula. It is also one which moves the shoulder joint. After this, you will see five nerves which go to the upper arm, of which three are large, and lie one next the other, and the fourth is small. This nerve is nearer the surface of the body than those others. The fifth massive nerve then makes its way into the deeper parts. In Book III of this work I have described how these nerves distribute themselves to the whole of the upper limb, that is, in the Book in which I reported to what region of the upper arm there mounts the small nerve [*intercostobrachial*] between the ribs and how it is distributed in the skin there. You can see all these details clearly only when you expose those structures which I mentioned above in the way which I have described for you.

I now proceed to the discussion of the nerve-pairs arising from the spinal cord, starting with the assumption that you have already exposed and finished with these structures. I have given an account of one after another [of these nerves] from the commencement without taking into account my present point, since my intention has been to give an
307 inclusive survey and a general summary of the nerves going to the scapula, to the shoulder, and to the upper arm. Yet there is here something that we must of necessity relate before commencing the discussion of these pairs of nerves. It is that, whereas we always find that nerves come to these regions which we have mentioned, nevertheless we do not find that the plexus which the nerve-pairs form with one another after their origin is of one and the same form in all animals. Since this is so, we shall describe only what is often to be found and seen in the combination and plexus of the nerve pairs, and we shall leave out the account of what is only seldom seen, since for our requirements in the exercise of the healing art we find but little use for an intimate knowledge of and acquaintance with such combinations and plexuses. An example of that was the point I mentioned previously in Book III regarding the little fingers of the patient who had sustained paresis and defective sensibility here. For there was nothing in that that makes it necessary for us to go profoundly into this matter and to acquire for ourselves full and accurate knowledge of the nerve that supplies the fingers that had met with this injury, and to find out whether it comes from the eighth or the ninth pair. For the treatment and cure of such injuries can be completed, and the desired result obtained, without our having to make so exhaustive and rigorous a study. Thus the remedial means which are applied to the site of the injury envelop both vertebrae together. And since this is so, it is enough for us to know for certain that the nerve upon which the injury fell is a branch of one or other of these two pairs. But that you should know of one nerve branch from which pair of the two it arises, is of no advantage to you with regard to what you need to treat the injury.

CHAPTER 5. THE SIXTH AND SEVENTH CERVICAL NERVES.

Of the sixth pair of the nerves arising from the spinal cord.[1] The origin of the sixth pair of nerves arising from the spinal cord is below the fifth *308* vertebra. It is much more substantial than any of the pairs which lie above it. A single nerve goes on from this pair on each of the two sides, the right and the left, and you should know for certain that whatever you see on one side of the body, you will find exactly the same thing when you turn your attention to the side opposite. Consequently, I will confine my discussion here to one of the two nerves. My starting point in that is what follows. I say that the nerve whose origin comes after the fifth vertebra at once picks up the one which lies higher up than itself, that is, the one of which I spoke previously. And at the blending and junction of these two is the origin of the upper component of the nerve which goes to the diaphragm. But the one which originates from the junction of the two nerves which we mentioned, breaks up on the spot into three subdivisions. You see the uppermost of these proceeding to the parts of the scapula which lie at the neck of the shoulder. Postpone enquiring as to the way in which this division breaks up, with a view to investigating it later on. The second division of this nerve you will see proceeding to the deep excavated surface of the scapula, and you should leave the investigation of its division until you can study it later on. As for the third division, that is, the lowest of all, this has a twig smaller than the first which takes the direction towards the diaphragm. And this twig blends and joins up with the other one which I have previously mentioned. After this it blends and joins up with a single twig of the nerve which follows the sixth vertebra. I shall report to you somewhat later about this nerve in the place in which I deal with the seventh pair. Here, however, the discussion is still confined to the sixth pair.

From this pair [the sixth] there proceeds, as I described, a single nerve to the upper border of the scapula [*N. suprascapularis*]. Then another nerve goes to the deep excavated portion of the scapula. Do you also *309* start by following the first nerve which we have mentioned, after you have cleared away everything around it which is in close relation with

[1] Probably a scribal addition. B.T.

it, until you can see that it has begun to plunge and sink into the depth of the structures lying beneath the head of the shoulder. Now cut away the muscle which resembles the Greek letter Δ [*M. deltoides*], of which the principal mass of the shoulder flesh consists, and separate it from the site of its attachment to the upper arm. Then draw it upwards, so that it may not prevent you from studying the nerve [*N. suprascapularis*] which we are discussing. When you do that, you will find a ligament [*coracoacromial*] which connects the neck [*coracoid process*] of the scapula to the end of the partition wall [*spine*] which is found at its mid-point, I mean the end which projects upwards towards the 'head' of the scapula. Since these two bones that we have mentioned have something like a single common root, an angle is formed there after the fashion of the figure which I will demonstrate for you below,[1] where the point α is the place where the origin of the two processes of the scapula commences. Of the two processes one, that is, the neck [*coracoid process*] of the scapula is represented by the line αγ, and the end of the partition wall which lies in the middle of the scapula, that is, the part which is called the eye of the scapula, is represented by the line αβ. You should understand that the point β is the acromion itself. Consequently there must be an angle at the point α between the two lines βα and αγ. Now the nerve of which we are speaking passes through this angle past it and beyond. In order that it should never at any time be drawn upwards to the line αβ, or else forwards, a ligament is interposed there which comes from the line αβ and runs to the line αγ. This is a thin ligament of the nature of a fascia, yet strong despite its tenuity [*ligamentum coracoacromiale*]. It binds down
310 this nerve, which it embraces at the junction of the lines βα and αγ, nor does it allow it to pass through and beyond, abandoning the place where it should be. And when you divide this ligament, you see that the nerve becomes slack so that you can examine its branches which are distributed to the musculature lying above the scapula; between them lies the partition wall which is at the middle of the scapula. This is the musculature of which I taught you that it stretches the head of the

[1] No intelligible figure is given in the Arabic text, but the description clearly refers to a triangle of which two sides (αβ, αγ) are formed by the bony processes of the scapula, and the third (βγ) by the ligament which connects them. B.T.

humerus upwards and at the same time moves it slightly to the side [*abduction* at the *shoulder joint*]. And to this musculature come sensation and massive power from this nerve.

So far as concerns the other nerve [*posterior cord*], of which I said that it goes to the hollow excavated part of the scapula, now follow it up similarly after you have detached and removed from it everything that lies around it and hinders its inspection, whether this be a connective tissue [*fascia*] or, in general, any structure at all that lies near to it. You will see that from this nerve, as it proceeds, three branches spring off to the hollow excavated part of the scapula [*subscapular nerves*], though you will find on rare occasions that there are only two of these branches. Then that part of the nerve which still remains over [*circumflex nerve*] mounts upwards to the shoulder joint beneath the neck of the scapula. Thus a nerve reaches to the neck of the scapula on each of its two sides: from above comes the nerve [*suprascapular*] of which we spoke previously and which is distributed to the upper muscle of the shoulder joint, and from below comes the nerve [*circumflex*] which we are discussing. Of this latter one branch divides and breaks up in the muscles [*M. teres major* and *M. teres minor*] which ascend from the lower [*axillary*] border of the scapula to the shoulder. But its principal part mounts to that muscle which resembles the letter delta of the Greek script, that is, Δ. Its course runs below the neck of 311
the scapula, close to the superficial aspect of the joint, where it makes contact with and joins the deltoid muscle. You can see that a branch from it also distributes itself to the adjacent muscle [*M. teres minor*]. But all the rest of it that remains over runs outwards to the skin [*upper lateral cutaneous nerve*] and is distributed to the outer and upper part of the upper arm, in a superficial stratum.

Now recall to your memory that the nerve which comes after the fifth vertebra divides up into three branches, after it has been joined by a branch from the nerve which comes to it from those that follow the fourth vertebra. You have already heard about the distribution of two of these branches. We shall go on to discuss the remaining branch, that is, the third, of which I said that it is interwoven with one of the two branches of the nerve which follows the sixth vertebra. In the discussion on which I am about to embark you shall hear how this nerve reaches to the commencement of the upper arm, after first having heard on that subject a point which I have still to make. This is that the division of which I said that it causes the nerve to break up into three branches after the union of the two pairs mentioned, I mean the fifth and the sixth, is not always to be found occurring in this way. For sometimes it divides into two branches only. I will tell you later what the position is with regard to the division of this pair and of the others, and with regard to their interlacement, and I will give an account of what normally happens there. Now proceed with us to the dissection of the seventh pair of nerves, and assume that these things function in this way.

Of the seventh pair of the nerves arising from the spinal cord.[1] We have already said that the third division of the nerve of the sixth pair blends and unites with one of the two divisions of the seventh pair. That is one of the facts which indicate that this pair becomes doubled
312 immediately after its origin. Accordingly make this now the starting point of your study of the nerves of the seventh pair. Each of the two parts of this pair of nerves splits into two divisions as it climbs upwards. Of these two divisions one, that is, the upper one of the two, blends and unites with the lower division of the nerve which comes after the fifth vertebra, as I described previously. And at this blending and union there branches off from it immediately a small twig which extends to one after another of the muscles which are in close relation with it. Investigate this twig and its origin after you have previously traced the large nerve when it extends to the upper arm. But this nerve does not reach the upper arm as a single, still isolated nerve which has not divided. On the contrary, it divides immediately after that small twig which I have previously pointed out. And now one of its divisions, the large one, makes its way to the head of the muscle lying at the front of the arm, and its other division divides into two branches. Of these, one, that is, the upper of the two, makes its way over the upper arm below the nerve which I mentioned previously and of which I said that it reaches to the origin of the muscle lying on the front [of the arm]. But the lower of the two blends and unites with a twig of the nerve of that pair which follows after this. Then, after blending and uniting, it divides again into two nerves of unequal size, and both of these extend to the

[1] Probably a scribal addition. B.T.

arm. Of these two the upper one is the more slender, and the other, that is, the lower one, is far thicker. And so it comes about that the sum total of all those nerves which traverse the axilla and proceed to the arm amounts to four as counted up to here in our discussion. Each one mingles with the others in the same way that the nerves of the neck are interwoven [*cervical plexus*]. But the former [*brachial plexus*] mingle with one another in a much more intricate manner, and are much more
fully dispersed than the latter. That is because the nerves emerging from *313*
these vertebrae wander onwards to far distant places, and in addition they are suspended without any firm attachment or stability. For in their blending, their combination, and their union with each other, they acquire strength, both individually and collectively. One example of that is that you can see plainly that the two pairs which we mentioned previously, I mean the sixth and the seventh pairs, are interwoven not only in this manner but in others also. For I have already said shortly before this that on not a few occasions I have seen how the sixth pair, after the preceding pair has united with it, divides up into three divisions. Again, once in a foetus I saw that it divided into two divisions, and one of these, the uppermost of the two, divided once again into two. The upper of these divisions ascends to the place which we mentioned before, in regard to the diagram and figure that I gave you, where I said that the root of the neck of the scapula [*coracoid process*] lay. But I have seen the other twig blend and unite with the half of the seventh pair, after it has divided into two. Similarly the other half of the first division blends and unites with the other division of the seventh pair. And before its blending and union there branch off from it the three divisions which go to the hollow excavated part of the scapula. We have often seen this branch also divide and ramify immediately after its first division, and we have also frequently seen this happen after it has passed on a short way. Once we saw a single nerve springing out and dividing itself into three branches, while on another occasion we saw this emerge as two nerves, one of which then divided into two. Again, on a few occasions we saw, as I have described, two small nerves connect closely with the
hollow excavated part of the scapula and join with it. But invariably *314*
in all apes we have seen these twigs branch off from the far-extended nerve. You will also observe there the nerve which descends from the

sixth pair after it has mingled with the seventh. It ramifies on its way to the top of the shoulder. You will recognise that that happens to it only by means of a thorough investigation of the great [main] mass of the nerve-fibres which [here] blend and unite.

And now, after the two portions of the sixth pair and the two portions of the seventh pair have blended and united, as we have described previously, there becomes visible in all apes a nerve-branch [*circumflex*] which goes to the main mass of the musculature of the shoulder. The position with regard to this branch is that either more is found in it from the sixth pair than from the seventh, or, alternatively, one finds in it an equal contribution coming from both pairs, I mean the sixth pair and the seventh pair. After the blending and the union of the two branches of the sixth pair of nerves with the seventh, two nerves arise. One of these two, that is, the upper, divides into two branches. And of these two branches one pursues the path which the [parent] nerve has followed from its commencement, passing across the hollow excavated part of the scapula until it arrives at the head of the shoulder as I have described previously, and it travels on beneath the neck of the scapula to cross the outer aspect of the joint. But the other branch of this nerve, that which lies higher up, blends and unites with the pair which comes after the seventh vertebra, as will soon be described to you.

Now, however, I pass on to the description of the other nerve, the remaining one of those two of which I said that they arise in common
315 from the two pairs which blend and unite with one another, I mean the sixth pair and the seventh pair. I say that from this nerve there branches off immediately a nerve [*lateral pectoral*] which goes to the two muscles which ascend from the sternum to the shoulder joint [*M. pectoralis major, two heads*]. It then proceeds on from this part, and in its course it joins and unites by means of a twig it has, which runs transversely, with another nerve [*medial pectoral*] from the next pair, with which we shall shortly deal. And after this twig has branched off from it, it passes on and reaches the upper arm, close to the vein which reaches it after traversing the axilla. As for the nerve of which I said that it associates itself with the pair following the seventh vertebra, that is, the nerve of which I have promised to speak soon, at the point of its union and junction there immediately branches off from it a small twig which

proceeds in a downward direction, and divides in the great muscle behind the axilla [*M. latissimus dorsi*]. It then passes straight onwards and so comes to the upper arm a little below the twig of which we spoke. At times this twig, which proceeds to the great muscle, has a branch which joins and connects with it and which comes from the origin of the nerve following the eighth vertebra.

CHAPTER 6. THE EIGHTH CERVICAL AND FIRST THORACIC NERVES, WITH FURTHER CONSIDERATION OF THE BRACHIAL PLEXUS.

Of the eighth pair of nerves arising from the spinal cord.[1] The place of
origin of the eighth pair of the nerves arising from the spinal cord is
after the seventh vertebra. Immediately after its first origin there blends
and unites with it that pair [*first thoracic nerve*] which follows it. Consequently, when you see that, you may think what is found in this place
is a single nerve-root, if you have not completely removed from the
origins of these nerves the structures which surround them. In this
situation also there is the artery which comes to the arm, and similarly
the vein which comes to it as well as those of the offshoots which spring
from the two of them after the fashion of the branches from a tree.
Some of these are the ones which branch off in the axilla itself. And
since this is so, you must act very deliberately and remove all that *316*
surrounds them, taking care that none of these veins and arteries is torn,
and that their surroundings are not filled with blood. I have already
told you that in the dissection of the bodies of apes the blood gushes
out, even when you have anticipated this, and have strangled the ape
in the previous evening, and proceeded to dissect it on the next
morning.

These nerves thus blend and unite with each other as soon as they emerge [from the respective intervertebral foramina]. And this is the chief reason which leads one to imagine at first that what arises after the seventh vertebra is only a single massive nerve, with which no other is combined. But such is not the case, since there is a single nerve there whose origin is clear and which comes from the first intercostal space. This nerve [*first thoracic*] blends and unites with that other one

[1] Probably a scribal addition. B.T.

at their place of origin. The unified nerve which is formed from both these two, after it has gone forward a little way, divides again and blends and unites with those ones which are higher than it and which originate from the sixth pair, so that frequently, when I have explored and examined this part, I have thought that the nerve which is third in position of the nerves of which I have said that they come to the arm, is directly opposite the nerve whose origin comes after the eighth vertebra.

Now this nerve, which occupies the third place among those that overlie the upper arm, is very much stouter than all of those others. Next to it in stoutness comes the last of them, and then the second of
317 the first two nerves. There is here a fifth nerve, more slender than all of these, and it is the one whose path lies between the third and fourth nerves in a superficial position. But I treat my discussion, so far as I deal with this nerve, generally and inclusively, as you will always observe that these pairs blend and unite with one another immediately after their origin, and that after that blending and union, the pair which is higher than them divides.

Two massive nerves also come to the upper arm, which travel straight onwards, opposite these pairs. One of them is the nerve of which I said that it is the third in order and position, and this breaks up in the outer lateral musculature of the whole of the upper arm, and the other nerve, that is, the one which follows this, proceeds to the inner head of the upper arm. Further, I have actually seen the nerves mentioned so related that the one of them which proceeds to the inner head of the upper arm was standing, as it were, straight over against the nerve whose origin comes after the seventh vertebra. Frequently, also, it stands over against the nerve whose origin comes after the eighth vertebra, and now and then it has an equal contribution from both nerves associated with it. You know from what I have said about this nerve that occasionally I have thought of the other one, which lies higher up than this, that it comes wholly or for the most part from the eighth pair, sometimes however from the ninth pair, and on another occasion from both together. Now just as one of these two, that is, the lower [*ulnar nerve*], proceeds to the medial epicondyle of the arm, so also the upper one [*radial nerve*] passes in the direction of the lateral

epicondyle, and it twines itself round the humerus, from the hinder
region, at the place from which originates the main mass of its smaller 318
anterior muscles. And on its course to the arm there springs from it immediately beyond the plexus a twig [*medial pectoral nerve*] which makes its way across the interior of the axilla and goes to the great muscle which extends from the anterior surface of the thorax to the upper arm [*M. pectoralis major*].

Now, however, I return to my discussion, and recommence the account of these two pairs of nerves with which I am dealing, since that arrangement should ensure clarity of explanation. I say, then, that the two last pairs of nerves of those which proceed from the spinal cord to the arm, blend and unite with one another at the spot at which they first emerge [from the intervertebral foramina]. Then they again separate from one another as two nerves, and each of the two blends and unites itself with the nerves which come from the seventh pair. It is clear that this pair comes after the sixth vertebra. And further a branch from the pair which comes after the fifth vertebra often blends and unites with that pair which comes after the seventh vertebra.

But now, since the blending and union take place in many different ways, and are not always to be found arranged in the same pattern in all apes, I have come to the conclusion that nothing that might prove useful can result from their intensive investigation. What is of use here is this, that you should know from which pair originates each one of the nerves which extend to the scapula and to the upper arm. We must now first specify the total number of these nerves and the order in which they are positioned. For in accordance with that we shall act in the judgements which we pass on the things which are constantly or most frequently to be seen. I say that what is always to be seen is the ordinal sequence of these nerves in their situation. The first of them all is a nerve of moderate dimensions, which goes to the upper region of the
scapula [*N. suprascapularis*]. The second, following after it, comprises 319
three small nerves which go to the hollow excavated surface of the scapula [*Nn. subscapulares*]. The third thereafter is another nerve [*N. circumflexus*] which goes to the main mass of the flesh of the shoulder. And after the passage of this nerve come four nerves which distribute themselves to the musculature of the whole arm. Besides

these there is still another, a small fifth nerve which branches off from the union of two other pairs [of nerves]. The fibres of this nerve stand as it were in a direct line exactly opposite the nerve whose origin comes after the eighth vertebra. Now no branch of this nerve distributes itself to a muscle at all. It is just the same in regard to the one which originates from the second intercostal space. But those other four nerves are distributed to the muscles of the whole arm, as we have indicated in the third book of this work. What I have described to you regarding the course of the nerves that have been mentioned, I have seen in all apes in the order and series which I have given. But I have never seen each one of them come off constantly from one and the same pair of nerves arising from the spinal cord. For the first of them is a nerve which takes its origin from the point of junction of the fifth with the sixth pair. And most frequently I have seen the fascicles of this nerve travelling over against the fifth pair. Occasionally I have thought that a slender twig reached it from the sixth pair also. Of the fifth pair too I have sometimes thought that after its blending and union with the sixth pair it again broke off from it by means of the nerve of which I spoke previously and by means of one of the two nerves that go to the diaphragm. For the fifth pair broke up and its union disintegrated
320 so that these two nerves proceeded out of it. Another time, I thought that it contributed something to the sixth pair, and yet again on another occasion, that it received something from it [the sixth]. Often it neither gave nor received anything, but simply combined and united with it.

Thus from this plexus, when it comes about in this way, the first nerve ascends to the upper part of the scapula. But as for the nerve-shoots which go to the hollow excavated part of the scapula, I have constantly been of the opinion that they are, as it were, parts of the sixth pair, and never receive anything from the seventh pair. I have thought, however, that they received a slight [contribution] from the fifth pair, through the blending and union of fibres. As for the nerve [*circumflex*] which comes after these and goes to the main mass of the shoulder flesh, you will see that most of it, that is, its bulk, comes from the sixth pair, just as the first nerve which goes to the upper arm is, for the most part, shared in common by both nerve-pairs, I mean the seventh and eighth pairs, and that the main bulk of that nerve, the second which comes after this, comes from the eighth pair. Of the two remaining nerves, however, most of their bulk derives from the two remaining pairs. In general I have seen these nerves in the state which I have described, but again, rarely, I have seen them not conform to it. Nor is there any great advantage to be gained by a thorough and intensive investigation of points like this.

In Book III of this work I have already described in a previous discussion the course of those nerves which come to the upper arm. But to the great muscle [*pectoralis major*] of the sternum two small nerves pass [*pectoral nerves*]. One of them lies directly in line opposite the seventh pair, and the other lies in line with the eighth pair, not far 321
beyond its origin and emergence. Then, after the two have blended and united with one another, they distribute themselves in that muscle. And a branch runs from each through and beyond to the muscle at the sternum, I mean the one proceeding upwards, and to the special muscle of the first rib, whose origin comes from the clavicle [*M. subclavius*]. Of it [this muscle] I also believed previously that the nerve came to it from the seventh pair. That was because the union of the pairs and their interlacement make their composition indistinct and uncertain and render it impossible to make a thorough investigation, so as to learn their direct course. Now above these nerves lies another one near the root of the sixth pair, and this goes to the great muscle of the thorax, which is attached and joined to the scapula [*M. serratus anterior*]. It is my custom to name this muscle often, 'the muscle common to the scapula and the thorax'. Generally you will see, in the bodies of apes, each one of the two (I mean the right and the left side) nerves of the diaphragm arising from two roots or heads of which one usually comes from the sixth pair just in the place where lies the root of the first of these nerves that extend to the scapula. We said already earlier that this nerve lies over against the fifth pair. But the origin of the other head or root, which is more slender and smaller than it, goes out from the second nerve which is found here, and which has its origin in the sixth pair. This head is a part of the nerves that pass to the diaphragm [*N. phrenicus*]. The second head is, as we have said, more slender and smaller than the first. At times I have also seen a third head which originated from the nerve that follows those ones in the bodies of the

animals which we have already mentioned. In the bodies of other animals, however, of the class of quadrupeds, you will see that the nerves of the diaphragm have, in general, three roots or heads. We
322 have already said that to the massive muscle, of which the fleshy material of the axilla consists, a special nerve is attached behind this place [*nerve to latissimus dorsi muscle*]. And if you observe carefully, you will see that this nerve sometimes proceeds from the fibres of the eighth pair. It passes last of all the nerves which are related to this muscle, after many nerves have gone to it on its way from below upwards.

Consequently I have decided, when I have brought to an end this work on which I am engaged, to deal in another work with the subject of how many heads the nerves that go to each muscle possess. And there I shall also describe the distribution of the nerves in all the bodily parts. But in this present work I have produced a simple account, without reservations, of the points that have been mentioned.

You must, then, remember what I said to you about the first and second branches of these pairs, namely that the first branch ascends upwards [*N. suprascapularis*] to the musculature which surrounds the septum in the middle of the scapula, and that the second branch distributes itself to the hollow excavated part of the scapula [*Nn. subscapulares*], but the third branch goes to the muscle on the main mass of the flesh of the shoulder [*M. deltoides, N. circumflexus*]. From this nerve I have sometimes seen a branch which proceeded to the upper muscle which opens out the elbow joint. And I said also that its end comes through to the skin, for it is distributed on the external aspect of the upper arm.

CHAPTER 7. THE THORACIC NERVES.

Of the remaining pairs of the nerves arising from the spinal cord.[1] After the seven vertebrae which we have mentioned before, twelve others, whose situation is dorsal to the thorax, are joined to them. The origin
323 and the emergence of the nerves from the spinal cord take place in the neck through foramina and orifices shared between each pair of vertebrae which meet one another and articulate with each other. With

[1] Probably a scribal addition. B.T.

the exception of the first two, all these are alike to one another in regard to their contribution to the production of the common foramina or orifices between all those parts. But among the vertebrae behind the thorax you will see that the lower one is the less excavated. And this pattern occurs constantly amongst all these vertebrae, and it gradually increases until the nerve can almost pass through and emerge from a single vertebra, that is, the upper of the two. In the lumbar vertebral column, that is, the region of the five vertebrae which come after those of the thorax, the whole nerve does in fact emerge from that vertebra which lies above, especially in the last of them.

Now in regard to the nerves which come out from between the vertebrae, there are some details which are shared in common by them all and which embrace them all, and some which are peculiar to each one of them. As for the characteristics which they share in common, one of them is that after the emergence of each one of these nerves from the vertebrae, one branch immediately goes from them to the dorsal side, as we have described with regard to the nerves which emerge from the neck, and the other branch proceeds to the ventral aspect. Another of those details is that all the branches which go backwards enter the vertebral musculature [*long dorsal muscles*] and the other muscles which have their heads and origin in the vertebral column. These muscles, which lie behind the thorax, are the two muscles of the scapula and, thirdly, the upper muscle of the thorax, that is a muscle resembling fascia. It is evident and well known that the disposition of all these structures on each of the two sides, I mean the right and the left, takes place after one and the same fashion. Yet another common detail is that all the nerves which come to the front side [ventral or anterior aspect] from the spinal cord in the vertebrae behind the thorax, pass in *324*
the spaces between the thoracic ribs. And in their course they pass close to those ribs which are situated higher up, especially at their places of origin. Besides these common characteristics I will now describe to you point by point what distinguishes the individual nerves one after another, as soon as I have sorted out and distinguished between the various kinds and divisions of these special details. There are, among these details, some which may properly be called peculiar, in that they apply to individual nerves by themselves, whichever these may be.

Others belong to three or four or to a certain number of nerves. Now I will first describe to you those details which are peculiar to individual nerves.

I say that the first nerve of all those which I mentioned in the foregoing discussion originates and rises from a foramen and passage shared in common by the eighth and the ninth vertebrae. It comes into relation with the first rib, and then immediately turns upwards and mounts up on its own until it passes this rib. After it has reached this place, it goes out to the external parts in the direction of the axilla, and blends and unites with that nerve which comes before it. I have described a little earlier how these two in the axilla pass onwards to the upper arm, and distribute themselves in the structures of the arm. This, then, is something which distinguishes this nerve and is peculiar to it alone. As for the other nerve, it comes out from the second of the intercostal spaces and proceeds to the upper arm. Of the behaviour of this nerve also I have already instructed you before now. But of the nerves of the intercostal spaces which follow this, the one which comes out of the third space distributes itself in the superficially placed parts of the axilla. And the nerves coming from the fourth, fifth, sixth and
325 seventh intercostal spaces all distribute themselves in the slender muscle which travels in the axillary cavity and ascends to the shoulder joint. Their other branches go outwards to the surrounding skin. In regard to this muscle [*latissimus dorsi*] I said earlier that the anatomists have overlooked and ignored it because it is usually reflected together with the skin. Following the order of these nerves which we specified, and belonging to their group, come the nerves which run along the intercostal spaces and mount from the thorax [*Nn. intercostales*]. At the false ribs they reach the muscle [*latissimus dorsi*] which ascends up to the shoulder joint. This muscle is the largest of all those which move this joint, and it covers all the parts of the axilla which lie behind and without [laterally]. I have already said that a branch arises and goes to this muscle from the nerve which, together with a vein and an artery, comes to the arm. There is still another, a second, series of nerves here. These are the ones which penetrate and come out from the intercostal spaces [*lateral cutaneous branches*]. The place at which they arise lies near the mid-point of each rib, and they distribute themselves in the muscles

overlying the thorax. After their ends [terminal branches] have perforated the muscle they branch out in the skin covering the muscles.

As for those ribs which are connected with the sternum, the nerves lying between them travel along the several spaces which are found between every two ribs, and beyond these until they reach the sternum, together with the veins and arteries which meet and connect with them. Then they go out to the sternum outside the thorax [*Nn. cutanei anteriores*] and blend and unite with the endings of the nerves which belong to the second group of which we said that they distribute themselves to the muscles overlying the thorax and that their endings, after they have pierced the muscles, ramify in the skin covering the muscles [*Nn. cutanei laterales*]. But as for the nerves which lie in the ribs that are below these, their endings distribute themselves in that muscle
[*rectus abdominis*] which is the most massive of all the four muscles of 326
the abdomen, and the one which lies outside all these others. Of all the nerves in the intercostal spaces, the shortest is the first, because the first of the intercostal spaces is itself shorter than any of the others. And furthermore, this nerve gives off no branch at all externally in either of the two series.

Now ascertain for yourself and study thoroughly all the courses of the nerves and their paths to the exterior of the thorax which I have enumerated here, so that if ever you have to cut through a rib or to perform in that region some other surgical operation which requires you to divide a bone, you may know precisely the spot at which the nerve comes out. Accordingly after you have assured yourself on this point, open the thorax, and ascertain carefully the situations of these nerves in the thoracic cavity. That you will only see by means of the following method of dissection. Go to the spot at which that portion of every rib which is ossified ends, and where the cartilaginous part begins, and in this precise spot make an incision which runs from above downwards longitudinally, and let the incision pass across the whole of the ribs in their succession. It is understood that the incision is made in duplicate on both sides of the thorax, I mean one on the right side and one on the left side [of the sternum]. Now in the place where the ends of the two incisions run out, let the knife go across from one end to the other. Then grasp the margin of this incision, and draw upwards

the whole sternum in the direction of the neck of the animal, including
327 with it the parts of the ribs [still] attached to it from both sides. If you do this properly you will see the thoracic cavity, one on each side, and you will see that the membranes which divide the thorax at its mid-point surround the pericardium and, together with it, the heart also. You will then clearly see that a vein and an artery lie close to every nerve that is to be found in the intercostal spaces. And when you like to detach the membrane also which envelops the ribs from within and is known as the inner membrane of the ribs, you will then be able to observe the vein, the artery and the nerve in every intercostal space and to see them bare and denuded. Further, you can be still more thorough in your examination, if you want, by cutting away a single one of the intercostal spaces and separating it completely from the thoracic structures, of which we said that they would become visible after the [first] incision. Then you must separate the two sides of the thorax, and draw one of the two upwards, and the other downwards. Occasionally you may bend backwards whichever rib you like, one rib, if you want, or more. If you do so, then you will get a good view of the nerves at the root of the ribs, running from above downwards [*sympathetic trunk*]. Of these nerves some [anatomists] believe that they are branches of the sixth pair of nerves coming from the brain. We have already mentioned their place of origin in the preceding Book, where we were dealing with the nerves which have their origin in the brain. We have also described how they traverse the thorax and what relationship exists be-
328 tween them and the nerves which run through and out of the intercostal spaces, and by means of what kind of dissection you can see them clearly.

CHAPTER 8. THE LUMBAR AND SACRAL NERVES.

But now let us take in hand the parts lying below the thorax, and you must here learn the point which I am making. It is that, though the number of the vertebrae of the neck and the thorax in the bodies of apes and men is one and the same, this is not true of the lumbar vertebrae. For in these vertebrae the ape resembles the other animals which I started by dividing into six classes. All these animals have in the lumbar vertebral column seven vertebrae, as has the ape, and behind the thorax they have twelve vertebrae, as has Man.

Since this is so, then the nerves whose origin springs below the diaphragm from the spinal cord found in the lumbar vertebral column, must of necessity be of greater mass in the bodies of men, but in the remaining animals, and also in the apes, they must be small. That is because although these animals have two [lumbar] vertebrae in excess, yet they have the same number of origins of nerves which go to the legs as has the human body. Since this is so, then understand that the similarity of the ape to Man in regard to the origins of these nerves of which we wish to speak, does not lie at the twentieth or twenty-first vertebra, but at the twenty-second. That being so, you should understand also that what you see in the dissection of an ape at the twenty-second vertebra is to be found at the twentieth vertebra of the human body. What you see at the ape's twenty-third vertebra is found at a man's twenty-first. Similarly also, what is to be seen at the ape's twenty-fourth vertebra is precisely what is found at the twenty-second
human vertebra, and what is found at the ape's twenty-fifth vertebra 329
is found at the twenty-third vertebra of a man. In the same way you will find that the last remaining vertebra of the spine is in Man the twenty-fourth, in the apes the twenty-sixth. And with regard to the foramina, and the channels in the 'wide bone' the arrangement is the same in both. The 'wide bone' is also, as I have said previously, called the 'greatest bone', that is, the 'cross' [*sacrum*]. Now you will see in the bodies of apes that in the three vertebrae which come after the diaphragm, I mean the twentieth, twenty-first and twenty-second vertebrae, lie the origins of nerves that are not large, and these are bifurcated as well. One of these nerves ascends to the muscle lying on the abdomen [*M. transversus abdominis*], I mean the muscle which runs transversely and is the first [encountered from within] of the inner muscles, and to the oblique muscle lying on it [*M. obliquus abdominis internus*]. A small offshoot from it also breaks up in the structures which are adjacent to it. But the other nerve breaks up and ramifies in the musculature of the vertebral column and in the muscle which draws downwards the last thoracic ribs [*M. serratus posterior inferior*], and in the origin of the great muscle [*M. latissimus dorsi*] which passes up to the shoulder joint and extends as far as to the exterior part of the axilla. Both the loins also, that is, the muscles which attach themselves to the

vertebrae inwardly [*M. psoas, M. quadratus lumborum*], receive branches from these nerves. Now all the nerves which we have mentioned [*Nn. intercostales, Nn. lumbales*] unite themselves with those nerves [*sympathetic trunk*] which descend from the brain. We have already mentioned this junction in the place where we dealt with the anatomy of those nerves. As for the nerve whose origin is at the twenty-second vertebra, a branch comes from it to the one which springs out after it.
330 Further, it also blends and unites with the two nerves springing out above it, the one joining with the other, as is the custom of these nerves, namely to unite with one another at all the vertebrae, as we informed you previously. As for the twenty-third vertebra, all these details which we have previously described to you will be found there.

From this vertebra comes the origin of the nerves which go to the lower limb. To the nerve which originates at the twenty-third vertebra, there runs a little nerve from the preceding one, as we have described, and thence it passes on, descends and unites with that nerve which originates from the twenty-fourth vertebra. Of the total of three nerves which come to the leg, one travels in the external part of the vertebra. Then it is joined by another nerve from the one which originates from the twenty-fifth vertebra, and afterwards it proceeds to the great foramen which pierces the pubic bone, that is, the foramen which one calls 'that which resembles a gateway' [*foramen obturatum, N. obturatorius*]. The second of these nerves, after it has blended and united with another, from that nerve whose origin comes from the twenty-fifth vertebra, travels in the muscle which goes to the lesser of the two processes of the femoral shaft [*trochanter minor and M. psoas*], and a twig springs from it to this muscle and to the muscle which lies at the hinder side beneath the skin [*M. gluteus*]. This muscle of the femur is analogous to the muscle of the shoulder [*M. deltoides*] which constitutes the principal mass of the flesh of the shoulder. But the third nerve, which is somewhat more obliquely inclined than these, travels at first high up on the outer aspect of the vertebra. Subsequently it passes beyond the nerve branch that descends to the second nerve and mounts on the femur at the muscle which lies on its anterior side aspect [*N. femoralis*].
331 As for the nerve whose origin comes from the twenty-fifth vertebra, one branch goes from it to the nerve which comes to the foramen

piercing the pubic bone [*obturator foramen*] and another branch goes to the nerve which comes to the prominence of the groin. The remainder of it, after it has blended and united with the nerves whose origin follows after this, arrives at the outer region of the leg where it is adjacent to the coccyx. But the nerve whose origin comes from the twenty-sixth vertebra passes on outwards together with the first of the nerves springing from the sacrum, and travels to the hip-joint. Near the coccyx it blends and unites with the nerve whose origin comes after the twenty-fifth vertebra. And from these nerves there spring off branches like the branches of trees, and these go to the muscles which lie around the hip-joint. A small branch goes to the nerve which is the first to have its origin after this. These are small nerves.

All these nerves blend and unite with those which originate from the sacrum, and they distribute themselves to all the various organs near the sacrum and to the uppermost of the muscles of the hip-joint. It is from these nerves that, in part, sensation, and in part, sensation accompanied by voluntary movement, is imparted to the urinary bladder, to the genital organs, that is to say, in the woman the uteri and in the man the penis, to the rectum, to all the various fasciae found there, to the muscles of these organs which we have mentioned, and to the skin which envelops them.

Thus all these organs always receive from these nerves which we have mentioned sensibility and mobility, a thing which you will also invariably see in the four 'heads' [principal mainstems] of the nerves which go to the leg, I mean the stem which is found at the obturator foramen [*obturator nerve*], the stem which passes at the side [*inferior gluteal and posterior femoral cutaneous nerves*], the stem which lies near
the anterior muscle [*femoral nerve*] and the stem which lies outside the 332
hip-joint [*greater sciatic nerve*]. In the third book of this work I have already described how these stems distribute themselves to the whole lower limb. But so far as concerns the interrelation of nerves which spring out from the vertebrae, this does not come about constantly in one and the same fashion, just as the interrelation of those nerves which traverse the axilla, and continue on to the arm, is not uniform. But the difference between them in their association is small here as it is there. Furthermore in the knowledge of this relationship and its distinctions,

there lies no usefulness for anyone who seeks to practise medicine, even though he investigates it very thoroughly, and pursues it in the most searching fashion, a point which we have explained with regard to the arm also. But as far as concerns the collateral combination of the nerves, which exists in all the individual parts of the muscular system, not only in the muscles which we have mentioned, but also in the muscles of the whole of the body, of this I will inform you in another treatise, in which I intend to describe which muscles possess a single nerve-root and which possess more than one. Similarly I will instruct you in the special anatomy of the remaining organic structures to which nerves make their way, and tell you what the aggregate mass of those nerves is, what their total number may be, and to which parts of those organs they distribute themselves.

End of the Fifteenth Book, and therewith the final conclusion of this excellent, outstanding work, which is one of the compositions of a man who performed marvellously, and revealed extraordinary things, the master of the earlier surgeons, and the Lord of the more recent savants, whose efforts in the practice of medicine have been unequalled by any of the prominent since the days of the learned and great Hippocrates—I mean Galen. May God Almighty be merciful to him!

INDEX

All references are to page numbers

Index

Index

Index

Index

Index

For EU product safety concerns, contact us at Calle de José Abascal, 56–1°, 28003 Madrid, Spain or eugpsr@cambridge.org.

www.ingramcontent.com/pod-product-compliance
Ingram Content Group UK Ltd.
Pitfield, Milton Keynes, MK11 3LW, UK
UKHW010348140625
459647UK00010B/908

* 9 7 8 1 1 0 8 0 0 9 4 4 7 *